Germany s
Russia problem

MANCHESTER
1824

Manchester University Press

Germany's Russia problem

The struggle for balance in Europe

John Lough

Manchester University Press

Published by Manchester University Press
Oxford Road, Manchester M13 9PL
www.manchesteruniversitypress.co.uk

British Library Cataloguing-in-Publication Data
A catalogue record for this book is available from the British Library

ISBN 978 1 5261 5150 6 hardback
ISBN 978 1 5261 6923 5 paperback

First published 2021
Paperback published 2022

The publisher has no responsibility for the persistence or accuracy of URLs for any external or third-party internet websites referred to in this book, and does not guarantee that any content on such websites is, or will remain, accurate or appropriate.

MIX
Paper from
responsible sources
FSC® C013604

Typeset by
Servis Filmsetting Ltd, Stockport, Cheshire
Printed in Great Britain
by CPI Group (UK) Ltd, Croydon CE0 4YY

Contents

Acknowledgements

The origins of this book go back more than thirty-five years to my days as an undergraduate at Cambridge University where I had the good fortune to benefit from Irina Kirillova's brilliant teaching of nineteenth-century Russian literature. From her I first learned about the deep cultural relationship between Germany and Russia. Similarly, Jo Whaley's mesmerising lectures and supervisions on the revolutions of 1848 opened my eyes not just to a key moment in European history but also to the notion of Germany's *Sonderweg* (special path). As a young policy analyst, I profited hugely from the knowledge and guidance of Chris Donnelly, Head of the Soviet Studies Research Centre at Sandhurst who in 1988 identified the need to recruit a German speaker, believing that 'something might happen' in the German Democratic Republic. Less than a year into the job, I was covering the collapse of the Berlin Wall and the process that led to Germany's reunification. It was a thrilling experience and formative at the same time.

During my time as NATO's first representative in Moscow (1995–1998), I had the extraordinary privilege of being based at the German Embassy after it became NATO's Contact Point in 1996. Ernst-Jörg von Studnitz, Germany's outstanding ambassador, and his staff provided wise counsel and taught me much about the way Germany approaches Russia. In this respect, I am indebted also to Colonel Manfred Diehl who worked alongside me to improve

Acknowledgements

the Russian public's understanding of NATO. His commitment to building trust-based relations with Russia combined with his affection for the country set a fine example. It was painful to see him expelled from Moscow in 1999 and branded a 'German fascist' by a senior Russian Defence Ministry official at the start of NATO's air campaign against Yugoslavia. My German colleagues at NATO Headquarters who worked on Russia and Ukraine, especially Ulrich Brandenburg, Jürgen Schulz and Christof Weil, also contributed greatly to my understanding of Germany's approach to its 'East'. I am particularly grateful also to BP Germany's government affairs team who were excellent colleagues throughout my time at TNK-BP (2003–2008) and gave me valuable insight into Germany's energy relationship with Russia and the place of the Russian market in the thinking of German business.

Over recent years and during my research for this book, I have benefited greatly from conversations with many German officials who have taken the time to debate Russia and policy towards it. Unfailingly courteous, they have always offered an informed viewpoint and been willing to listen to another perspective. I am also especially grateful to Hannes Adomeit, Marieluise Beck, David Crawford, Judy Dempsey, Liana Fix, Hans-Joachim Falenski, Ralf Fücks, Michael Harms, Martin Hoffmann, Wilfried Jilge, John Kornblum, Stefan Meister, René Nyberg, Alexander Rahr, Irina Scherbakowa, Jan Techau and Reinhard Veser, who have regularly shared their views and broadened my knowledge. John and René, two outstanding ambassadors of their countries to Germany and in René's case to Russia as well, also took the trouble to comment on the manuscript. My sincere thanks to them as well as to Duncan Allan and Janet Gunn who also offered invaluable guidance on ways to improve the overall text. Wolfgang Brett, Roger Golland and Philip Vorobyov kindly reviewed individual chapters and provided helpful feedback. James Sherr, friend and colleague for over three decades, deserves special thanks for so frequently acting as a sounding board and allowing me to tap into his

Acknowledgements

unparalleled understanding of Russia's conduct of foreign policy. I am also indebted to Tatiana Parkhalina, Lilia Shevtsova and Konstantin von Eggert, all of whom who I first met over twenty-five years ago. Their breadth of knowledge and subtle insights have contributed greatly to my understanding of Russia and its relations with the West. Sadly, Charles Dick, who mentored me in my early days at Sandhurst and read the full manuscript, did not live to see it published. His extraordinary knowledge of history helped me greatly during the drafting process and his shrewd comments on the text were immensely valuable.

I carried out the initial research for this book at NATO Defense College in Rome in the autumn of 2017 thanks to a visiting fellowship generously offered by its Research Division. I am grateful to all those at the College who made my stay so pleasant and productive.

I must also thank my editors at Manchester University Press, Tom Dark and Alun Richards, for making the production process so smooth and straightforward, and especially the series editor, Andrew Monaghan, for his cheerful encouragement and advice. My copy-editor Doreen Kruger made a daunting task appear easy.

My heartfelt thanks go to Suzy and Heidi for their understanding and company during the writing process that coincided with the first months of lockdown and other restrictions related to the COVID-19 pandemic in 2020. Over more than thirty years, Suzy has borne my interest in Germany and Russia with patience, fortitude and an abundance of good humour. Her eagle eye and grammatical rigour improved the draft manuscript enormously.

The book is dedicated to the memory of my late father William Lough (1914–2000), a brilliant linguist, who taught me German and helped me take my first steps in Russian. His knowledge of the literature of both countries and his descriptions of visiting Germany in the 1930s and the USSR in the late 1950s sparked my curiosity at a young age and inspired a passion.

Redbourn
July 2021

Introduction

Germany's relationship with Russia is the most important link between the western world and the largest country on the European continent. As the western-led global governance order established after 1945 continues to erode as part of a natural process of evolution, Germany's interests are increasingly in conflict with Russia's goals to re-balance the international system and renegotiate Europe's security arrangements agreed at the end of the Cold War. As Europe's reluctant 'indispensable power', Germany finds itself increasingly responsible for shaping western policy towards Russia as America reduces its role in European affairs in a world in which the West has lost considerable moral authority over the past two decades. For a country that only regained full sovereignty in 1990 after forty-five years of post-war division, this is a hugely challenging task, one made much harder by its deep and troubled history with Russia.

Unlike Germany, Russia has not lost the art of strategic thinking. As a power that sits astride Europe and Asia, it has suffered for centuries from internal weakness related to its size and its economic backwardness. This has bred an impressive capability to harness its strengths and apply them to relations with its more powerful competitors. The Putin administration's success in recent years in deploying power in Ukraine, Syria and Libya reflects this tradition, as does its identification of divisions in western societies and its readiness to exploit them. These efforts have caught western countries off guard, creating confusion and muddled responses. Unconditional surrender and occupation in 1945 put an end to German strategic thinking and led to its outsourcing to Washington as the Federal Republic (FRG) took its place on the front line of Europe's defences against the Soviet bloc. This did not stop the FRG having policy goals, including reunification, but 'grand strategy' was not its domain. Not surprisingly, Germany is now struggling to adapt to the game that Russia is playing at the strategic level. For Germans, the spectacular end of the Cold War had promised a different era in which military force and the 'right of might' would be absent from European affairs in a concert of common values and interests.

Instead, Russia has used military force to change borders, and Europe now finds itself without a functioning arms control regime and with a severely impaired system of confidence-building measures to manage relations with Russia. The US withdrawal in 2019 from the treaty arrangements limiting the deployment of US and Russian intermediate-range nuclear forces in Europe in response to Russian violations was a further sign of the deterioration of the security order in Europe. At the same time, Germany has run down its armed forces since the end of the Cold War, leaving them improperly structured and embarrassingly ill-equipped to contribute fully to NATO's core task of collective defence. Lamenting Germany's current lack of a deterrent against countries such as Russia, the chairman of the Munich Security Conference Wolfgang Ischinger recently noted, 'We are the masters of soft power. But soft power without hard power is like a football team without a goalkeeper.'[1]

This book examines what lies behind the challenge facing Germany in formulating effective policy towards Russia. A complex mixture of cultural biases, instincts and sensitivities built up over centuries of involvement with Russia conditions the way Germans view the country and interact with it today. The traumatic experience of the twentieth century that involved two large-scale wars punctuated by collaboration as pariah states in Europe and forty-five years of Cold War confrontation with Germans on both sides of the dividing line have left a particularly deep mark on the German national psyche. A sense of guilt for Nazi crimes inflicted on the peoples of the USSR is ineradicable.

In contrast to the USA and even some of its European allies, Germany cares about Russia. History has given Germans an acute understanding of the importance of Europe's relationship with this vast country that is conflicted about its own identity and the extent to which it is European. Germany's largest bilateral embassy in the world is in Moscow with sizeable political and economic sections and a large military staff. It has over thirty-five accredited journalists in Moscow, many with considerable experience of the country.[2] The largest Goethe Institute in the world is in Moscow and the German Academic Exchange Service's largest support programme is focused on Russia.[3] Germany also has a fine tradition of academic scholarship on Russia. Yet for over twenty years, successive German governments conducted highly consistent but ineffective policies towards Moscow based on the belief that a combination of expanded economic relations and maximum possible dialogue with government and society would help guide Russia along a path of reform leading to its admission to the family of like-minded democratic European nations. Guided by wishful thinking, Germany closed its ears to the message from liberal-minded Russians and Central European governments among others, that Russia was heading in an entirely different direction far removed from the one it wished to see. In its stubborn quest for 'strategic partnership', Germany inadvertently ended up supporting the emergence of a Russian regime hostile to its interests and values. In other words, its policy did not just fail. It was counter-productive. It legitimised and reinforced a deeply corrupt and increasingly authoritarian and repressive Russian system, emboldening it to deploy force against its neighbours and to attack western institutions.

This is an unpleasant reality for German policymakers, businesspeople, civil society leaders and others who sincerely believed that by showing understanding for Russia and cultivating relations with it, they were acting in Germany's and Europe's best interests. Of course, Germany was not alone in misreading the development of Russia and facilitating the emergence of a system in Russia willing and able to confront the West. The UK, for example, has also been a significant enabler of today's Russian system by closing its eyes to the origins of Russian money flooding into London and by helping to integrate into the West members of the new Russian nobility who express anti-western positions at home. Similarly, US authorities ignored the rise of the Russian mafia in New York and its role in the extensive money-laundering operations of Russian organised crime. These oversights accelerated the criminalisation of the Russian state. The Obama administration's 'reset' policy towards Russia failed because it was based on a misreading of Russian interests and motivations. Several western governments also believed that in a 'post-modern world' their interests were ultimately convergent with Russia's and that Moscow believed the same. In their view, this meant that they should be able to reconcile differences with Russia. However, in Germany's case, its deep historical experience and knowledge of Russia and its plethora of carefully nurtured contacts across so many different sectors of Russian life should have made it obvious by the late 1990s that its approach was unrealistic and needed to change. Instead, Germany chose to remain in denial about the direction of Russia until the annexation of Crimea in 2014.

The premise of this book is that Russia in its current condition and configuration poses a serious threat to the stability of Europe. Russia's authoritarian system is weak at home and yet strong enough to be a revanchist power, one able to fill power vacuums created by the USA and its allies in Africa, the Middle East and parts of Central America. Turning its back on Europe, Russia has moved closer to China, apparently ready to accept being its junior partner in the absence of allies to counter-balance Chinese influence. The focus of Russia's leadership is on survival. It sees the restoration and upholding of Russia's international status as essential to the process of securing its rule, prioritising it over the need to equip Russia for a new economic and political age dominated by climate change, digitalisation and other disruptive forces. The rise of Asia, the disorientation of the USA and its allies as well as the tarnishing of western values and the fractures in western societies all offer short-term gains for a Russian leadership fearful of reform at home but confident of its strength abroad. This has encouraged an ill-conceived policy of aggression towards Ukraine that could easily have triggered a wider European conflict in 2014 when it annexed Crimea and deliberately destabilised south-eastern Ukraine. In the process, Russia has needlessly made an enemy of a people with which it shares a strong cultural affinity, consolidating Ukraine as a political nation that no longer sees its future in close alliance with Russia. The 'return' of Crimea to Russia is meagre compensation for forcing Ukraine on to a pro-western path of development and seriously aggravating relations with the EU and NATO. Moscow's flat-footed reaction to revolution in Belarus in the summer of 2020 pointed again to poor decision-making and limited crisis management capabilities. The Lukashenka regime had been living on borrowed time for years beforehand and danger was looming. Further misjudgements of this kind are likely to increase rather than decrease as the Russian system closes further in on itself in pursuit of greater resilience to outside threats.

With substantial foreign currency reserves, generously financed security forces, and no serious signs of dissension among the elite groups, the current Russian system does not face immediate threats to its viability. The revision of the Constitution in 2020 to allow Putin to serve two more terms has, for now, removed a large measure of uncertainty about what could happen after 2024 when his current term ends. Some parts of the economy such as agriculture, e-commerce and IT are developing fast and demonstrating considerable innovation. However, Russia's current leaders have neither the vision nor the ability to extend this isolated dynamism to the rest of the economy. Overall investment levels remain low, the country is losing ground technologically and its best brains continue to leave in search of better opportunities. The resemblance of Moscow and St Petersburg to modern European cities is Russia's latest Potemkin façade. Behind it, there still lies the same endlessly large, ramshackle country where many regions live in a different historical age with high levels of poverty, poor infrastructure and atrocious public health provision. The euphoria around the 'return' of Crimea that united the Russian public in 2014 and gave the Putin administration a much-needed popularity boost is now a distant memory. It will be hard to replicate a similar public mood over the coming years. Instead, Russia's poor economic performance looks set to continue amid general stagnation reminiscent of the USSR in the 1970s, as some of the system's key players, including Putin himself, increasingly sound old and out of date. The revolution in transportation that is beginning to gather pace around the world is a clear threat to Russia's hydrocarbon exports, which remain a mainstay of the economy. Consequently, Russia is likely to be increasingly vulnerable to shocks. Its hollow political institutions offer no cushion. Change may come suddenly, uncontrollably and violently, with unpredictable consequences for the 'shared neighbourhood' between Europe and Russia, and for Europe itself.

Deeply shaken by Russia's annexation of Crimea, German policymakers are gradually waking up to this danger but struggling to develop mitigating policies. Germany does not just face a Russia challenge. It has a Russia problem of its own because of its difficulties in clearly seeing Russia's direction of development and drawing the correct conclusions. A vicious circle is at work since Germany's own Russia problem accentuates the challenge posed by Russia. This book seeks to explain how Germany's inherited historical experience and attitudes towards Russia have shaped its policy thinking since 1990 and continue to do so despite a sharp shift in response to Russia's actions in 2014. Russia casts a shadow over Europe that exposes Germany's historical complexes about it since Germans and Russians have a contradictory history going back centuries, one that has included peaceful interaction as well as extreme violence.

For over two centuries, Germans were insiders in Russia, unlike the British and the French. They were part of Russian life and culture.[4] This closeness no longer exists. However, the consciousness that it once did is still present on both sides. History has taught Germans to respect and fear Russia as a military power while admiring its culture and its people. At the same time, defeat by the Red Army in 1945 and the experience of the Cold War when communism posed an existential threat to the FRG have embedded a deep desire to achieve lasting reconciliation with Russia as it did with its western neighbours. After 1990, this aspiration translated into policy encouraging the use of carrots instead of sticks in response to bad Russian behaviour as Germany sought a 'peaceful order' *(Friedensordnung)* in Europe, one that included Russia. The instinct behind this behaviour is still alive today. It tells Germans to avoid confrontation with Russia because of the danger of war and to seek where possible to accommodate its interests. The roots of this thinking go deep into history. German commentators regularly quote the words attributed to Wilhelm 1, King of Prussia (1861–71) and Kaiser (1871–88) who built up a formidable army but avoided initiating war. He famously warned that 'friendship and harmony should be sought with the Russian Tsar'. The risks from doing otherwise were great, he said, and 'nothing was to be gained' from them. At the same time, he noted that 'one should not trust the Russians too much'.[5]

For German policymakers today, Russia's readiness to have an adversarial political relationship with Germany and disrupt its alliances while continuing to sell it gas and buy its goods is disturbingly counter-intuitive. To them, it makes no sense for Russia to turn away from Europe and sacrifice a relationship with Germany that brought it clear advantages in the past. After all, Germany lobbied for the G7 to expand to include Russia. It consistently went the extra mile in both the EU and NATO to encourage its allies to show sensitivity to Russia. For example, it played a key role in 2008 in blocking the US proposal in NATO to give Membership Action Plans to Georgia and Ukraine. It also took on the burden of justifying the Nord Stream pipelines designed to bring gas directly from Russia to Europe. Moscow's apparent indifference to damaged relations is even more bewildering since Putin likes the country and takes a deep interest in it. Worse still, Russia is attacking Germany indirectly by fanning divisions within the EU and NATO and weakening its strategic anchors.

To explain Germany's default instincts in dealing with Russia requires examining the two countries' intense and dramatic history of relations. Chapter 1 provides an overview of this complex *Sonderbeziehung* (special relationship), outlining how ties between the countries were highly productive and mutually beneficial when their interests were aligned and disastrous when they were not. It explains the remarkable influence of Germans on Russia's cultural and economic development over the centuries, including the role of Germans in government. Catherine the Great's epic reign (1762–96) remains the finest example of this, despite her considerable efforts to distance herself from her German origins, but Germans were also instrumental over a far longer period in shaping Russia's education and healthcare systems as well as its army, not to mention its literature and philosophy. The rise of Prussia dramatically changed the political map of Europe and led to it joining Russia to partition Poland, a pattern of cooperation between Germans and Russia that re-emerged after the First World War and led to the Molotov-Ribbentrop Pact in 1939. The diabolical mutual attraction between Nazi Germany and the USSR inevitably resulted in confrontation between them, and on an unimaginable scale. Not surprisingly, Hitler's invasion of the

USSR and the Wehrmacht's catastrophic defeat by the Red Army continue to weigh particularly heavily on German thinking about Russia, as does the forgiveness shown by so many Russians to the German nation after the war. The post-war division of Germany and Germans' experience of being on the front line in the East–West conflict has left a deep mark of its own. For many Germans, there is a causal link between the role of *Ostpolitik* in reducing tensions in Europe and the eventual demise of the USSR. This explains in part the continuing German conviction that trade relations can serve as a lever to reduce tensions in relations with Russia and align interests.

Chapter 2 examines some of the main trends in German thinking about Russia over the centuries. Stereotypes matter because they reproduce themselves through generations and influence relations between states. A turbulent history has shaped conflicting views of Russians among Germans, contributing to the contradictory relationship between them. Germans have oscillated between viewing Russians as Asiatic and barbaric on one hand, and pure and unspoilt by western influence on the other. Similarly, Germans have thought of Russia as both uncultured and cultured, regressive and progressive and as a partner and an enemy. For a nation that prizes rationality, these irreconcilable views buried deep in the national psyche create discomfort when thinking about Russia. It is harder, therefore, for German policymakers than for their British or American counterparts, for example, to discuss how to live with a confrontational Russia when their instincts are to avoid confrontation. Germans lack the detachment of others who have been less intimately involved with Russia and have not experienced a romantic fixation with it. As part of their historical conditioning, Germans have an emotional connection with Russia, one that can easily obstruct clear thinking about it. It is perhaps ironic that in Russia, Germans have a reputation for being logical thinkers and lacking emotion. In this respect, the issue of Russia is one of Germany's weak points.

Chapter 3 looks at the impact of Germany's reunification on views of Russia. It explains how this miraculous outcome occurred more by chance than because of a conscious policy of benevolence on the part of Moscow towards Germans. Reunification is associated with a time when it seemed that a united Germany was fully reconciled with both its western and eastern neighbours and at peace with Russia. This was a luxury version of Mikhail Gorbachev's 'Common European Home' that included the unexpected addition of NATO membership for the whole of Germany. In historical terms, it was the shortest of unsustainable moments when the USSR was in retreat, close to unravelling and ready to make sacrifices in relations with the West to gain time. This was Russia's second Brest-Litovsk of the twentieth century. Consequently, Germans' gratitude to Moscow for reunification, while understandable, is exaggerated. Gorbachev's decision to allow the USSR's satellites to go their own way had made the process unstoppable. Germany's good fortune lay in the fact that the speed of events outstripped Moscow's ability to keep up and excluded the possibility to use force to save the country at least temporarily. In addition, Gorbachev accepted the western arguments that it made sense to integrate a united Germany into NATO and imposed his view on the Politburo. Even if Russia's current leaders would not have followed the same logic and despise Gorbachev for allowing the USSR to disintegrate, they are still happy for Germany to feel a sense of obligation towards Moscow for making reunification possible. The emotions associated with the issue form another part of Germans' historical conditioning and provide a pressure point for Russia in its dealings with Germany.

Chapter 4 surveys Germany's Russia policy from 1990 to 2014 and shows how successive governments stuck to the idea that Russia was a partner in Europe and were prepared to disregard its backtracking on democracy and its violation of human rights and tolerate the development of a form of capitalism incompatible with rule of law. A key measure of Russia's progress was the growth of trade with Germany. Berlin continued to believe that economic development would promote good governance and rule of law as though Russia could fall back on an earlier legal culture as Germany had done after 1945. The election of a German-speaking president in 2000 seduced Berlin into believing that relations could not be better. It shut its eyes to the Kremlin's closure of privately owned media, its progressive stifling of political opposition and civil society and its subversion of the country's legal system to consolidate power and facilitate self-enrichment. At the same time, German policymakers failed to heed the warning signs as high commodity prices injected adrenalin into the Russian system, stimulating it to begin challenging western policy and propose renegotiating the principles of European security agreed at the end of the Cold War. Berlin also failed to see that the EU posed a challenge to Russia in the 'shared neighbourhood', setting the scene for the dramatic breakdown of relations over Ukraine in early 2014.

Chapter 5 analyses Angela Merkel's re-calibration of policy towards Russia in response to Russia's actions in Ukraine. With limited support from the Obama administration, Germany showed impressive leadership in the EU by achieving consensus on the need for strong political support for Ukraine and economic sanctions against Russia. The abandonment of previous orthodoxies in dealing with Russia was shocking to many *Ostpolitik* generation practitioners but received surprisingly broad public backing, including from business. German policymakers cleverly fashioned an EU policy towards Russia, invoking the spirit of NATO's Harmel doctrine of the 1960s that combined dialogue and deterrence and was a precursor to détente. For presentational purposes, this was important. It helped secure acceptance of the policy change in both Germany and other EU countries that had reservations about sanctioning Moscow. It suggested that Europe was not in full-scale confrontation with Moscow and was in fact keen to avoid such an outcome.

This mixed signal could not disguise the fact that Germany was starting to emerge from its two decades of conscious denial about the direction of Russia. It was now beginning to face up to the real version of Russia rather than the one it wanted to see. However, its limitations were also on show. German efforts to negotiate a peace process in Ukraine achieved only the semblance of one. In practice, Russia did not see sufficient incentives to change its policy. Despite its firm stance on sanctions, Germany showed that it had not given up on expanding energy relations with Russia. The government's support for the new Nord Stream pipeline designed to double the capacity of direct gas deliveries to Germany indicated that its new approach to Russia retained an important old element. This policy prioritised the interests of German industry in cheap gas supplies over the security interests of Ukraine, the prime loser from the diversion of gas through the new pipeline. It also ignored the EU's energy security strategy as well as the objections of its central European neighbours united in their vigorous opposition to the project. By doing so, Germany unwittingly became Moscow's accomplice in placing additional pressure on Ukraine and undermined the credibility of the EU's and NATO's resolve to resist it.

Chapter 6 reviews the economic relationship between Germany and Russia and demonstrates that even before EU sanctions in 2014, it was under-developed and far less important to German business than commonly assumed. It explains how the gas relationship has changed significantly in recent years because of the EU's success in forcing Gazprom to adapt to its regulatory framework. This was a major irritant in the EU's relations with Russia and contributed to the breakdown of relations over Ukraine. For all Germany's fine words about increased trade helping to promote good governance in Russia, in some cases major German businesses engaged in systematic corruption in Russia. Such double standards have been a gift to Russia's leaders, reinforcing their view that western values are not for real and that German business is prepared to compromise them if the price is right. Beyond the gas relationship that is set to decline over time, the false notion that the Russian market is a major destination for German exports strongly influences views of how to manage relations with Moscow.

Chapter 7 discusses the little-researched issue of Russian influence in Germany. The country has long been the target of Russian 'soft' power operations and espionage but since 2014, it has experienced the use of some new 'harder' instruments of influence, including disinformation and cyberattacks. For now, Russia appears content with its level of 'soft' power penetration. German discussion of the subject has paid little attention to Russian influence through well-established networks in the mainstream political parties as well as business. Not surprisingly, the issue is extremely sensitive and Germany's intelligence agencies do not openly discuss it. The left-wing party Die Linke, with its roots in the former GDR holds some positions on Russia close to those of the far right Alternative für Deutschland. Together, the two parties' different ideological sympathies with Russia provide an important additional form of influence in Germany focused on the large Russian German community. For now, Russia has used disinformation tactics only sparingly. Cyberattacks on the government and the Parliament have shown Moscow's capabilities in this area. However, its decision not to deploy stolen data in the 2017 federal election suggested that it viewed its existing level of influence as sufficient and did not see the need to interfere in the election process, as it had in France, the UK and the USA.

Chapter 8 considers the outlook for Germany's handling of relations with Russia against the background of Russia's likely development as well as the factors influencing its view of Russia and the instruments it has available to counter undesirable Russian behaviour. It is essential that it invests more in defence after more than twenty-five years of reaping a 'peace dividend'. Germany's thinking about the current Russian system is gradually evolving as it confronts more evidence of its criminal nature and practices, a process accelerated by the poisoning of the opposition politician

Alexei Navalny with Novichok in the summer of 2020. However, it is not clear to what extent Berlin is ready to change its approach and create greater capacity to deter and resist Russian pressure.

The concluding chapter argues that to manage the challenge posed by Russia, Germany must rediscover the ability to design strategy. To do so, policymakers must define policy goals based on interests not emotions.

The central argument of this book is that the complex psychological inheritance of its history with Russia is key to understanding how Germany conducts its Russia policy today. Interestingly, the subject has not attracted attention as an area of research in either Germany or Russia or any other country, possibly because it requires an approach beyond the confines of traditional academic scholarship that weaves together the different disciplines of history, culture and contemporary foreign policy. It is perhaps easier for an outsider with knowledge of both countries to take the plunge and offer a view. The motivation behind the book is to encourage German policymakers to examine their own instincts towards Russia and question some of their policy judgements. What felt to Germans like the right approach after 1990 quickly turned out to be flawed, and still it remained in place for another two decades. Germany's admirable achievements in building such extensive links with Russia in so many areas of Russian life were not enough to stop Russia turning against Europe and estranging itself from Germany. The much-trumpeted economic relationship, including increased purchases of gas, did not help either. Efforts to integrate Russia into Europe backed by Germany's distinctive brand of 'soft' power were insufficient.

Understanding Germany's vulnerabilities as well as its strengths in dealing with Russia is an essential step to increasing Europe's resilience against Russia's efforts to divide and disrupt it, and, by extension, to encouraging Russia's future leaders to put the country back on a reform track.

1

The weight of history

Commonalities, complementarity, connectivity

No other foreign country can match the depth of Germany's historical interaction with Russia. The Swedes, the English, the French and even the Scots have all left their mark on Russia, but to nothing like the same extent as the Germans. Beginning in the seventeenth century up to the start of the First World War, Germans played a key role in Russia's state administration and made extraordinary contributions to the development of its economy, science, education and military system. Until the catastrophes of the twentieth century, the overall relationship between Germans and Russians was, for the most part, peaceful and mutually beneficial. It demonstrated an unusual degree of complementarity between neighbouring peoples shaped by fundamentally different historical forces. Germans have left an indelible imprint on the Russian mindset and language while German culture has played an unparalleled role in contributing to Russia's sense of European identity and vocation. At the same time, Germany's deep connection with Russia has shaped Germans' sense of who they are as a people and where they belong in Europe. In short, this relationship has deep and complicated roots that make it special for both countries.

Etched into the popular Russian memory over centuries are images of Germans as a foreign people who were different from

Russians. Немец (nemets), the Russian word for a German, appears to come from немой meaning dumb, and may have originally referred to all Northern Europeans who first came into contact with Russians. The same word exists in almost all other Slavonic languages suggesting that Germanic peoples were among the first to interact regularly with Slavs. To the Russians they encountered, Germans became known as people who smelt because they smoked tobacco. They were capable and punctual but also rational and pedantic. They ate meat in large quantities but were miserly. They paraded their superiority and spoke Russian badly. Yet even if they found few friends and were the butt of jokes, they were valued. As the Russian proverb notes, 'the German has a tool for everything'. Other sayings include: 'The German gets to the result by reasoning – the Russian using their eyes (i.e., by copying)' and 'A fox is cunning – but a German more so'.

For all these positive qualities, there were deficiencies too. The historian and statesman Alexander Turgenev (1784–1845), a life-long admirer of German culture, expressed frustration at the difference in character between Germans and Russians: 'somehow the Germans do not have a heart ... they are cold and without feeling'.[1] This perception of Germans in Russia persists to this day, perhaps magnified by the enthusiasm expressed by Germans beginning in the nineteenth century for the 'Russian soul' and the image cultivated by Tolstoy and others of the childlike simplicity, kindness and generosity of the Russian peasant. For an outside observer, it can be tempting to conclude that because they are so different, Russians and Germans see in each other qualities that they lack in themselves.

Commonalities have reinforced complementarity. In addition to their close interaction, Germans and Russians share the historical experience of the struggle to protect themselves and find their balance between East and West in the absence of clear geographical borders. In both cases, the absence of natural defences created vulnerability to invasion by external powers during periods of weakness. Russia's Time of Troubles in the early seventeenth century and the extreme devastation experienced by the German lands in the Thirty Years War (1618–48) are examples that had a profound influence on the history of each country. The East–West dichotomy is a staple theme of Russian history exemplified by the nineteenth century dispute between Slavophiles and Westernisers about Russia's identity and the most suitable model for its development. In Germany's case, the issue was how to reconcile the conservative instincts of the ruling class in Prussia gained from their historical experience of looking east with the influence of enlightenment ideas from the West. The 1848 revolution and the failure of the Frankfurt Parliament marked the collision of these two forces. Prussia and Russia shared a common allergy to the 'revolutionary disease' and took steps to suppress its spread. Their systems of government and bureaucratic cultures bore considerable similarities up to the mid-nineteenth century. Prussian military organisation has left a particularly strong mark. The goose-step still practised in the Russian Army today originated in Prussia in the eighteenth century. By contrast, the *Pickelhaube*, the pickaxe helmet that became a defining feature of the German army in the early years of the First World War was a Prussian import from Russia.

The intimacy of cultural contacts is a striking example of the successful complementarity in relations between the two countries, and a further indicator to Germans, as they view Russia today, that the relationship between the countries is special. In art, music, literature and philosophy, there has been unrivalled exchange and cross-fertilisation. Paradoxically, the 'Russian soul' so admired by German writers and philosophers in the early twentieth century owes its origins in Russia to the export of German cultural romanticism by the philosopher Friedrich Wilhelm Joseph von Schelling whose works exercised a deep influence on the philosophical debate in Russia for generations.[2] Romantic nationalists in Russia took inspiration from German ideas of defending the ancient community (*Gemeinschaft*) against the new society (*Gesellschaft*) possibly because they too feared the social consequences of industrialisation. Both Germany and Russia were laggards in this process at the time. The works of Goethe, Hegel, Heine and Schiller had enormous impact on the development of Russian intellectual thought, not to mention Marx and his contribution to a Russian brand of communism.

Another revealing indicator of the close cultural connectivity and mutual understanding that has existed between Germans and Russians is the appeal to both of the literary double, or doppelgänger. The German writer E. T. A. Hoffmann (1776–1822) was among the first to use the traditional doppelgänger motif in the novel form of a character questioning his or her own identity rather than the traditional case of mistaken identity. The split personality double would later appear in the form of Raskolnikov in Dostoevsky's *Crime and Punishment* (1866). Hoffmann's works that contrasted dream and reality also influenced the writings of Chekhov and Gogol[3] and, through them, later generations of authors.

German influence on the Russian language is also particularly striking. Hundreds of German loan words are still in everyday use. Бинт (Binde/bandage), бутерброд (Butterbrot/sandwich, галстук (Halstuch/tie), шахта (Schacht/mine, штраф (Strafe/fine), шприц (Spritze/injection), штука (Stück/piece), штурман (Steurmann/navigator and цейтнот (Zeitnot/lack of time) are notable examples. Even the word for French (французский) has a German root. A German researcher has detected nearly 195 German words in current use in the language of the Russian mining sector.[4] Peter the Great's visits to German mines during his travels in 1711–12 prompted the recruitment of German mining specialists to work in Russia. In addition, bureaucratic Russian shares many features of its German equivalent with its long sentences and impersonal constructions, which often create a similarly peremptory tone. Despite differences of word order, both languages often translate well into the other helped by their similarities. The Russian German Jakob Karlovich Grot who taught Tsar Nicholas II Russian and German compiled the first Russian academic dictionary and is regarded as the father of Russian grammar.

The mark left by Germans on such wide areas of Russian life is testimony to an astonishing achievement of soft power not diminished by Hitler's invasion of the USSR. Erich Maria Remarque's novel *Drei Kameraden* (*Three Comrades*) first published in 1936 was very widely read in the USSR in translation in the late 1950s. At the same time, West German writers such as Heinrich Böll, Günter Grass and Siegfried Lenz also became widely available in translation. The Soviet authorities looked favourably on them because they criticised social conditions in West Germany. Böll's novella *Das Brot der frühen Jahre* (*The Bread of Those Early Years*) enjoyed huge popularity among a Soviet readership because of the perceived resemblance of the characterisation of its hero to the style of Dostoevsky.

These connections are the result of close contact between Germans and Russians over centuries. The pattern has been remarkably consistent. Germans have transferred culture, knowledge, skills and technology, contributing significantly to the Europeanisation of Russia. Their openness to Russian culture and its influence on them has been a major factor in persuading Germans that Russia is a European country that straddles both Europe and Asia. Germany's sense of discomfort today at Russia's turn towards China at the expense of Europe reflects a deep-seated conviction built up over hundreds of years that there is natural complementarity between Germany and Russia and their relationship is a defining feature of Europe, one that is vital to its completeness and its overall stability.

For example, Rüdiger von Fritsch, Germany's highly regarded ambassador to Russia from 2014 to 2019, has described how his work in Moscow was guided by the principle that there is no alternative to good relations between Germany and Russia.[5] For non-Germans, particularly Russia's close neighbours, this is a troubling assumption. After all, good relations between Berlin and Moscow in 1939 brought about the partition of Poland between them and assigned the Baltic states, Finland and Romania to a Soviet sphere of influence. In any case, Germany's relations deteriorated sharply with Russia in 2014 after Russia's aggression against Ukraine, showing that there was indeed an alternative. Germany could not have good relations with a country that in its view had committed a serious violation of international law and undermined the basis of European security. Furthermore, the quality of relations is a measure of the extent to which diplomats can align interests and cannot be reduced to a principle. However, placed in a historical context, von Fritsch's argument is explicable to Germans. The need for harmonious ties is a product of Germany's experience of dealing with Russia at close quarters over centuries and signals an awareness that the relationship is fragile and misalignments potentially perilous.

The tumultuous events of the twentieth century in Germany's relations with Russia continue to exert great influence on German thinking today about Russia because of their extreme contradictions and their legacy of violence. However, the preceding centuries of largely peaceful contact between Germans and Russian make the tragedies of their twentieth-century experience even more remarkable and are vital to understanding Germany's instinctive efforts to pursue mutually beneficial ties with Russia.

The role of Germans in Muscovy and the early Russian Empire

Austria and its history of ties with Russia aside, it was not until the rise of Prussia as a major power in the mid-eighteenth century that interstate relations between Germans and Russians became a factor in European diplomacy. By contrast, as a significant maritime power, England, for example, established close ties with

Russia as early as the 1550s when Ivan the Terrible sought a military alliance with Elizabeth I. The first indication of Prussia's significance as a player in Europe was during the Seven Years War (1756–63) when Prussian and Russian interests briefly came into conflict. In 1772, they coincided in the first partition of Poland. Before the emergence of Prussia, Germans had traded with the Russian lands through the Hanseatic League and over time, they increasingly migrated to Russia to fill skills shortages. This practice started in the mid-sixteenth century and lasted over three hundred years.

Ivan the Terrible relied on a German military engineer to blow up the heavily defended fortress of Kazan[6] that led to its capture in 1552. His capture of Livonia in 1558 led to Livonian Germans entering the service of the Tsar and settling in Moscow. These Baltic German nobles were descendants of the Teutonic Knights who had started their colonisation of the region in the twelfth century. Boris Godunov (ruled 1598–1605) was the first Russian ruler to recruit Germans from the German lands. His emissaries travelled to the old Hanse city of Lübeck to recruit doctors, metalworking specialists, cloth makers and other artisans to settle in Russia. Godunov himself had six highly paid German doctors.[7]

The Romanovs' successful claim to the throne in 1612 led to three centuries of pronounced German influence in Russia. The 'German' suburb of Moscow established a century earlier expanded after 1650. Peter the Great (ruled 1696–1725) was a frequent visitor in his formative years, allegedly to meet with the daughter of a German jeweller.[8] After defeat against the Swedes at Narva in 1700, Peter began his first recruitment campaign for foreign specialists to assist in the overhaul of the armed forces and the Russian state. His closest adviser in the process was a Baltic German nobleman.[9] Germans were prominent among the first foreigners to come to Russia to take up Peter's offer and included ship carpenters, engineers, metalworking specialists, sail makers and others. German mining specialists were particularly sought after. German doctors and apothecaries made a name for themselves as part of Peter's effort to improve the health of naval personnel. German educational specialists played an important role in developing the school system. In 1703, a Latin School opened in Moscow under the direction of two Germans. This was the prelude to the establishment of an Academy of Sciences in 1724. German scholars again played a leading role in its work in return for generous salaries and subsidised living expenses.[10] The German presence at senior levels in the government and the army became particularly strong towards the end of Peter's rule. Germans too were involved in the construction of the Winter Palace and the Peterhof Palace in St Petersburg. As in Moscow, a German suburb took shape in the new capital.

From 1710, Peter instituted a marriage policy that would establish dynastic links between Russia and the German principalities up to the Bolshevik Revolution. For his nieces and children, he chose only connections with the houses of the German princes since the Catholic Habsburgs would not convert to Orthodoxy. With the marriages to Germans came retinues of personal tutors, doctors and service personnel that expanded the German presence at the Court. With his conquests of the Baltic provinces beginning in 1704, Peter brought Baltic Germans under the Russian Crown. The Baltic German elites were well educated and, in many cases, quickly made successful careers often as officials in St Petersburg. Over the next 200 years, they and their descendants would go on to play a particularly influential role in Russia's administration and the army.

Aged 15, Sophie Auguste Friederike, Princess of Anhalt-Zerbst, smelled power and chose to marry Peter III. She would become Catherine the Great (ruled 1762–96), and has been widely regarded as one of Russia's greatest leaders. Following Peter the Great's example, she summoned foreigners to Russia to assist in the process of modernising Russia and expanding its power, offering them special status, including exemption from military and civil service as well as tax incentives. Many farmers and artisans came from the over-populated southwestern German lands or from Hesse that had suffered particularly during the Seven Years War.[11] They settled in the Volga region and later the newly acquired provinces of 'New Russia' after war with the Ottomans. After a slow start, the settlers successfully modernised agricultural practices and established communities that grew dramatically over the next century. Catherine also recruited doctors, scientists and military specialists from Germany. At the same time, she kept her distance from Prussia and the other German principalities and tried to dilute the influence of Germans at the Court. Her relations with Britain, for example, were much closer.

Alexander I (ruled 1801–25) understood the need to protect Russia's territorial acquisitions in the south by developing them economically with the help of foreigners. An edict in 1804 offered opportunities in Russia not just to farmers but also to a wide range of other professions, including tailors, cobblers, carpenters, blacksmiths, potters, weavers and masons.[12] The recruitment campaign proved successful in Germany. The economic presence of Germans in the cities increased notably and they began to assimilate. The routing of Napoleon's Grande Armée after its invasion of Russia in 1812 and the Russian army's role in Napoleon's defeat at Leipzig in 1813 brought Alexander prestige as the 'Saviour of Europe', not least in Prussia whose army had suffered a humiliating defeat by French forces at Jena in 1806.

The increasing role of Germans in the Russian state

Nicholas I (ruled 1825–55) was the product of a Prussian-Protestant upbringing, and a great admirer not just of the Prussian Court but also the Prussian army, in particular.[13] Under his rule, relations with Prussia became particularly close. By his brutal suppression of the Polish Uprising in 1830–31, he established a reputation as a supremely reactionary leader. He relied heavily on the advice of officials of German descent, especially the Baltic German, Count Benckendorff, who became head of the secret police. He and several other Russian Germans, including the Foreign Minister Nesselrode symbolised the highly repressive policies of Nicholas's reign. Officials of German origin became particularly prominent in the state bureaucracy and army. According to one calculation, they held 57 per cent of senior positions in the Foreign Ministry and 46 per cent in the War Ministry. Similarly, one third of officers in the army and navy had German heritage.[14] In parallel, the German communities in St Petersburg and Moscow were growing and becoming more prosperous. German doctors, mineralogists and pharmacists had formed their own associations.[15] In Moscow, some professions were mainly in German hands. In addition to doctors and chemists, these included bakers, cake makers and sausage makers.[16]

Parts of Russian society viewed the expanded influence of Germans with concern. From exile in Paris, the political philosopher Alexander Herzen, born of a German mother, railed against the repressive nature of Nicholas's rule and his reliance on 'Russified Germans' and 'Germanicised Russians'.[17] His criticism reflected a growing view by 1850 that Germans had created a state within a state[18] and presaged increasing unhappiness among pan-Slavists and nationalists who were deeply opposed to Prussia and Bismarck. They started to raise questions about whether the German settler communities had profited from the Crimean War by supplying food to the army. In the 1880s and 1890s, this would become the basis for accusing the Russian Germans of a lack of loyalty.[19] Paradoxically, Prussia's refusal to join the Anglo-French coalition in the Crimean War had prevented a crushing defeat of Russia.

Alexander II (ruled 1855–81) adored Prussia and Germany. He had received a strongly Prussia-orientated education[20] and married a German princess. Officials of German heritage would also play a major role during Alexander's reign: the Baltic German Ferdinand von Wrangel, the Minister of the Navy after the humiliation of the Crimean War, laid the foundations for naval reform. Count Sievers was one of the architects of general military conscription. Germans too were involved in developing the reform that led to the emancipation of the serfs.[21] The zemstvo, the new institution of local government, was strongly influenced by the experience of Prussian self-administration bodies. Many prominent writers of scientific literature and articles in quality newspapers during the reform years were of German origin[22] while many regional governors and vice-governors were also German Russians. Count Berg who had been instrumental in putting down the revolution in Hungary in 1849 was redeployed to Poland in 1863 to suppress the rebellion there.

Increased German economic presence

Siemens and Halske became the first major German company to establish a significant role in Russia. It was the beneficiary of a trade boycott by Britain and France since both were in dispute with Russia over its control of the Danubian principalities. The company received a contract in 1853 to build telegraph lines to improve the Empire's communications as it expanded its power to the south-west. By 1855, it had installed 9000 km of lines – just in time for the new system to report the loss of Sevastopol.[23]

The 1860s marked a fresh attempt to attract foreigners to settle in Russia to support the growth of domestic industry. Many German businesspeople and manual workers took up the offer. The St Petersburg Industrial Exhibition in 1870 provided evidence of the strong presence of German Russian companies in the fast-expanding economy. For example, German Russians owned 14 out of 37 of the best-known wool-spinning plants.[24] Four out of six of the major cement factories had German Russian owners,[25] and among the 127 largest mechanical- and machine-building factories, at least 47 were German.[26] Meanwhile, the numbers of

German settlers in the Ukrainian lands were growing rapidly. They would reach 400,000 by the end of the century.

Bismarck and Russia

Germany's unification under Prussian leadership dramatically changed the political map of Europe. It created increasing tensions that personal links between Kaiser and Tsar could no longer manage on their own. Otto von Bismarck, the 'Iron Chancellor' of the German Empire (1871–90), knew Russia well having served there as Prussian ambassador in the early 1860s. King Friedrich Wilhelm IV sent him there to take a proper look at Russia and assess its suitability as a military ally.[27] Bismarck learned Russian and quickly saw that the country was undergoing deep change and that the unassailable authority of the Tsar and the traditionally pro-Prussian position of the Romanovs faced internal challenge. He singled out Foreign Minister Gorchakov as an influential player who did not share the Kaiser's pro-German sympathies and was prepared to deal with France. He regarded him as his mentor in diplomacy.[28]

Russia's humiliation at the Congress of Berlin in 1878 when Bismarck accommodated British interests by denying Russia the opportunity to expand its naval power fuelled growing anti-German sentiment at home. In vain, Alexander surrounded himself with conservative loyalists of German origin as the terrorist threat grew. This only fuelled resentment among the intelligentsia. After Alexander's assassination in 1881, Bismarck noted that Russia's acquiescence in Germany's annexation of Alsace-Lorraine in 1871 was the personal decision of Alexander, contrary to the pro-France sympathies of Russian society.[29] At the end of the Franco-Prussian War, the Kaiser had written an emotional note to the Tsar professing lifelong gratitude for not contesting the annexation.[30]

By this time, Bismarck had long since formed the view that revolution in Russia was on the horizon. Although he adopted harsh banking sanctions against Russia in late 1887 in a dispute over customs tariffs, his policy towards Russia was generally cautious. He avoided being drawn into the controversy in Russia around the status of Baltic Germans and later the settlers in western Russia. The pan-Slavists had started to bang the nationalist drum and whipped up anti-German sentiment. He also famously saw the dangers of war with Russia because of its climate and the ability of Russians to pull together. He remarked in his memoirs that a defeated Russia would be Germany's born enemy, and one in need of revenge.[31]

For all Bismarck's calmness and pragmatism in dealing with Russia, his record is more complicated than many German commentators today suggest. They tend to overlook his insensitivity towards Russia's wish to settle independently with Turkey at the end of the Russo-Turkish War as well as the cooling of his relationship with Gorchakov whom he treated brusquely at the Congress of Berlin in 1878. Bismarck also did not reciprocate Russia's readiness to allow Prussia to agree its own terms after defeating Austria-Hungary and France.

Growing tensions in relations

Alexander III (ruled 1881–94) did not share his father's enthusiasm for Prussia and disliked the influence of German Russians in the running of the state. His reign coincided with a marked rise in anti-German sentiment in Russian society, partly the result of Prussia's much increased power through the unification of Germany but also in response to the growing prosperity of the German communities in cities and the countryside. A media war broke out as German nationalists and pan-Slavists clashed over the place of Germans in the Russian Empire. Some nationalist circles in Germany had visions of the German settler communities in Russia as strategic bastions in a German empire that would stretch to Persia and India.[32] The pan-Slavists responded by directing their fire at the 'Germanisation' of Russia's western and southern provinces and the issue of land ownership. This coincided with a dramatic reorientation of Russia's diplomacy in Europe when it established a military convention with France in 1892 followed by a full alliance in 1894. Its purpose was to counter the Triple Alliance (Austria-Hungary, Germany and Italy) and prevent Germany from dominating Europe.

Under the reign of Nicholas II (1894–1917), relations between the Russian and German governments remained friendly until 1904–5 despite growing tensions in the Balkans and Germany's pursuit of a more aggressive foreign policy. Both sides were keen to avoid direct conflict. The Kaiser helped fuel the Russian fleet on its journey from the Baltic to Asia to fight Japan. His logic was that conflict between Britain and Russia in Asia could strengthen Germany's position in Europe. He also saw the possibility that defeat for Russia would break the Franco-Russian alliance. However, Nicholas's main foreign policy preoccupation was the expansion of Russia's position in Asia although he was deeply concerned about how the potential collapse of the Ottoman Empire might affect Russia's access to and from the Black Sea.

Meanwhile, trade boomed in both directions from the 1890s. Between 1892 and 1896, German exports to Russia almost doubled as heavy industry supported the rapid expansion of the Russian railway system. Imports from Russia more than doubled mainly because of increased demand for grain as Germany's population continued its remarkable growth. However, after the Russo-Japanese War, French, not German investment houses were Russia's main source of foreign loans although German exports to Russia were five times greater by 1903.[33] Berlin instructed a leading German banking group not to participate. This was an indication of Germany's increasing estrangement from Russia as differences over alliances increasingly came to the fore despite the friendly personal relationship between Nicholas and Wilhelm as third cousins.

A tragic symbol of the close ties between leaders amid fraying relationships between their states is the photograph of Nicholas and Wilhelm in Swinemünde in August 1907 observing joint naval manoeuvres: the Tsar is wearing a German naval uniform, the Kaiser a Russian uniform.[34] In 1913, there was still an eerie calm as the Romanovs celebrated 300 years of rule and Wilhelm marked twenty-five years on the throne. Both countries had shifted to rearmament and nationalist voices were becoming stronger. In Russia, a small group of radical socialists believed a future world war could bring about world revolution. In Germany, a second generation of 'All Germans' had come to the fore with visions of Germans displacing Slavs in European Russia and forcing them back behind the Urals.[35] A major collision of interests was in the making.

First World War and Revolution

When the First World War started, the worst fears of the pan-Slavs seemed to have materialised. They had predicted for decades that Germany's historical destiny would lead it to subjugate Russia. Naturally, Russian attention turned to Germans in Russia, in particular the Empress Alexandra Fedorovna. Born Princess Alix of Hesse-Darmstadt, she was in fact half-English, the granddaughter of Queen Victoria. As a Christian philanthropist, she made great efforts to care for the sick and later the war wounded, yet she never found favour in Russia. Her deep commitment to her adopted Orthodox faith did not overcome the perception that she was 'German'.

After the war began, the mood in Russia turned viciously anti-German. In May 1915, as German forces advanced further into Russian territory, crowds in Moscow went on the rampage for two days, looting German shops, businesses and houses.[36] The previous year had seen the wrecking of the German Embassy in St Petersburg, now bearing the de-Germanised name of Petrograd. Nevertheless, 300,000 German Russians served in the Russian

Army during the war and some 15–20 per cent of the General Staff and the officer corps were of German origin.[37] When Nicholas visited the front in 1914, four out of the 11 staff officers accompanying him were German Russians.[38] The German population in Russia had grown rapidly since the mid-1890s. By 1914, it had reached close to 2.5 million. Alongside the 600,000 Germans in the Volga region alone, there were over a million in the Black Sea region and Poland.[39]

German efforts to hasten Russia's defeat led to the fateful decision to facilitate Lenin's return by train from Switzerland to Russia via Germany and Sweden. The February Revolution had accelerated the loss of morale and discipline in the Russian Army as it too became afflicted by 'dual power'. Soldiers' committees sprang up alongside the traditional command structure. However, the 7,000,000-strong army did not disintegrate since the Provisional Government succeeded in broadcasting a message that soldiers needed to defend the Revolution and that peace would come later. To keep up the pressure, German strategists searched for a radical group that could create greater confusion in Petrograd. Their aim was 'a little inconclusive civil chaos' rather than revolution even if the Bolsheviks offered the enticing prospect of bringing Russia to its knees and incapacitating it over the long term.[40]

Despite Lenin's resistance to alliance with other groups, German negotiators decided that he was their best bet and eventually persuaded him that their intentions were genuine. There is no evidence that Lenin received direct German financial assistance but there can be little doubt that some of Berlin's extravagant support of a propaganda effort to unite the Russian underground helped the Bolsheviks among others. The October Revolution and Lenin's ruthless determination to sue for peace surpassed the expectations of the German officials who had designed the plan for his return. The Brest-Litovsk Treaty signed on 3 March 1918 ended Germany's war in the east on extraordinarily generous terms, as the Bolsheviks ceded 780,000 square kilometres of territory and 56 million people, around a third of the population of the Russian Empire.[41]

Meanwhile, Berlin had shown little interest in the fate of Germans living in Russia, starting with Princess Alix herself and her children. The government ignored requests to assist the Tsar's family, leaving them to an obvious fate in the hands of the Bolsheviks. The 165,000-strong German population in the Baltic provinces played a role in securing independence for the Baltic states in 1920 but, as in Bessarabia where Germans numbered around 80,000, found themselves marginalised and deprived of their formal social status. The 500,000 Germans living in Poland were beyond Moscow's reach after the war with Poland in 1920. This left 600,000 Germans in briefly independent Ukraine. German troops had entered Ukraine in spring 1918 and deployed along a line all the way from Volhynia in the west to Rostov in the east, bringing calm and order.[42] Their withdrawal in late 1918 led to civil war and left German settlers unprotected against the vicious attacks of Nestor Makhno's forces, who pillaged and destroyed entire German villages. There were 120,000 Germans living in the Caucasus, the majority in its northern areas. Like their neighbours in the Ukrainian lands, they found themselves in early 1918 part of a short-lived independence project. The Transcaucasian Federative Republic lasted until the Red Army restored Moscow's control three years later. German troops had even entered Tiflis in 1918 and stabilised the situation for the local German community.[43] The Volga Germans tried in vain to negotiate a special status with Stalin, the then Commissar for Nationality Affairs, but were rebuffed. He imposed loyal leaders tasked with rooting out class enemies among them. An 'autonomous' Volga German republic was established within the USSR in 1924 and lasted until 1941 when its population of 400,000 was exiled to Siberia and Central Asia after Hitler's invasion. An estimated 300–350,000 Germans in the USSR later died during the Bolsheviks' collectivisation[44] of agriculture while the Germans in cities, typically, first generation arrivals from before the war, suffered marginalisation and a loss of social status followed by exile in 1941.

Two outcasts find common cause

Lenin could separate his disdain for the Prussian Junkers and the German bourgeoisie from his admiration for German discipline and organisation that had enabled Germany's rapid industrialisation. He wanted the USSR to emulate these impressive results. He viewed Russia and Germany as 'two halves of socialism – next to each other like two chicks under the single shell of socialism'.[45] When his optimism about the prospects for a radical socialist revolution in Germany proved unfounded after the failure of the Spartacist Uprising and the demise of the short-lived Bavarian Soviet Republic in 1919, he saw the tactical need to cooperate with the Weimar Republic. Aside from the economic motivation, there was also a joint interest in contesting the terms of the Versailles peace treaty. Both countries opposed its resurrection of Poland, while it also imposed on Germany extensive disarmament obligations and crippling reparations. Russia did not participate in the treaty negotiations since it had concluded a separate peace agreement with Germany and withdrawn from the war. Germany was also not at the table.

The Rapallo Treaty signed between Germany and the USSR on 16 April 1922 on the margins of the 34-nation Genoa Conference undermined the possibility of the Western powers coopting Germany into an alliance against Russia. The US diplomat and historian George Kennan viewed the treaty as 'the embodiment of the profligate carelessness with which the Western democracies treated the moderate and well-meaning elements' in the German government.[46] A combination of a reparations bill beyond Germany's means and a decision by the League of Nations to maintain the industrial part of Silesia within Poland contributed to pushing Germany to conclude a treaty with the Bolsheviks.

Strongly opposed by France and Poland, this was the first major international agreement signed by Germany after the war and signified its emergence from humiliating isolation. It established full diplomatic relations with Soviet Russia and cancelled mutual claims. The German government was careful, however, not to be the first to recognise the Bolshevik regime. It still hoped to renegotiate the terms of Versailles. However, restoring economic relations held considerable attractions for the German side because of its acute economic problems.

Berlin's caution had not prevented the start of secret military cooperation with the Bolsheviks in 1921.[47] An agreement signed in August 1922 gave the Reichswehr access to training facilities in the USSR for its air and tank forces banned by Versailles.[48] In return, it provided training for the Red Army officer corps and access to German military industrial technology. An air base opened at Lipetsk in 1924, followed by a chemical warfare facility in Saratov in 1927–28 and a combat vehicle centre in Kazan in 1930. This cooperation was mutually productive and lasted until 1933 when Hitler came to power. It included joint work by German and Soviet specialists who together reverse engineered foreign military equipment and worked on the development of new weapons systems. Major German companies such as Albatros-Werke, Blohm & Voss, Krupp and Junkers were able to manufacture artillery, aircraft and even submarines on Soviet soil. General Heinz Guderian, a pioneer of tank warfare and Hitler's adviser on the Eastern Front, was one of the first graduates of the Kazan centre. The Lipetsk facility, memorably depicted in the recent German TV series *Babylon Berlin*, was vitally important for the development of the Luftwaffe, and according to one estimate, may have saved Hitler ten years in creating a modern air force.[49] Underpinning this military cooperation was a joint antipathy to the terms of Versailles in general, and to the independence of Poland in particular.

At a political level in Germany, fear and loathing of the Bolsheviks on the right coexisted with admiration for their cause on the left. This contributed to the splintering of the Social Democratic Party (SPD) and the subsequent rise of the German Communist Party (KPD). The Bolsheviks' achievements as a revolutionary force inspired admiration in none other than a young Josef Goebbels, later Hitler's long-standing Minister of Propaganda.

Contributing also to this contradictory background was the strong interest in parts of German industry in resuming trade relations that had flourished before the war. Between 1908 and 1913, exports to Russia had grown by a staggering 49 per cent, with imports up 34 per cent. Germany accounted for 47 per cent of Russia's overall imports.[50] During these years, AEG and Siemens, in particular, were profiting handsomely from electrification projects in Russia while heavy industry and the machine-building sector were also enjoying the boom. In the 1920s, some of the largest companies pushed hard to rebuild trade links with Russia. This together with the desire of part of the Reichswehr to build links with the Red Army provided an important impulse to pursue the Rapallo Treaty. However, developing trade proved harder than expected, not least because of the political situation in Germany, the threat hanging over the Ruhr as well as inflation. The Soviet government was also short of hard currency and forced to pay in grain. Nevertheless, in 1928, 30 per cent of German machine-building exports went to Russia.[51] As economic conditions in Germany worsened, the Soviet market was a lifesaver for parts of industry. In 1931, the USSR accounted for 53 per cent of German exports of metalworking machinery. That year, a German trade delegation visited the USSR and was amazed at the progress of industrialisation. In 1932, 75 per cent of exports of metalworking machinery went to the USSR, together with 54 per cent of pumps and 84 per cent of cranes.[52] The same year, the value of Germany's exports to the USSR was four times Britain's and fifteen times America's.[53] From 1923 to 1932, the USSR was Siemens largest export market.[54] However, after 1933, exports fell quickly as the Germany economy shifted to rearmament although German companies continued to export to the USSR up to the beginning of 1941.

The same companies that traded with Russia before 1914 were the ones that advocated re-establishing links after the revolution and succeeded in gaining state credits. Some recognised that by trading with the USSR they were strengthening the Soviet system. Others thought that continued trade would bring a lifting of the foreign trade monopoly and restoration of private property. Foreign Minister Stresemann argued that by trading with the USSR, Germany would keep it close to Europe and increase the chances of its evolution.[55] These arguments are strikingly similar to those of parts of the German industrial lobby and their political supporters after the imposition of EU sanctions against Russia in 2014.

Hitler and Stalin: fatal attraction

As Stalin and Hitler consolidated control at home, the inevitability of collision between the two regimes grew. Each was trying to position itself to take advantage of the delicate balance of power in Europe that was changing in response to their emergence as systems hostile to the West. Germany's non-aggression treaty signed with Poland in 1934 marked the start of a cat and mouse game by Hitler to expand German influence, short of provoking an alliance between the USSR and the Western powers. They were on opposing sides in the Spanish Civil War (1936–39) but did not come into direct conflict. As early as 1933, as Berlin stopped military cooperation with Moscow, the Red Army Commander, Mikhail Tukhachevsky, later purged by Stalin, had summed up the duality in the relationship between the Red Army and the Reichswehr. Noting the friendly relations between the two armies but the political differences between their countries, he warned the Reichswehr not to underestimate what the Red Army had learned and its ability to fight.[56] In 1937, Tukhachevsky, widely regarded as the Red Army's top thinker fell victim to an elaborate conspiracy dreamed up by Gestapo Director Reinhard Heydrich that used falsified documents to persuade Stalin that the Red Army leadership was planning a coup against him. An orgy of bloodletting followed that decimated the Red Army officer corps. Awaiting trial and execution, Tukhachevsky worked on a military strategy, allegedly noting that Hitler would attack the Soviet Union 'in spring 1941 with up to 200 divisions'.[57]

Even if they ultimately misread the other's immediate intentions, the personal chemistry between Hitler and Stalin was remarkable. Each admired the other's ruthless consolidation of power. Stalin praised Hitler's murderous purge of his enemies during the Night of the Long Knives in 1934, calling his actions 'very correct and far-sighted'.[58] *Mein Kampf* was required reading for the Politburo not just for the purposes of knowing an enemy.[59] Stalin had effectively helped Hitler to power by designating the Social Democrats as the German Communists' main enemy and not Hitler. For his part, Hitler expressed admiration for Stalin's economic policy, praising it for its lack of 'humanitarian fuzziness'.[60] He called Stalin 'a guy of genius' because of 'his ability to deploy human labour in an astonishing way'.[61] It was hardly surprising that two authoritarian regimes studied each other's tactics and learned from the other's experience. Hitler's demonstration of how it was possible to purge enemies without consequences from abroad may well have encouraged Stalin in his bloodletting. The murder of Stalin's rival Sergei Kirov in December 1934 marked the start of a process that culminated in the Great Terror of 1936–38. German Communists who had fled the Nazis were among the victims. The Soviet authorities killed more members of the Politburo of the KPD than the Nazis, with only a third of the party's leading figures who took refuge in the USSR avoiding execution or death in the Gulag.[62] In 1939–40, the NKVD handed over 800 Austrian and German Communists to the Gestapo.[63] Margarete Buber-Neumann, wife of a prominent German Communist executed during the Purges, went from the Gulag to a Nazi concentration camp where she spent five years. She concluded that the philosophies that created the two systems were the same.[64]

For all their ideological and cultural differences, the German and Soviet dictatorships shared an affinity and a common language. This was clear during the remarkably rapid negotiation of the Molotov-Ribbentrop Pact, the non-aggression and friendship agreement concluded in August 1939 that also contained a secret protocol dividing Poland between Germany and the USSR. Both Hitler and Stalin held professional diplomats in contempt and had appointed foreign ministers who had no background in traditional diplomacy and flouted its norms. Ahead of the negotiations, the Germans sent signals that they were intent on concluding an agreement quickly and a personal telegram from Hitler to Stalin ensured that Stalin received the German delegation on arrival. According to Count von der Schulenburg, the German ambassador at the time, Stalin had never participated in negotiations and avoided contact with foreigners.[65] It took just three hours to agree terms.[66] To celebrate the signing of the agreement, Stalin toasted Hitler's health. Foreign Minister Ribbentrop later remarked that, in the Kremlin, he had felt as if he had been together with 'old national-socialist party comrades'.[67] Of course, both parties understood that the pact was a strictly tactical alliance ahead of inevitable conflict between the two. The logic of Germany's development under Hitler was eastward expansion of the Reich to provide natural resources and *Lebensraum*. Stalin's error was to assume that it offered him a longer breathing space. He had hoped that by averting a German–Soviet war, Hitler's armies would turn to France and meet greater resistance than they did.

Nazi Germany had proved that it was in a class of its own in its dealings with the USSR. No other country in Europe had relations of this depth and intensity with the USSR, increasingly feared not just because of its hostility towards western democratic systems but also because of its readiness to kill its own people. Even if reports of artificial famine in Soviet Ukraine had met with initial disbelief abroad, the Purges and the show trials simply underlined the determination of the Soviet leadership to consolidate its rule with total disregard for the human cost and their standing in the world.

Crimes in common in Poland

To his dying day in 1986, Foreign Minister Molotov denied the existence of the secret protocol. The Soviet authorities finally admitted its existence fifty years after its signature. The debate as to why Stalin chose to enter a pact with Hitler continues to this day. In December 2019 at a meeting of leaders of the Commonwealth of Independent States, an irate President Putin launched into a televised diatribe against Poland and its pre-war western allies in response to a European Parliament resolution passed months earlier. The resolution blamed 'the two totalitarian regimes' for concluding an agreement that 'paved the way for the outbreak of the Second World War'.[68] Putin argued that the Polish government had conspired with Hitler to dismember Czechoslovakia and that through their joint inaction, epitomised by Britain's appeasement policy, the Western powers had not just left the USSR exposed – forcing Stalin to agree terms with Hitler – but also made war inevitable.[69] He could have added that the new partition line in Poland largely followed the Curzon Line first proposed by Britain as Poland's eastern border at the end of the First World War.

Of course, Putin did not discuss the USSR's actions in Poland, and later the Baltic states, Bessarabia and Finland when Stalin took Hitler's invasion of Poland as a cue to lay claim to reconquer more of the territory ceded at Brest-Litovsk. Nor did he refer to the joint victory parade held by the invading German and Soviet forces in Brest-Litovsk on 22 September 1939, an event airbrushed out of history by the latest Russian official accounts.

The two invaders used disturbingly similar approaches to subdue their respective Polish conquests. The Gestapo and NKVD set to work to 'decapitate' Polish society, arresting, deporting and murdering the elements considered capable of resisting German rule. For the Germans in one half of Poland, it was the intellectual classes as well as the Jews; for the Soviet authorities in the other half, it was the class enemy. Hitler viewed the destruction of the 'upper levels' of a nation as a pre-condition for its enslavement. His racist policies aimed to extinguish Polish culture and replace it with superior *Germanentum* as part of his mission to establish an expanded 'German state of the German nation'. This made the Polish intelligentsia the top target.

As allies between September 1939 and June 1941, the German and Soviet authorities together killed an estimated 200,000 Polish citizens and deported a million. Gestapo contacts with the NKVD had preceded the signing of the Molotov-Ribbentrop Pact and they continued after the division of Poland. Four conferences took place between September 1939 and March 1940 to discuss issues of Polish resistance, but no historical evidence of direct coordination of operations has surfaced. The NKVD was better at keeping its operations secret. It killed over 21,000 members of the Polish officer corps and deported their families to inhospitable locations in Soviet Central Asia. Stalin's executioners used German-made pistols. During the Second World War when evidence of the murders at Katyn first came to light, the Soviet authorities blamed the deaths on the Germans. Subsequent investigations showed that the Germans could not have been responsible since the territory was not under their control at the time. The USSR never acknowledged its responsibility. In 1992, Moscow finally admitted that the Soviet authorities carried out the killings. In a macabre touch, Stalin had replied to an effusive telegram from Hitler expressing birthday wishes in December 1939 by noting that 'the friendship between the peoples of the Soviet Union and Germany, cemented in blood, has every reason to be solid and lasting'.[70]

Warning signs ignored by Stalin

Stalin and Hitler were both playing a tactical game to alter the balance of power in Europe to their advantage. Stalin was well aware of Hitler's views of Bolshevism and the USSR expressed in *Mein Kampf* and re-confirmed after 1933. Both leaders had been too busy with other issues in the mid-1930s to pay the other much attention although the warning signs of conflict were present. Germany and Japan had left the League of Nations. With their departure, the USSR performed an about turn and joined the organisation in 1934 that it previously denounced as pursuing 'imperialist' policy. It was expelled in 1939 after it attacked Finland.

While Hitler was re-arming and preparing the remilitarisation of the Rhine, Stalin was distracted by the danger of an internal power struggle that climaxed with the Purges in 1937–38. This was against a background of Hitler's speeches mentioning German plans to take control of the natural resources of Ukraine, the Urals and Siberia, perhaps part of a manoeuvre to signal to Britain and France that Germany's goals were to the East.[71] If he saw conflict coming as he later contended, Stalin did not see it on the immediate horizon. Instead, he made sure that the USSR kept Germany supplied with vital materials that helped sustain its war effort on the Western Front. In 1940, 52 per cent of the USSR's exports went to Germany, including 75 per cent of its oil exports and 77 per cent of its grain exports. From 1940 up to 22 June 1941, 72 per cent of Germany's imports came via the USSR with 64 per cent of its exports going the other way.[72] Remarkably, a Nazi delegation attended the May Day Parade in 1941 and was officially greeted by Defence Commissar Timoshenko who just weeks later after the German invasion became Chairman of the Soviet Forces High Command.

Germany's invasion of the USSR

Operation Barbarossa brought Germans and Soviet citizens into a war on a scale never experienced before in Europe. The Wehrmacht advanced 800 km into the USSR along a 1,650-km front in just three months. German military planners had expected to achieve their ambitious war aims before the onset of winter. The Nazis ultimate objective was to move Germany's eastern border 1,000 km to the east, expelling 41 million people beyond the Urals and enslaving the 14 million who were to remain. The *Generalplan Ost* foresaw a thirty-year process for 'Germanising' the conquered territories.[73] As the Wehrmacht swept forward, Stalin raised the possibility of territorial concessions but Hitler rebuffed him. The extraordinary subsequent mobilisation of the Soviet system and the peoples of the USSR that vanquished the invading armies and contributed so greatly to the defeat of Nazism remains an unparalleled achievement of human courage, sacrifice and ingenuity. The *Untermenschen* depicted by the Nazis rose to defeat the strongest military machine in the world not simply by out-numbering it, but by outsmarting it. The Red Army reorganised itself after a series of catastrophic defeats in 1941–42 to wage war on a scale incomprehensible to German commanders. While the Wehrmacht was winning occasional tactical battles, it was losing campaigns because of its errors, the Red Army's greater numbers and its ability to outmanoeuvre it through a superior grasp of operational art. The human losses were immense for both sides, albeit far greater for the USSR. During the war, the Red Army conscripted 34.4 million men while 1.2 million women served in combat roles; 17 million soldiers perished. The Wehrmacht conscripted around 17 million soldiers from 1939 to 1945 and sustained overall estimated losses of 3.8 million on the Eastern Front, over two-thirds of its overall total losses in the Second World War.

The USSR's civilian losses of around ten million point to the fact that for the Nazi leadership, this was *Vernichtungskrieg*, a war of annihilation, with deliberate disregard for the norms of warfare. A special decree on military jurisdiction on the occupied territories freed the Wehrmacht to execute civilians without judicial procedure. There were special guidelines ordering the immediate shooting of political commissars. Four SS *Einsatzgruppen* totalling 3,000 men were part of the invading force with the purpose of murdering Communist Party officials, including, of course, Jews. Their brief expanded to include the extermination of all Jews. Just as the Bolsheviks had forced the peasants into collective farms through a policy of starvation, the Nazis also had their own Hunger Plan that envisaged starving 30 million people and destroying the USSR's industrial base. Implementing the Hunger Plan on that scale proved impossible because the Germans were unable to exercise the necessary degree of control. Yet they starved the citizens of major cities most notably Leningrad (over one million dead) as well as Kiev and Kharkov. As they retreated, German forces carried out a scorched earth policy with a ferocity that shocked some Wehrmacht officers.

Hitler's Final Solution emerged from the invasion of the USSR and the discovery that it was possible not just to emulate the mass executions pioneered by the NKVD but to put it into practice on a far larger scale. Equally, the Nazis learned from the Gulag that there was value in enslaving people before killing them. They even discussed sending Jews from Europe to the network of Gulag camps north of the Arctic Circle. It was possibly not surprising that two such violent totalitarian regimes used some of the same methods to wage war against their enemies. However, according to his daughter, Stalin had believed in a long-term alliance with Germany and had been deeply disappointed by Hitler's betrayal. He repeatedly said after the war that 'together with the Germans, we would have been unconquerable'.[74] He was not referring to Nazi Germany because he knew the two systems could not coexist peacefully.

Bond of spilt blood

Hitler's fateful invasion of the USSR has left far more than a deep, ineradicable scar on the relationship between Germany and Russia. The bond of spilt blood between the two peoples has no parallel elsewhere. It is a tribute to the forgiving attitudes of many Soviet citizens that West Germans were able to rebuild relations with the USSR relatively quickly after the war. In a remarkable demonstration of Moscow's willingness to turn the page, a Soviet military band played the West German national anthem when Chancellor Konrad Adenauer visited Moscow in 1955. Victory in war makes it easier to move on, but there are probably additional reasons for this. The first is that Soviet society had experienced what a murderous dictatorship can lead its people to do. Soviet Ukraine, for example, had lived through a vicious civil war followed by the Great Famine. The conquest of Germany and the establishment of the GDR as a monument to the USSR's victory over the Nazis also gave meaning to the human sacrifice while ideology assisted in the process: it was possible to view the German working classes as having been corrupted and exploited by class enemies.

While Russia under its current leaders has little interest in overcoming its twentieth-century past, indeed its efforts to gloss over Stalin's crimes point in the opposite direction, Germans continue to enjoy a benevolent attitude. Official Russian rhetoric speaks of 'fascists' in Ukraine, and hints at fascist tendencies in Estonia and Latvia with reference to the treatment of the 'Russian-speaking' communities in both countries, yet it never describes Germany or Germans in these terms. Sometimes what is not said in relations between countries is a powerful message in itself. Just as Germans have developed over the centuries deep insight into Russian psychology, the same applies to Russians' understanding of Germans. Forgiveness for the criminal actions of an early generation of Germans and a refusal to tar their descendants with the same brush create a sense of debt and obligation. As such, they are valuable mechanisms for psychologically conditioning today's Germans and influencing their behaviour.

The tradition of the May Day Victory Parade in Moscow, complemented in recent years by the 'Immortal Regiment' marches where Russians hold placards showing the faces of their descendants who fought in the campaign, is a constant reminder for Germans of how the war instigated by Germany has shaped the identity of the Russian nation and its historical memory. While Belorussians and Ukrainians suffered disproportionately during the war because of the occupation and the extreme levels of violence inflicted on the civilian population by the Wehrmacht as well as the SS, for Soviet historiographers, there was no differentiation because these were citizens of the USSR. The suffering and the heroic feats of war belonged to the Soviet people even if it had been necessary to light the fires of Russian nationalism to mobilise the full energies of the country. This Soviet narrative has had consequences for the ways in which Germans both East and West learned to remember the war. By equating Russia with the USSR, they have encouraged Germans and others to think of Germany as having inflicted devastation and suffering predominantly on Russians when this was not the case even if Russians accounted for most Red Army deaths.

As the American historian Timothy Snyder has observed, the centre of this war of annihilation was Soviet Ukraine. Three million inhabitants of Soviet Ukraine died in the Red Army and 3.5 million were the victims of German killing policies during the occupation.[75] The USSR was pushing on an open door because Germans considered these territories to be historically part of Russia. This has consequences detectable today in how German foreign policy thinking approaches Belarus and, particularly, Ukraine. The aftermath of Ukraine's Euromaidan Revolution in 2014 revealed long-standing weaknesses in both German government structures and academia in terms of knowledge of the country and its history. Berlin, like some other European capitals, had tended to view independent Ukraine through the prism of Moscow, inevitably exposing it to bias and distortions. In the same vein, Russia's depiction of Euromaidan as a 'coup' mounted by Ukrainian nationalists touched a nerve in Germany because of sensitivity towards the issue of nationalism, not just because of Germany's Nazi past but because Germany played a role in developing Ukrainian nationalism as a tool of its occupation policy there.

Collaboration, prisoners of war, *Ostarbeiter*

The USSR had good reason to want to camouflage other aspects of the war. The degree of collaboration between an invading army and the local population was unprecedented. Some 1.1–1.2 million Soviet citizens served on the German side, including the Vlasov 'Russian Liberation Army'. The so-called *Hilfswillige* or *HiWis* were volunteers drawn from prisoners of war and the local population. Even groups of Cossacks served on the German side – a considerable irony given their place in German folklore as a terrifying symbol of the Russian invader. Representatives of all Soviet nationalities collaborated. The largest number were Russians (around 400,000) followed by Ukrainians (around 250,000) and Kazakhs/Central Asians (180,000).[76] There were two main reasons for the remarkable number of defections to the German side: first, an estimated 25 million Soviet citizens had died during the twenty-five years before the German invasion because of civil war, artificial famines and the Purges.[77] These experiences clearly did not encourage loyalty to the Soviet regime. Second was the Germans' treatment of prisoners of war (POWs); the Bolsheviks had denounced the 1907 Hague Convention on the laws of war and boycotted the 1929 Geneva Conference that gave birth to the Geneva Convention. They feared that the prospect of humane treatment for Soviet prisoners of war would sap the Red Army's will to fight. This gave Hitler a justification beyond his contempt for Slavs and his ideological hostility to the USSR to ignore international norms in Germany's treatment of Red Army prisoners.

Of 5.8 million Soviet POWs, around 3.3 million perished, mainly of starvation and disease. Starvation of Soviet POWs was part of the Hunger Plan. Through a filtering process to identify 'dangerous' individuals, the Germans sent some POWs for execution in concentration camps. By comparison, in the First World War, the Central Powers captured around 2.4 million Russian Army soldiers but only 70,000 died in captivity and efforts to encourage desertion were unsuccessful.[78] Collaboration therefore offered many prisoners the only possibility of survival. After the mass surrenders in the first weeks of the war, Stalin had issued the infamous order No. 270, spelling out the 'need to liquidate 'cowards and deserters' and requiring all officers and soldiers to fight to the last or face execution on the battlefield.

Even if they could stay alive in captivity, Red Army soldiers who had surrendered had little to lose.[79] Some Wehrmacht officers expressed concern at how they were required to treat Soviet POWs, notably Admiral Canaris, head of the Abwehr, who formally raised the issue with his superiors but to no effect. The death rate for German POWs was high but not at the levels of their Soviet counterparts. During the war, the Red Army captured an estimated 3.2–3.5 million German soldiers. Around 1.1 million died or never returned.[80] Of the 91,000 captured at Stalingrad only 6,000, mainly officers, made it back to Germany. These crimes against humanity unite both Germans and Russians and are part of their collective suppressed memory. Little historical research has taken place on either side into their joint responsibility for the deaths of 4.5 million soldiers.

The Soviet authorities also regarded as collaborators the roughly 2.75 million Soviet citizens[81] taken to the Reich for forced labour from the 60 million population of the Soviet territory occupied by Germany and its allies. At the outset, some volunteered in the erroneous belief that they would escape the severe food rationing that followed the invasion, yet the vast majority were compelled to go to Germany. Once there, often working in factories of major companies such as Daimler-Benz, Farben, Siemens and Volkswagen, they found themselves treated as the lowest category of foreign worker and underfed to the point where they were sometimes unfit for work. The majority of the so-called *Ostarbeiter* returned to the USSR at the end of the war as part of the Yalta repatriation policies but suffered discrimination for decades for their alleged complicity. This extended even to small children who had accompanied a parent or relative. Although many *Ostarbeiter* experienced humiliation and abuse in Germany, others reported humane treatment.[82] Only in the 1990s did the *Ostarbeiter* finally receive status in Russia as participants in the Second World War. The fate of the Nazis' forced labour policies attracted attention in West Germany in the 1980s and became a central focus in its efforts to confront the past. This led to the creation of a compensation scheme funded by the government and industry worth 10 billion deutschmarks that belatedly brought recognition of their suffering to an ageing group of *Ostarbeiter*. As a result, today's generation of Germans is more able to talk about the enslavement of Russians, Ukrainians and others by the Nazis than its great grandparents, some of whom directly witnessed these practices, but remained silent about them. Historical awareness can skip generations. For example, Continental, one of the world's largest car part makers, published details of its use of 10,000 forced labourers during the war only in August 2020.[83]

Memories of the Red Army's invasion

The Red Army's behaviour in Central and Eastern Europe in 1945 is legendary. Throughout history, victorious armies have raped and pillaged, but the advancing Soviet forces took these practices to a new level in several countries, particularly in Germany. There is no firm data available, but Miriam Gebhardt, author of a recent book on the lasting effects of sexual violence at the end of the war, estimates that between 1945 and 1955, there were overall close to 900,000 cases of rape in occupied Germany, and that around two-thirds of them took place in the Soviet zone.[84] Others suggest that the number in the Soviet could be closer to two million.[85] By the end of 1946, the population of the Soviet zone was around 17 million compared to over 40 million in the western zones. One of the victims in the Soviet zone was Helmut Kohl's wife, Hannelore. She was just 12 years old when several Red Army soldiers raped her as she fled westwards with her mother. Thrown out of a window after the attack, she suffered a long-lasting spinal injury as well.[86]

A combination of factors explains the extreme levels of sexual violence perpetrated by the Red Army in Germany: anti-German propaganda, revenge for the behaviour of the Germans in the USSR and the loss of moral values in society under Bolshevik rule. Some perpetrators had criminal backgrounds; others had been in combat without leave for nearly four years. All had witnessed the scorched earth policy of the retreating German forces. There are also indications that Stalin officially tolerated rape and looting in Germany.[87] Grigory Pomeranets, a young Red Army lieutenant later noted in his memoirs: 'Of course, the Germans were scum, but why copy them? The Army humiliated itself. The country humiliated itself. This was the most terrible thing during the war.'[88] Another Soviet officer horrified by what he saw was Lev Kopolev. He received a ten-year jail sentence for 'bourgeois humanism' after speaking out about the Red Army's crimes in East Prussia but was rehabilitated after Stalin's death. After emigrating to the FRG in 1981, he became a major intellectual figure there renowned for his exhaustive ten-volume study of Germans' perceptions of Russians and Russian perceptions of Germans going back 1,000 years.

If the numbers of victims of sexual violence are disputable, their effect on Germans' psyche is not. The brutality of the Red Army towards the civilian population has left a deep mark that has passed down the generations. Marta Hillers' diary account of her experiences as the Red Army entered Berlin in 1945 originally published in 1953 was reprinted fifty years later and became a bestseller. The 12 million Germans who fled westwards after experiencing expulsion from their homes in Poland and Czechoslovakia also brought their own stories of how Soviet forces behaved. However, the Red Army sometimes showed generosity and respect for culture. As the author Harald Jähner relates in a recent account of life in Germany at the end of the war, Soviet soldiers also occasionally astounded Germans with their 'impulsive warmth of heart', inviting them to victory celebrations and spontaneous parties. The Commander of the Thuringia Military Administration paid a high-profile visit to the Goethe-Schiller Monument in Weimar in the summer of 1945.[89]

Legacy of victory

The Red Army's storming of the Reichstag was the start of the USSR's emergence as a global power and the defeat of a nation that had dared to think itself more powerful and culturally superior to Russia. Shortly afterwards, complementing its advances westward, the USSR moved into North-East Asia seizing Manchuria and providing support to the Communists in the Chinese Civil War. The spirit of the USSR's spectacular defeat of Germany lives on in the confidence that Russian leaders and diplomats still feel in dealing with their German counterparts. The bombastic Stalinist architecture of the Russian Embassy on Unter den Linden in Berlin is a monument to victory. Russia's continued need for its own *amour propre* to define itself as a victorious power in the absence of competing achievements over the past seventy-five years allows Russian diplomacy to play on German discomfort with its past and to try to keep Germany conscious of its place in history as a defeated nation rather than a country transformed by that experience. For reasons of political correctness, Germans find themselves forced to play along and are at pains to avoid giving the impression of moral superiority. Yet the scale of Germany's Second World War trauma is at its most visible in its relations with Russia, and far more so than with its West European allies with which it can express itself more directly and assertively. For its part, the Russian side understands the game. It does not need to raise its voice in dealing with Berlin in the way it sometimes does, for example, with London, Paris and Washington.

The division of Germany

Germany's post-war relations with Russia mark a new and complicated chapter in the history of bilateral ties. Stalin's predecessors could only have dreamt of subduing Germany by occupying historic Prussian lands and establishing a new German state in the form of the German Democratic Republic (GDR) led by Moscow-trained German Communists. The failure of the Potsdam Conference in 1945 to agree the future of Germany beyond occupation made division of the country inevitable as relations between the USSR and the Western powers deteriorated and Washington and Moscow battled for global influence. Germans found themselves on the front line between East and West and the competing ideologies of both as the Cold War intensified. Anti-communism drove the integration of the FRG into western security structures and hastened its rearmament as the USSR threatened to expand its zone of influence into Western Europe. In 1952, in a bid to prevent the FRG joining the newly created North Atlantic Alliance, Stalin had proposed creating a neutral unified German state but had met with resistance from the USA. His goal was control of all of Germany. Washington insisted on free elections under UN supervision in the full knowledge that this would be unacceptable to Moscow. The incorporation of the SPD into the Socialist Union Party (SED) formed in 1946 by merging the KPD with the SPD had purged it of what the Soviet authorities regarded as unreliable elements, destroying the prospects for social democracy in a part of the country where it enjoyed a strong following. Communists who had survived the 1930s in the USSR experienced again an atmosphere of mutual suspicion and the search for Trotskyites, fascists and agents of imperialism. Some suspects went on trial and received long sentences in the Gulag.

The 'Moscow' Germans epitomised by Walter Ulbricht, the first GDR leader, had learned how to establish a Stalinist state supported by the tools of repression. In 1947, the Soviet occupation authorities established a political police in contravention of the rules of the Allied Control Commission. Kommissariat 5 was formally part of the criminal investigation department of the People's Police. It set about hunting down Nazis, anti-communists and social democrats with such energy that a lack of prison space led to the reopening of facilities at eleven former concentration camps, including Buchenwald and Sachsenhausen.[90] Kommissariat 5 would develop into the GDR's powerful state security service, the Stasi, one of the largest secret police organisations in the world relative to the size of the population. Throughout its existence, it maintained its repressive Stalinist culture of unlimited power in the search for class enemies and agents of western 'hostile organisations'.

As the two new German states consolidated, their respective citizens rapidly acquired sharply contrasting identities. The westernisation of FRG society took place alongside the Sovietisation of GDR society transforming both politically and economically, encouraging each to identify as the antipode of the other. Millions of Germans fled the Soviet Occupation Zone and, later, the GDR bringing with them direct experience of the system taking shape there.

From the Berlin airlift to the Wall

Stalin showed clumsiness in Germany from the outset of occupation with his economically damaging reparations policy that stripped the Soviet zone of industrial capacity and shipped it to the USSR. The pattern continued in 1948 with his failed attempt to force the western Allies the USA and British authorities to withdraw the new deutschmark from Berlin. The subsequent airlift and the determination of West Berliners to stand alongside the western occupying powers against the USSR forced him into a humiliating retreat and revealed to Germans the limits of Soviet power. However, its violent suppression of the June Uprising of 1953 as labour tensions flared across the GDR showed its determination to uphold its rule. This crisis and its outcome finally removed any possibility of German reunification that had briefly moved on to the agenda again after Stalin's death.

The Khrushchev 'thaw' brought some relief for the GDR. The USSR ceased taking reparation payments and no longer required it to pay for the presence of Soviet forces stationed there. At the same time, Moscow secured an important concession from Bonn with far-reaching consequences. Adenauer travelled to Moscow in September 1955 and agreed to establish diplomatic relations in return for the release of 10,000 Germans imprisoned in the USSR. Most were POWs who had received long sentences in the Gulag for war crimes together with several civilians convicted of offences in the GDR. The return of the 10,000 that included a small number of individuals later found guilty in the FRG of serious war crimes was a sensation and one of the high points of Adenauer's long rule. Video footage showing the emotional ceremonies in October 1955 when returnees were reunited with their families captures the disbelief in FRG society that the men were still alive. In his negotiations with Khrushchev, Adenauer used a surprising approach. As a west-facing Rhinelander, he had no personal affinity with Russia and no personal reference points with Khrushchev. He responded to Khrushchev's theatrical bullying style by shouting back. Remarkably, he even dared to raise the issue of the behaviour of the Red Army in Germany in 1945 when he responded to a Khrushchev monologue on the actions of German forces in the USSR. A translator mistakenly translated his words *entsetzliche Dinge* (dreadful things) as 'atrocities' (злодеяния) and caused Khrushchev to fly into a rage and shake his fist. In response, Adenauer grabbed Khrushchev and yelled. 'Who signed the Hitler-Stalin Pact? You or I?' Khrushchev later told one of Adenauer's aides that the Chancellor was 'a great man'.[91]

After the suppression of the anti-Soviet revolution in Hungary in 1956, the building of the Berlin Wall in 1961 was the next international flashpoint in the Cold War. Poorly prepared and high on medication, the new US president John F. Kennedy had suffered a mauling at his first meeting with Khrushchev in Vienna in June that year. The subject of the talks was allied rights in Berlin. Ulbricht was pushing Moscow hard for permission to close the border. Khrushchev saw the bigger opportunity to threaten to make access to West Berlin subject to control by the GDR and conclude a treaty-based division of Germany on advantageous terms for the USSR that would weaken the credibility of US commitment to Western Europe. Khrushchev terrified the young US president and his delegation by mentioning three times in one meeting the possibility of war.[92] Khrushchev correctly sensed that Kennedy would not stand in the way of the GDR preventing its own citizens from travelling to West Berlin to arrest the haemorrhaging of the East German population. Over 2.5 million people had moved to the West since the establishment of the GDR and they were leaving in greater numbers attracted by higher wages and better standards of living generated by the West German economic miracle. The GDR was facing an existential threat from its own citizens. Ulbricht's rigid Stalinist policies were largely responsible, forcing Moscow to agree to East Berlin's proposal to build a wall to lock in its own population. It would become the symbol for the next twenty-eight years, not just of a divided Germany but of a divided Europe.

Adenauer kept quiet. He had resigned himself to the fact that the FRG needed to play the long game and that its integration into western economic and security structures (*Westbindung*) would eventually make reunification possible because of its strength relative to the GDR. However, Berlin's Mayor Willy Brandt fired off an impassioned letter to Kennedy accusing the western allies of endorsing the 'illegal sovereignty of the East Berlin government'[93] and calling on the USA to respond, including by strengthening the US military presence in West Berlin. Kennedy was livid that a city mayor felt able to address him in this way but he heeded the advice. The despatch to West Berlin of General Lucius Clay as the US President's representative in Berlin was a bold move. As the former Military Governor for the US Zone in Germany, he had commanded the Berlin airlift and enjoyed cult status among West Berliners. His insistence on enforcing allied access rights to East Berlin could have triggered war when US and Soviet tanks faced each other down at the Friedrichstrasse border crossing in October 1961. Khrushchev saw the danger and gave Kennedy a way out. For Adenauer personally, the Berlin crisis proved costly as voters punished his lame response to the building of the Wall. The Christian Democrats (CDU) lost their majority in the September elections in 1961 forcing them into coalition, while the Social Democrats now with a non-Marxist programme under the new leadership of Willy Brandt secured the highest number of votes. The Berlin crisis had left its mark not just on the map but on West German politics as well. It also reinforced fears among Germans on both sides of the border that they were at the centre of a potential war between the superpowers. Similar angst would return in the 1980s on both sides as each deployed intermediate-range nuclear weapons.

Ostpolitik

Willy Brandt and his press secretary at the time, Egon Bahr, were the pioneers of a new West German approach to managing relations with the USSR and its Eastern European satellites later known as *Ostpolitik*. Its goal was to overcome the division of German in small steps. The policy remains the subject of fierce debate in Germany today. As early as 1963, Brandt and Bahr were speaking of 'common security interests' between East and West and arguing that change in Germany's eastern neighbourhood would only be possible if the USSR allowed it. Christened *Wandel durch Annäherung* (Change By Getting Closer), the idea behind the policy was to create greater stability for the FRG by recognising the status quo while not ruling out reunification. Critics called it *Wandel durch Anbiederung* (Change by Ingratiation) because of its perceived approach to Moscow. The new approach also reflected the fact that the international environment had changed for the worse after the USSR had acquired a second nuclear strike capability, adding to fears of a superpower confrontation in Europe. It dovetailed with NATO's new policy of deterrence and dialogue that emerged in the 1967 Harmel Report. After Brandt became foreign minister in 1966, he began laying the groundwork for the policy shift and aroused controversy at home – particularly among Christian Democrats – as well as nervousness in some western capitals. Opponents spoke of a 'new Rapallo'. There was particular concern not just in the FRG but also among its allies about the idea that a new European security system without military alliances could provide a path to reunification. This had a distinct whiff of Stalin's proposal in 1952.

After becoming Chancellor in 1969, Brandt was ready to move fast to exploit the USSR's desire to improve political and economic relations with the West after the Warsaw Pact invasion of Czechoslovakia the year before and its continuing problems with China after the Sino-Soviet split. Although Washington had

encouraged the CDU leadership to take a more flexible attitude to relations with the USSR, it was alarmed at the speed
with which Brandt was moving forward with negotiations on a
treaty to 'normalise' relations with Moscow. President Nixon
and his National Security Adviser Henry Kissinger worried
that the FRG might lose its commitment to Western European
unity and that Moscow might pursue détente with just the
Europeans.[94] Despite its scepticism, Washington assured the FRG
government that it was supportive of the process. Skilful West
German diplomacy led to the signing of the Moscow Treaty in
August 1970 and the Warsaw Treaty at the end of that year. The
FRG now recognised the Oder-Neisse line as Poland's border
with Germany as well as the inviolability of the intra-German
border.

Yet it had cleverly kept open the possibility of German reunification through a separate letter delivered to the Soviet government on the day of the treaty signing. Twenty years later, this
would provide an all-important diplomatic basis for reunification.
The next challenge was to regularise the status of West Berlin.
The negotiations on Berlin brought the USA to the table as one
of the four controlling powers. Its wider interests in strategic arms
reduction and the USSR's desire for an anti-ballistic missile agreement gave it the leverage to achieve favourable results from the
Berlin talks. The Quadripartite Agreement signed in September
1971 included significant Soviet concessions, among them a commitment not to impede traffic to and from West Berlin. The next
stage in the *Ostpolitik* process was the most controversial for the
FRG and led to the signing of the Basic Treaty with the GDR
in 1972 signifying de facto recognition of the GDR. It met bitter
opposition from the CDU and its Christian Socialist Union (CSU)
allies in Bavaria. *Ostpolitik* had effectively normalised a profoundly
abnormal situation, namely the existence of two German states as
parts of opposing military alliances. Yet this approach was at the
centre of the process that led to the signing of the Helsinki Final

Act in 1975 and the establishment of mutually accepted security principles that rested on recognition of the division of Europe within existing borders but with the possibility to change borders peacefully by agreement.

The economic dimension

Enhanced economic cooperation with the USSR and its allies was another tangible result of *Ostpolitik*. NATO's ban on the export of large-diameter steel pipes to the USSR to slow down the construction of major oil and gas pipelines gave way to pipe exports by West German companies to the USSR and imports of Soviet oil, natural gas and enriched uranium. The first gas imports arrived in 1973 in a gas-for-pipes deal and were part of a policy that the FRG saw as confidence building. In 1969, the FRG's Foreign Ministry believed that it would be desirable to have up to 20 per cent of the FRG's gas supplied by the USSR[95] as part of an effort to reduce the FRG's dependence on gas imports from the Netherlands. Under Brandt's successor, Helmut Schmidt, the policy continued. Schmidt travelled to Moscow in 1974 to sign a major economic agreement. When détente ended abruptly in 1979 with NATO's double track decision on nuclear weapons and the USSR's invasion of Afghanistan, the Chancellor headed to Moscow with a business delegation that led to the financing and construction of the Urengoy pipeline and the doubling of the FRG's gas imports from the USSR. Schmidt strongly supported increased dialogue at difficult times, holding three meetings with Leonid Brezhnev during his term as tensions between the West and the USSR increased. In response to the controversial gas deal strongly opposed by the USA, he famously said: 'The usual business with the Soviet Union needs to continue, but it should not be business as usual.'[96]

Ostpolitik in perspective

A mythology has built up in Germany, particularly in older SPD circles, around the achievements of *Ostpolitik* and the belief that it was the single most important factor in ending the Cold War and achieving the long-term goal of reunification. Bahr himself immodestly suggested that without *Ostpolitik* neither Mikhail Gorbachev nor Boris Yeltsin would have made it to the Kremlin.[97] As the US analyst Angela Stent has argued, the USSR's détente policies undermined the stability of the GDR because a less confrontational era made it impossible to calibrate the triangular policy of the past when Moscow could play off Bonn against East Berlin.[98] This was not the intention of *Ostpolitik*. While the policy undoubtedly played an important role in reducing tensions in Europe and put human rights on the East–West agenda, it is fair to ask at what cost. Arguably, the relaxation of tensions bought time for the Soviet system and prolonged its hold over Central Europe.

Critics point to the SPD's discomfort with the emergence of civil rights groups in Czechoslovakia, Poland and other countries after the signing of the Helsinki Final Act that threatened the stability that *Ostpolitik* sought to create. It appeared to prefer dealing with Communist governments rather than their citizens who wished to enjoy democratic rights. A product of its time when democratic changes were not on the horizon, it later became a synonym for accommodation if not appeasement. Its emphasis on achieving *Verständigung* perhaps best translated as 'mutual understanding' persists today in the belief not restricted to SPD circles that if only Germany keeps talking to Russia's leaders, it will eventually find a form of words on which both sides can agree. The history of *Ostpolitik* weighs heavily on Germany's approach to dealing with Russia today.

Germans' experience of being on the military front line during the Cold War has had a deep influence on public attitudes towards defence in general and nuclear weapons in particular. This explains the pacifist tendencies in parts of German society today and the public's reluctance to invest in defence in the absence of a clear military threat. NATO's Cold War defence posture came to rest on the policy of flexible response that included multinational conventional forces stationed in the FRG alongside the Bundeswehr, backed up with US tactical nuclear weapons deployed on FRG territory and the strategic nuclear capabilities of the US, France and the UK. The issue of modernising short-range nuclear missile systems deployed by the US army in Germany gave rise to the grisly saying: 'the shorter the range, the deader the Germans'.

Soviet peace propaganda had a field day in the FRG as a strong peace movement took root in the early 1980s in protest at the deployment of US Pershing 2 missiles fuelling anti-American sentiment and support for 'Europeanisation' of East–West relations. The SPD even proposed full diplomatic recognition of the GDR and formal abandonment of the goal of reunification to preserve the peace in Europe.[99] US President Ronald Reagan's harsh rhetoric towards Moscow and the shooting down of the Korean airliner by a Soviet fighter jet in September 1983 were the backdrop to a NATO command post exercise code-named 'Able Archer' that some historians believe brought the world closer to nuclear war than the Berlin and Cuban crises. Evidence emerged later suggesting that the Soviet leadership genuinely believed that NATO was preparing to launch a nuclear strike on the USSR.[100] The exercise possibly also started a process that led to the end of the Cold War as Reagan, supported by the British Prime Minister Margaret Thatcher, dialled down their language towards the USSR and intra-German trade ties intensified as the Soviet economy went into sharp decline.

Chancellor Helmut Kohl won a resounding election victory in March 1983 and was the first Western leader to visit the new Soviet leader Yuri Andropov just a few months later. This was only the fifth visit to Moscow by a West German chancellor, and the Soviet side was clearly keen to see whether Bonn's *Ostpolitik* might change in response to the increasingly tense East–West relationship. If they expected changes, Kohl disappointed them, by keeping strictly to the line of his predecessors albeit as noted by one observer 'with a different facial expression and a different vocabulary'.[101] According to one authoritative account, Andropov had played a crucial role in managing the backchannels in communication with the Kremlin that had allowed *Ostpolitik* to develop under both Brandt and Schmidt.[102] The East German leadership could sleep tight in the knowledge that there was no change on the horizon. Yet neither Moscow, nor Bonn, nor East Berlin could be ready for what was to start happening less than two years later as Mikhail Gorbachev, the new Soviet leader, began his efforts to reform the USSR that would lead inadvertently to the resolution of the German question and the collapse of the USSR (see Chapter 3).

Conclusions

It is impossible to interpret Germany's policy towards Russia today without a firm sense of the extraordinarily deep and complex history of interaction that binds the two countries and the degree to which their shared experiences, positive and negative, has shaped them both. This history lives on in mutual perceptions. For example, in 2000, Alexander Rahr, a German of Baltic Russian origin who had spent his early career as an analyst at the US-funded Radio Free Europe/Radio Liberty station in Munich, published the first portrait of President Putin in German entitled 'Vladimir Putin: the 'German' in the Kremlin'. He wanted to persuade his audience that Russia's new German-speaking president was a Westerniser set to continue the tradition of Peter the Great and his successors who looked to Europe for sources of modernisation. For a long period, Chancellor Angela Merkel kept a portrait of Catherine the Great on her desk.[103]

The weight of history

No other European people has had such an intense relationship with Russia while also influencing its economic development and system of governance, not to mention its impact on Russian culture and thought. Russians showed their admiration for German talents and their desire to absorb them over centuries. Many of Russia's recognisably European features took shape over time by direct exposure to Germans who had the cultural ability to adapt to living and working in Russia. The skills that they brought and the opportunities that Russia offered formed part of a historical pattern of complementarity that still exists today through bilateral trade: Germany exports machinery and management skills in return for raw materials. It is not surprising, therefore, that Germans sense that they are better equipped in many respects to understand Russia and deal with Russians than other European countries. However, the word *Verständnis* (understanding) frequently used in discussion about Russia has become loaded in German discourse because the term *Russlandversteher* (someone who 'understands Russia') has come to describe Putin sympathisers and apologists. 'Understanding' in this context is a synonym for 'readiness to make allowances'.

With justification, the calamitous results of two world wars and the experience of having front row seats in the confrontation of the Cold War add to Germans' awareness that their relationship is special because Germans and Russians have been the best of friends and the worst of enemies. They have also brought out the best and the worst in each other, the former exemplified by the deep mutual admiration in cultural relations, the latter exemplified by the relationship between Hitler and Stalin in which they both fed off the other's evil genius. The Germans' guilt for the Nazis' crimes is part of their identity in the same way that the Russians' capacity to look beyond the war in relations with Germany is part of theirs. The tales of Soviet citizens who pitied German POWs and gave them food and clothing are a small part of this picture. However, it is noteworthy that the FRG and the GDR dealt with historical responsibility in different ways. The FRG's focus based on anti-totalitarianism was on the Holocaust symbolised by Auschwitz, while the GDR's focus based on anti-fascism was on the invasion of the USSR symbolised by Stalingrad.[104] Germans who grew up in the GDR also have the experience of living in a state designed on a Soviet model and an ability to communicate with Russians not shared by their West German counterparts. This adds to a sense of closeness to Russia and the ability to understand its complexity. Thousands of East Germans who studied in the USSR and learned Russian to a high standard are still professionally active in government, industry, media, politics and think tanks.

Arguably, Germans and Russians were destined to come into conflict because of their historically undefined borders and shared fear of encirclement that encouraged territorial expansion and led to overlapping spheres of interest. The slow process of unifying the German lands prevented this happening at an early stage. It also contributed to the numbers of Germans who saw the attraction of emigration to Russia. Yet when interests collided in the twentieth century, they did so with spectacular consequences. With their shared susceptibility to romanticism, both countries had simultaneously experienced the imposition of radical ideologies that made the risk of conflict inevitable albeit not with such extraordinary violence. Intelligence failures on both sides played a role in unleashing war: as Hitler later admitted, he would not have attacked the USSR if he had known how many tanks the Red Army had. Equally, if Stalin had trusted Tukhachevsky's early warnings and kept the Red Army leadership in place, the war could have ended much earlier and at vastly smaller cost for the USSR. Similarly, if their military cooperation of the 1920s had not taken place, neither Germany nor the USSR would necessarily have had the concepts to fight war with such intensity as they did.

The common experience of having suffered murderous dictatorships at the same time creates a unique and particularly deep bond between Germans and Russians even if as societies they have not explored it sufficiently together. The treatment of POWs on both sides during the Second World War is a case in point. However, recent collaborative efforts by Germans and Russians, for example, to better understand the fate of the *Ostarbeiter* points to an effort to address the ugly consequences of that process on both sides. The trauma of war and its aftermath mean that Germans can claim to have a closeness to Russia that others do not. Their consciousness of guilt, still actively encouraged by Moscow, contributes to this sensation. Equally, Russians know Germany in ways others cannot. To this extent, there is a deep underlying special relationship between the two countries; they have shared historical memory not just of successful cooperation and murderous destruction but of the fine line between them.

Germany's policy thinking about Russia today turns on this duality in history. Germany naturally seeks to have as much friendly contact with Russia as possible to calm its fear of confrontation, yet it must also be wary of becoming too close to Russia for fear of alienating its allies and destabilising itself. These conflicting instincts give Germany little room for manoeuvre in its Russia policy.

2

The development of German attitudes towards Russia

All peoples resort to stereotypes to describe others, usually as a means of self-definition. By saying what they are not, they confirm to themselves who they are. These clichés are important because they condition the ways in which countries communicate and react to signals from each other. Not surprisingly given the extremes of their history of relations, Germans and Russians have perceptions of each other that contain sharp contradictions. On the German side, there are consistent themes stretching back centuries of Russia as a frightening, backward, dirty, uncivilised country with 'Asiatic' and 'barbaric' features. Within these images, its people feature on the one hand as lazy, deceitful and frivolous, yet long-suffering, deeply religious, kind, hospitable and possessing pureness of soul. Russians, for their part, have traditionally thought of Germans as cultured, disciplined, highly organised, having high standards of cleanliness, industrious, attentive to detail and economically successful. At the same time, they have tended to identify Germans as dull, inflexible and prone to arrogance. Perhaps even more than most peoples in Europe because of Germany' deep impact on Russia's cultural development, Russians have justifiably struggled to understand how a *Kulturnation* that felt such empathy with Russia should suddenly view them as *Untermenschen* and try to drive them out of Europe through the cruellest of wars.

Baron von Herberstein (1486–1566)

The development of German views on Russia goes back to the sixteenth century and the remarkable insights into life in Muscovy, Novgorod and other neighbouring lands provided by Baron Siegmund von Herberstein, a Habsburg envoy to the Moscow court. In 1516–17 and 1525–26, he made long trips to the principalities that would soon form the nucleus of the Russian state, and in 1549 published his celebrated work *Rerum Moscoviticarum Commentarii* that played an important role in shaping thinking in Western Europe about the 'East'. It was the first detailed description by a European of the region's geography and its inhabitants. Herberstein spoke Russian and was able to communicate with a wide variety of people, including Vasily III, the Grand Prince of Muscovy (ruled 1505–33), father of Ivan the Terrible. Some of his thoughts on the political and religious practices he saw were particularly astute. He was struck by the Grand Prince's 'unlimited power over the lives and property of all his subjects'[1] and the acceptance by his people that Vasily was the executor of God's will. His most famous observation would find an echo among foreign observers over the following centuries as they struggled with the question of what made Russian political culture so different. 'It is a matter of doubt whether the brutality of the people has made the prince a tyrant, or whether the people themselves have become thus brutal and cruel through the tyranny of their prince.'[2]

Herberstein noted, in particular the terrible living conditions of ordinary people that he attributed to their status as 'slaves and serfs'. He commented that they were more inclined to 'subservience' than 'freedom',[3] perhaps the earliest recorded impression of how Russians seek a 'strong hand'. He commented on 'the custom with the Russians to be behindhand in everything, and never to have anything ready'.[4] He also related how a Russian woman married to a German blacksmith accused him of not displaying sufficient love for her. When asked what evidence she required of his love, she said that he had never beaten her. The blacksmith told von Herberstein that he administered a harsh beating and that after this, his wife 'showed much greater affection towards him'. He went on to beat her frequently.[5] This trope re-emerged in 2015 when the German television channel ZDF broadcast a profile of Vladimir Putin, and claimed citing West German intelligence sources that he regularly beat his wife Lyudmila.[6]

Some historians have argued that Herberstein and later observers of Russian life were hostages to their own values and prejudices and through their 'ethnocentricism' contributed to the creation of a warped picture of Russia by imposing their concept of normal on what they saw.[7] However, this argument disregards the fact that it was not just travellers' accounts that established a German mental image of Russians as a people inclined to brutality. For example, the dissolution of the Teutonic Order after Ivan IV's invasion of Livonia in 1558 left a deep mark. Eyewitness accounts recorded atrocities committed by Ivan's forces and captured towns and villages being burned to the ground. Muscovy now presented a threat to Germans in the same way as Turkey.[8] Over three hundred years later, the gory tales of terror inflicted on the local population by 'Russian-Tartar' forces, including the hacking to pieces of pregnant women and the impaling of babies on fence-post spikes, would make their way into the influential account of the Livonian Wars written by the national-conservative historian Theodor Schiemann.[9] A Baltic German, Schiemann established Eastern Europe research as an academic discipline in Berlin in the 1890s and became an adviser to the Kaiser on Baltic affairs.

Adam Olearius (1599–1671)

In the seventeenth century, the travel writings of Adam Olearius (1599–1671) helped to demystify the still largely unexplored Russian lands. Olearius (born Adam Oehlschlegel) was a mathematician, theologian and geographer. As an emissary of Friedrich III of

Schleswig-Holstein-Gottorf, he visited Russia in 1633 and 1636 as part of a commercial delegation bound for Persia. On his return to Gottorf in 1639, Olearius wrote an 800-page work, first published in 1647 drawing on his diaries and his cartological research. This significantly deepened knowledge in the German lands about Russia and further shaped views of its people as different from Europeans. Olearius repeated some of the already established motifs of Russian people as 'barbarians' born to be slaves, emphasising their crudeness and lack of education but also suggested they were sly and untrustworthy in their personal relationships.[10] Like Herberstein, he noted the ordinary people's wretched living conditions but also emphasised their uncleanliness. He drew attention to the problem of drunkenness and the tendency even among children to use bad language. He described Moscow as a dangerous city at night where thieves and murderers roamed and expressed astonishment at Russian men and women naked together in the bathhouse. Yet this was no superficial account. Its detailed picture at the time of the Russian system of government, its climate, its people and their lifestyles was unsurpassed.

Christian Weber (died 1739)

The Hanoverian diplomat Friedrich Christian Weber was ambassador to Russia from 1714 to 1719 and became another influential source of thinking about Russia. Between 1721 and 1740, his journal writings from his time in Russia appeared in three volumes under the title *The Changed Russia*. As a Russian speaker with a grasp of Russia's history before he took up his post, he was at pains to explain to his readers the extraordinary transformation achieved by Peter the Great within just twenty years, and its significance. His account discusses in detail the multitude of new institutions established by Peter, the establishment of a navy and the building of the new capital with 60,000 new houses where at the turn of the century, there had been just 'two fishermen's huts'.[11] He also provided a detailed picture of life in Moscow. Weber's work contributed to greater understanding of Russia's development that German historians began to document in more detail in the second half of the eighteenth century.

Divergent views

Despite the large numbers of Germans going to settle in Russia under Catherine, including prominent academics and other members of the educated classes, there are no notable accounts describing life in Russia and the cultural differences they experienced there. Instead, events further shaped German views of Russia. Some 180,000 soldiers from the Confederation of the Rhine states (for the most part from Bavaria, Saxony, Westphalia and Württemberg) served in the Grande Armée's Russian campaign in 1812. Only a fraction made it back home. The images of suffering of these mainly farmers' sons seared itself into German historical memory through returnees' accounts of their experiences, which provided sought after reading in the years that followed. The centenary anniversary of Napoleon's defeat prompted a huge wave of fresh interest in the literature of 1812.[12] The abiding images were the cold and snow of the harsh Russian climate, the vast distances, the poor living conditions of ordinary people and the fighting prowess of the enemy, notably the Cossacks who inspired especial dread.[13] Large parts of the German lands now had a previously unimagined connection with Russia that would remain deep in the popular consciousness. Yet to the East, by contrast, Prussia celebrated the Russian Army's routing of Napoleon and the end of a period of deep humiliation. If Tsar Alexander I had brought death to Napoleon's German conscripts and stood for hostility to free institutions, for Prussia, he was Europe's liberator. Once again, Germany's geography had spawned duality.

In German liberal circles, resentment at Russia's role in upholding the existing order grew in direct proportion to increasing appreciation of it in Prussia and Vienna. Under Nicholas I, Russia acquired the image of the 'Gendarme of Europe' because of the Tsar's willingness to put down revolution beyond Russia's borders. Perceptions of Russia among Germans were by now heavily politicised and there was little effort to distinguish between the Russian regime and its people. The crushing of the Polish Uprising (1830–31) set the stage for Russia's decisive intervention in Hungary in 1849 in an alliance with Austria and with the approval of Prussia. Yet even in Prussia, there were fears of a Russian invasion as rumours spread that Nicholas I had offered his cousin, Friedrich Wilhelm IV, military assistance to quell a liberal rebellion.[14] On 22 June 1848, the *Berliner Krakehler*, a satirical publication, carried on its front page a parody of the paranoia about Russia with the words 'The Russians Are Coming' printed ten times in increasing font sizes. In 1850, picking up the same theme, the poet and dramatist, Friedrich Hebbel, a lifelong Russophobe, penned his famous couplet: 'Deutsche zogen nach Rom, warum nicht Russen nach Deutschland? Jene waren ein Volk, diese sind nur ein Geschmeiss'[15] (Germans went to Rome, why not Russians to Germany? Those were a people, these are just vermin).

Baron von Haxthausen (1792–1866)

The French aristocrat Astolphe de Custine's biting observations on Russia under Nicholas I had appeared in 1843 and quickly found a German readership. He commented with amazement on how his impressions of the tyrannical system in Russia corresponded with Herberstein's recorded three centuries earlier.[16] De Custine described Russians as 'drunk with slavery'[17] and 'half savages' and condemned Russian civilisation as 'barbarism plastered over'.[18] He expressed horror at the low standards of medicine in Russia, noting that the German doctors in the service of the Russian princes were the only ones 'who would not assassinate you'.[19]

Despite his praise for Nicholas's reforms, the Russian government felt the need to present a different picture to a foreign audience and paid for a Prussian agricultural expert, Baron von Haxthausen, to visit Russia and report his impressions of the Russian countryside. Haxthausen had developed a reputation in Prussia as an expert on the ethnical and cultural diversity in the different provinces of Prussia. He showed particular interest in the distinctive traditions of communal organisation in the parts of Pomerania previously inhabited by Slavs.[20] An enemy of liberals at home because of his conservative views and fascinated by the Russian peasant commune (*obshchina*), he was an attractive proposition to St Petersburg. In 1843, starting in St Petersburg, he covered 7,000 miles in European Russia over six months travelling as far as the Caucasus and Crimea. His study of Russia's rural institutions published in three volumes in German between 1847 and 1852 was the first detailed study for a foreign audience of the Russian countryside and had considerable impact in both Europe and Russia. Haxthausen expressed admiration for the power of patriarchal authority in Russia as a natural stabilising force but was sceptical about how long it could last in the face of industrialisation and mass education.[21] However, unlike his predecessors, he was convinced that Russia belonged to Europe and that Russians were a European people destined to be an intermediary between Europe and Asia. He also saw a great future for it.[22]

The Crimean War and its aftermath

Russia's defeat in the Crimean War moderated perceptions of Russia among German conservatives and liberals alike. The menacing Russian giant suddenly had feet of clay and was no longer capable of upholding the status quo in Europe. As Russia entered a period of reform, Prussia-Germany emerged as the driving force of unification as conservatives and liberals found a modus vivendi. However, there was a bump in the road when Russia intervened again in Poland in 1863–64 to put down the latest uprising. Prussia briefly allied itself with Russia in support, causing anger among liberals, but left it to Russia to take action. This show of solidarity with Russia improved relations and contributed to Russia's neutrality in the Austro-Prussian War of 1866 when Prussia successfully challenged Austria for leadership of the German Confederation. Russia's restraint paved the way for unification. If in the past, Russia's behaviour had divided conservatives and liberals, it now aroused conflicting emotions among the latter.

As new technologies in communication, printing and transportation brought countries and peoples closer together, Germans were beginning to learn more about their eastern neighbour. German companies led by Siemens & Halske were discovering the Russian market and larger numbers of Russians were coming to study in Germany. The German spas were a top travel destination for wealthy Russians. Advertising for Russian goods brought new images and associations, stimulating curiosity about a country to which many Germans had moved but was still surprisingly unknown. At the same time, the rise of Russian nationalism with a pronounced anti-German tinge among both Slavophiles and Westernisers revived traditional images of Russia among Germans as an uncivilised country with a despotic system of rule. By now, the Baltic Germans who had fled Russification policies under Alexander III had formed an influential lobby group that depicted Russia as an oppressor and an enemy of Germany. Their Russophobia would later shape Nazi thinking about Russia.

A geography textbook published in 1908 captured a static picture of Russia that might have appeared centuries earlier: 'The unconquerable rawness of nature has conditioned them (the Russians) to frugality, patience and submissiveness ... The Russian tribes are half Asians. Their spirit is not independent, a sense of truth is replaced by blind faith … sycophancy, venality and dirtiness are genuinely Asiatic features.'[23]

This stereotypical picture contrasted with Russia's dynamic economic development and the effects of industrialisation on traditional social structures. As Haxthausen had feared, his utopian view of the *obshchina* as a unique source of stability for Russia as it entered a period of modernisation did not stand the test of time. Urbanisation was advancing rapidly and creating a proletariat. The clichéd depiction of Russia also ignored the impact of its cultural exports to Germany. The German reading public was discovering Gogol, Turgenev and Tolstoy and, thanks to Nietzsche, Dostoevsky. Russian music and ballet were also gaining popularity. However, the quelling of the 1905 Revolution showed that Russia was still a repressive autocracy, albeit a weakening one, while evidence of its cultural prowess challenged traditional notions of Germany's cultural superiority. The picture of its people was changing too as German social reformers found themselves drawn to Tolstoy's idealised portrayal of the Russian peasant together with Dostoevsky's intense evocations of the Russian 'soul'. For intellectuals searching for alternatives to western civilisation, the Russian people's poor but simple way of life, uncorrupted by western ways, and the role of religion in their lives became an increasing source of fascination. Major cultural figures such as the lyrical poet, Rainer Maria Rilke and the sculptor Ernst Barlach made trips to Russia at the turn of the century. Both experienced a deep and lasting spiritual impact from their encounters with Russia village life that shaped their later work. Rilke travelled to Yasnaya Polyana and met with Tolstoy and later described Russia as his *Wahlheimat* (chosen homeland), noting that Russia was the source of images that led to a 'breakthrough in his creative activity'.[24] For him, Russia was a country 'bordering on God'.[25] Likewise, Barlach spoke of the 'endless inspiration'[26] revealed to him in southern Russia, which led to a fresh start as an artist and global fame.

Twentieth-century extremes

The experiences of Rilke and Barlach were part of a dramatic evolution of views on Russia taking shape in German intellectual circles in the first decade of the twentieth century. As Gerd Koenen has noted in his masterly study of the contradictory thinking underlying Germany's fascination with Russia at this time, a new Russia myth formed around the idea of the Russian people and its great writers and artists as 'the true Russia' with their future ahead of them.[27] The shared experience of war, revolution and isolation that followed inspired a wide range of German artists and political thinkers to see common cultural causes in Germany and Russia's alienation from the West. Unbalanced by their own experience of turbulence in Germany, some lost their bearings. Thomas Mann spoke of the common affinity of the two countries' souls in relation to Europe, the West, civilisation, politics and democracy and the need for Germany and Russia to ally against 'Anglo-Saxonism'.[28] He saw the two countries going 'hand in hand into the future together'.[29] He and others who found themselves captivated by an intoxicating vision of spiritual complementarity nevertheless ignored Dostoevsky's concerns about the stability of future relations between Russia and Germany. The great Russian writer had seen conflict as inevitable.

After the start of the First World War, debates began in Germany on the country's role as a power in *Mitteleuropa* and the place of Russia in its future economic relations. This gave rise to the notion of *Zwischeneuropa*, the space between Germany and the Russian heartland, a natural area for economic domination by Germany and essential to its re-emergence as a power. The influential publicist Paul Rohrbach advocated a policy of establishing German-backed buffer states on Russia's western borders to constrain Russian influence in the East (*Randstaatenpolitik*). While the new myth of 'a community of souls' was counterpoint to traditional Baltic German views of Russia, some of the economic thinking was more consistent with them since it played to a German sense of cultural superiority. For example, in 1915, the prominent industrialist and war economy planner Walther Rathenau (1867–1922) who later served briefly as foreign minister sent a memorandum to General Ludendorff, Commander of German forces on the Eastern Front, arguing that Germany should re-align its post-war foreign policy towards Russia. He saw the possibility for Germany to finance Russian capital markets in place of France. Noting that Germany had no 'anti-Russian' interests, he viewed Russia as Germany's 'future sales market', one that the Middle East could not replace. He added in a revealing comment that Russia had 'national passions but no national feeling of honour'. It had 'loved all its conquerors in a way that a Russian peasant woman demands blows'.[30] Herberstein's influence was visible again.

Germany went to war with Russia in 1914 under the influence of propaganda that used old stereotypes to depict Russians as cowardly, cruel, dirty and uncivilised, with warnings of the danger to women and children of 'Cossack bestialities'.[31] Social Democrats, with their traditional anti-Tsarist views, found common cause with the conservative Baltic Germans, hardly their natural bedfellows, in their enthusiasm to defeat Russia. This consensus possibly explains how, despite the absence of a War Press Office at the start of hostilities, German media nevertheless took a highly consistent line in describing the nature of the conflict with Russia. Typical of this, a Munich newspaper called it a war of 'European civilization against despotism and barbarism'.[32]

The Russian Army's occupation of East Prussia gave German propagandists a field day as reports emerged of violence perpetrated by 'half Asian hordes' against the civilian population. According to one account, which could have appeared centuries earlier, 'They lived worse than wild animals … Old men, women and children were martyred to death in Asiatic beastliness. This was the culture that these murderers and incendiaries of the Peace

Tsar brought to the West: mutilated corpses and smouldering ruins and heaps of rubble mark their path.'[33]

A much-publicised dispute between two schools of thought on Russia took place in 1917 between the Baltic German medieval historian Johannes Haller and the academic, publicist and politician Otto Hötzsch. Haller viewed Russia as hostile based on its traditional political culture. Hötzsch saw it as a potential partner based on its role as a European power. Haller believed that without the German Russians, there would have been no modernisation in Russia. Hötzsch had earlier condemned the disproportionate influence of Baltic Germans on the shaping of German views of Russia. He believed that despite the limitations of the Tsarist system, Russia was still capable of modernisation using Western political and economic models. By successfully aligning its aspirations to be a world power with a more developed economy and culture, it would move closer to Germany.[34]

Even though Hötzsch's optimism about the ability of Russia to reform proved misplaced, he became a highly influential figure in the 1920s as he drove the rapid development of German Russian studies that made Berlin the pre-eminent world centre for Russia expertise. From the outset, he pointed to the need to consider Russia's development over the centuries as part of European history. As early as 1913, Hötzsch had called for expanding and intensifying contacts with Russia in all conceivable ways. He advocated establishing new journals and new university chairs to study the Russian language as well as Russia's history and geography, exchanges of scholars, as well as the creating societies to bring together people with an interest in Russia.[35] He also talked about the need to influence media reporting that often had a Baltic German bias.

The attraction of Russia after the Bolshevik Revolution

After the 1917 Revolution in Russia, the 'Bolshevik danger' replaced the 'Russian danger' in Germany as views of Russia took on a much more politicised form. This was inevitable given the Bolshevik hopes that revolution in Germany would establish a bridgehead for promoting world revolution. However, as elsewhere in Europe, the Bolshevik experiment aroused fascination and extreme Russophilia among parts of the German political and intellectual classes. For example, the writer Alfons Paquet thought of the Bolsheviks as the new Varangians who were interested in Germany not just because of its revolutionary potential but also because of a deep 'historical-cultural orientation' towards it. Like many others, Paquet had a vision of Germans continuing to play their traditional role of enriching the East with their 'organisational, engineering and pioneer spirit'.[36]

German observers did not fail to notice the significance of the Red Terror. As in other European countries, for some it was deeply repellent and a reminder of Russia's underlying 'barbarity', for others it was a sign of the true ambition of the Bolsheviks' goals and the fact that the ends could sometimes justify the means. German industry felt no squeamishness about doing business with Soviet Russia. In February 1920, Rathenau presented President Ebert with a memo on behalf of a group of major companies that argued in favour of placing 'trust in a natural community of interests' between Germany and Russia and accepting the Bolshevik invitations for German agricultural experts, railways engineers, mining experts and others to rebuild and modernise Russia's economic base. The memo finished with a statement that revealed the political thinking of German industry:

> Germany will either become a colony of the European Entente states and the object of their exploitation ... or it will succeed in realising the economic possibilities available in Eastern Europe ... Common adversities and Russia and Germany's common fate as defeated countries sit alongside the neighbourly relations and economic complementarities that link Central and Eastern Europe.[37]

The extraordinary interest bordering on infatuation with Russia in the 1920s reflected the ferment of political thinking in

Germany. *Kulturpessimismus* went hand in hand with a sense of humiliation and alienation from the West. Looking east was a natural response but it gave rise to an extreme range of views about the Bolsheviks and the prospects for Germany's relations with Russia. The philosopher Oswald Spengler, author of the influential book *Decline of the West*, struggled to reconcile a vision inspired by Dostoevsky of Russians as allies of Germans in their aversion to western capitalism with his own rejection of Marxism. However, he admired Lenin as a 'Caesar figure', painfully absent in Weimar Germany.[38] The cultural historian and Dostoevsky publisher, Arthur Moeller van den Bruck (1876–1925), was one of the radical nationalists who saw the mythical 'East' as the source of Germany's renewal. Like others, he found that Dostoevsky spoke to Germany's loneliness between East and West and the idea that it was a 'protesting country'[39] that had never wanted to be part of Western Europe and resisted the influence of ancient Rome for two thousand years. He saw Germans as one of the world's young peoples that together with America and Russia would be the powers of the future. Germany and Russia would be a *Schicksalsgemeinschaft*, a community of fate allied against the liberalism of the decadent West. Russia would recognise the error of its western orientation under Peter the Great and turn to Asia.[40]

Another prominent thinker who advocated an eastern orientation for Germany was the national Bolshevik, Ernst Niekisch (1889–1967). He played a central role in establishing the Bavarian Soviet Republic that lasted barely a month in 1919 and was a bitter opponent of the Versailles Treaty. For him, the Bolsheviks were the guardians of the Prussian collectivist tradition and Germany could only find its way back to itself through Moscow. A Prussian at heart, he believed that the Bolsheviks' extreme policies of violence at home were temporary and would soften if long-term Prussian-Soviet cooperation expanded.[41]

Nazi views of Russia

The Nazis had viewed the National Bolsheviks as a serious competitor. A purge of non-conformist elements of the national socialist movement began at the end of 1933 when Alfred Rosenberg, Hitler's ideologist and chief architect of racial theories, attacked Moeller van den Bruck personally along with other groups that claimed to be the fathers of National Socialism.[42] Rosenberg (1892–1946) was one of a number of Baltic Germans who shaped Nazi thinking about Russia uniting anti-Slav, anti-Semitic and anti-Bolshevik prejudices in a single picture. He was studying in Moscow in 1917 where he experienced the Revolution at first hand. He and Hitler initially resisted the idea, supported by the army, parts of industry and even sections of the Nazi Party, that Germany should cooperate with the Bolsheviks as a counterweight to the Versailles powers. They believed this would betray the struggle of the German and Russian peoples against Jewish domination and the only viable alliance option – a 'national' Russia without the Bolsheviks.[43] For them, Rapallo was not a case of two peoples coming together but of the Jews in both.[44] Hitler's discussion of *Ostpolitik* in the second volume of *Mein Kampf* published in 1927 recycled many Baltic German clichés about Russia but added an anti-Semitic element. Slavs had not built up the Russian state, but rather 'the Germanic element in an inferior race'.[45] Jews had displaced the Germanic core and Russians could not shake off the Jewish yoke on their own. Yet Hitler argued that the Bolsheviks would not be able to maintain their grip on Russia in the long term since they were 'leaven for its decomposition': 'The giant empire in the East was ready to collapse.'[46] Invoking the spirit of Bismarck, he argued passionately against allying with a state that was doomed. He predicted that alliance would not lead to the freedom of the German nation but a world war on German soil leading to the end of Germany. He spoke of the 'bestial cruelty'[47] of the Jewish Bolsheviks, seemingly distancing himself from the classic German depiction of 'Russian beasts'. For him, Jews were the source of evil in Russia.

The extreme disparity of German views on Russia during the Weimar years reflected the turbulence in German society in the aftermath of the war and the extraordinary changes underway in Russia as the Bolsheviks secured power. Germans were far from alone in Europe in having either strong pro- or anti-Bolshevik sentiments but their sense of being common 'outcasts' in Europe gave a practical sense of common interest and purpose that rested alongside the fantasies of intellectuals about a historically determined relationship of 'souls' that could inspire Germany's recovery. The Reichswehr's cooperation with the Red Army is an example of a marriage of mutual necessity where there was also a meeting of minds. Both shared an enthusiasm for offensive warfare and found a common language that rested on mutual professional respect. In other words, a combination of forces came together to drive the idea of Germany's *Ostorientierung* (Orientation to the East) – intellectual, commercial and military. At the same time, the Bolsheviks' creation of the Comintern and their influence over the German Communist Party (KPD) inspired traditional fears of Russia among German conservative- and middle-class circles, fanned in concert by radical Baltic Germans and 'White' emigré circles. The latter were highly active in Berlin after the Civil War. Anti-Bolshevik sentiment became more widespread in German society after Stalin branded German Social Democrats 'social fascists' in 1930 at the same time as the Catholic Church launched a large-scale anti-Bolshevik campaign. Some German Communists who visited the USSR in the late 1920s were less than impressed by what they saw: Willy Leow, Chairman of the Federation of Fighters for the Red Front, famously said after a visit to an industrial facility built during the First Five-Year Plan: 'The Russians should first learn to shit before they build industry.'[48]

The Nazis had taken the trouble to study Soviet propaganda techniques and used them to promote their anti-Communist message. They relied on first-hand accounts of life in the USSR even if the authors were not adherents of Nazi ideology. One example was an anthology published in 1935 of accounts by German and other foreign engineers who had worked in the USSR. The purpose was to discredit the Soviet authorities' claims of rising living standards and show the suffering of the population. It also served as a counterpoint to flattering accounts by fellow travellers such as the prominent writer, Lion Feuchtwanger, who visited Moscow in the winter of 1936–37 and wrote a paean of praise for the Soviet system, including the first show trials. Official German propaganda that accompanied the Spanish Civil War presented an image of Russia as an 'Asian' threat to European civilisation. In the same spirit, Edwin Dwinger, a writer of mixed German-Russian parentage who had been a POW in Russia during the First World War, joined the Nazi cause and published books for a mass readership about Poland and Russia that served as indoctrination tools for the SS. His books sold over two million copies. He supported genocide in Poland, but later came round to the idea that classifying Russians as *Untermenschen* was unhelpful and that Germany needed to win them over.[49]

Nazi racial theories about Slavs were confused. Before 1939, Hitler had shown a degree of respect towards Poles while reserving particular venom for Czechs who, in the view of many in Germany, had shown consistent disloyalty to the Austro-Hungarian Empire. Yet because they did not fight, Czechs fared much better under German occupation than Poles who were in a category close to Belorussians, Russians and Ukrainians. To varying degrees, these were *Untermenschen*. Hitler and his propaganda chief Joseph Goebbels routinely described Russians as 'beasts' and 'animals',[50] not terms they used for Belorussians or Ukrainians. As the war went on, racial policies became ever less clear. Russians fought on the German side despite Hitler's initial orders in 1941 that they should not do so, Ukrainians joined the SS and served as police and camp guards, and Cossacks went over to the German side, prompting the SS to speak of both having Germanic blood. The head of the SS, Heinrich Himmler, even concluded that Stalin must be a 'lost Nordic-German-Aryan blood type'.[51]

For the almost ten million Germans who fought on the Eastern Front, the propaganda images collided with reality and created a new set of images. The spectacular advances of the Wehrmacht and the unpreparedness of the Red Army suggested that Hitler had been right and that 'kicking in the door'[52] would bring about the rapid collapse of the USSR. The Red Army seemed to be in a poor condition to fight in terms of organisation and morale as evidenced by the spectacular scale of its surrenders in the opening phase of the invasion. However, instead of seizing the opportunity to bring the local populations to its side with an anti-Bolshevik message, the Nazis continued to foment their racially inspired picture of *Untermenschen* Slavs as their enemy. As Himmler wrote in 1942:

> 'The Untermensch – that biologically to all appearances completely identical creation of nature with hands, feet and a sort of brain, with eyes and mouth is nevertheless a quite different one, a dreadful creature, and just an approximation of a human being, with human-like facial features – intellectually and mentally, however, at a level below any animal.'[53]

War inevitably accentuates national stereotypes of an enemy by selectively emphasising weaknesses or perceived negative qualities. To vilify and dehumanise Slavs, Nazi thinking went to unexplored extremes beyond the common depiction of 'Bolshevik beasts' of the 1920s. It concluded that Slavs were not a race, and one racial expert even went as far as to suggest that 'Russians' did not exist.[54] The Nazis provided a new form of self-definition for a defeated nation that equated their superiority as a people over Slavs with superior cultural development and justified *Vernichtungskrieg* and the enslavement and colonisation of the peoples of the USSR as the defence of Europe against 'Asian barbarism'. However, as Koenen has observed, there was little coherence to the Nazi view of Russia, Bolshevism and the USSR under Stalin but rather an endless recycling of 'old or clearly mutually contradictory clichéd themes and topoi in a new composition'.[55]

As the fortunes of the war on the Eastern Front turned against Germany, notions of 'racial' superiority faded in propaganda, and fear of Bolshevism (albeit decreasingly 'Jewish' Bolshevism) came to the fore as the motivator of the war effort in the East. By the time of the defeat at Stalingrad, the German civilian population knew plenty about the destruction of the war and the tenacity of the Red Army soldier. The number of fatalities and soldiers missing in action as well as first-hand accounts delivered in letters and during home leave reawakened memories of 1812. War propaganda aimed at galvanising a fighting spirit added to fears about what the USSR could inflict on the civilian population. Therefore, it was hardly surprising towards the end of the war that millions of Germans fled westwards as the Red Army advanced, not seeing the USSR as a liberator. An old pattern was emerging again. Marta Hillers' diary entry for 20 April 1945 notes the envy of her Berlin neighbours for those in West Germany. 'No one says the word "Russians". The lips just won't say it.'[56] A week later, two Soviet soldiers raped her.

Post-1945 views of Russia

History always lives on, and the Germans' traditional mental images of Russia did not die with defeat in 1945 and four decades of living apart in two separate states. Anti-communism and resistance to 'totalitarianism' were central to the identity of the FRG and its integration into western political, economic and military structures. While perceptions of military danger ebbed and flowed, there was a consistent view across the political spectrum of the USSR as a security threat to the FRG and its allies, a country with a repressive political system, low economic development and poor living standards, and yet able to marshal its limited resources to rival the USA as a superpower. Similarly, there was recognition that the USSR possessed a significant cultural inheritance from pre-revolutionary times and had experienced a remarkable flowering of art, music and literature in the 1920s and 1930s before the onset of the Great Terror. In the 1950s and 1960s up to the start of détente, contacts between West Germans and Soviet citizens were severely restricted, closing channels of communication with the greater part of Germany that had been in place for over three hundred years. Especially after Stalin, the USSR took on the image of a 'puzzle' beyond the comprehension of those outside the country. The publication of Solzhenitsyn's *One Day in the Life of Ivan Denisovich* and other works during the Khrushchev thaw inspired renewed curiosity about the country. Some West German journalists' accounts began to fill in the picture. One of them, Klaus Mehnert, a student of Hötzsch, authored one of the first detailed explanations of people and their behaviour in the USSR. Published in 1958, *Der Sowjetmensch* (The Soviet Person), painted a sympathetic picture of Soviet citizens and their lives. Mehnert noted that during his travels of recent years, the friendliness of people had made the greatest positive impression on him.[57] This was a German writing barely ten years after the end of the war. At the level of popular culture, books such as Heinz Konsalik's *Der Arzt von Stalingrad* (The Doctor of Stalingrad) published in 1956, and later made into a successful film, showed how easy and acceptable it was to sustain clichéd images of Russians. Inspired by the stories of German POWs, it describes the heroics of a Wehrmacht surgeon who saves lives against the odds in a fictional POW camp, challenging the authority of his captors but earning their respect for his superior skills. Ten pages into the text, he instructs his assistant to take the anaesthetic away from a female doctor, adding, 'These beasts are no good for anything'.[58] The book sold four million copies.

With détente, the establishment of cultural and economic links and the development of tourism broke down some FRG images of the USSR as a hostile power. There was greater interest too in the study of Russian in schools and universities but, for most of society, the USSR remained a distant country even if its geopolitical presence was inescapably close in the GDR. The Pershing crisis in the 1980s reactivated fears about Soviet influence in Europe but firm political leadership and the reassurance of having military forces from several NATO countries on its territory, in addition to a capable army of its own, made the situation manageable. By contrast, two generations of GDR citizens grew up with the image of the USSR as the 'friend' of socialist Germans. The Society for German-Soviet Friendship became the largest public organisation in the country. Membership was a public duty rather than a statement of personal dedication to the USSR. From its establishment in 1947, it propagated the image of the USSR as a 'big brother', the superior, victorious partner whose achievements East Germans should strive to emulate. Unlike their counterparts in the FRG, GDR schoolchildren learned Russian as a first foreign language and grew up with exposure to Russian culture, including contemporary literature and music. Study in the USSR provided an opportunity for an elite group to further their careers and gain an unparalleled insight into living and working conditions in the USSR, allowing them to learn Russian to a generally far higher standard than FRG students of Russian. In some cases, the contrast with the GDR made a strong impression, with food shortages, poor infrastructure and inferior living conditions challenging the propaganda image of the USSR.

The Gorbachev factor

Over four decades as a 'junior partner' of the USSR, the GDR built up an extensive cadre of professionals across different disciplines with deep knowledge about the USSR and its peoples, together with practical experience of operating in the country. This has added an important ingredient to the mixture of inherited attitudes that condition German attitudes to Russia today that are easily overlooked since lustration policies excluded GDR officials from taking positions in united Germany's Foreign Office, Defence Ministry and security agencies. However, some used their knowledge to develop successful business careers. One was Matthias Warnig, a former Stasi officer, who made a career at Dresdner Bank after spying on it during his earlier life.[59] His personal friendship with Vladimir Putin led him to become an influential figure within the Kremlin hierarchy, managing the Nord Stream pipeline projects and sitting on the boards of several Russian state companies.

The speed at which Mikhail Gorbachev gained popularity with the FRG public as he began to improve East–West relations was astonishing. In November 1986, one poll indicated that 83 per cent of respondents believed that Gorbachev had already done more to reduce tensions than any previous Soviet leader. At the same time, another suggested that 90 per cent of West Germans believed that Chancellor Kohl had been wrong to compare Gorbachev as a PR practitioner to Goebbels and that 64 per cent believed the parallel was in any case wrong.[60] In February 1987, Foreign Minister Genscher asked that Gorbachev be taken at his word, causing nervousness in London and Washington.[61] One well-known television commentator saw in the new Soviet leader the return to the world stage of 'Jesus's vision of brotherhood and godly kinship of all men'. Another commentator spoke of Gorbachev 'restoring the archetypal holy order'.[62] Old romantic pictures of Russia from the turn of the century were reawakening, in part inspired by Gorbachev's wife, Raisa, whose dress sense and familiarity with western culture recalled pre-revolutionary Russia. Euphoria set in during their visit to the FRG in June 1989. An astonishing 80 per cent of West Germans believed in the success of his reforms, and 60 per cent viewed the USSR either favourably or with 'great sympathy'.[63] As his increasing popularity in the GDR showed, Gorbachev had touched a nerve in both Germanies.

Russia's path of development under Gorbachev's successors has not challenged established German views of the country. Boris Yeltsin's erratic rule quickly lurched from commitments to democracy and rule of law to the shelling of Parliament and establishment of a super presidency consistent with the tradition of strong rule. Similarly, the brutal attempt to bring Chechnya to heel was part of a broader pattern of disregard for civilian life and did not lead to a deterioration of bilateral relations. President Putin's attempts to entice the EU into a close relationship with Russia at the expense of the USA while bombing Chechnya and restricting civic freedoms fitted a broader historical pattern of a country unconcerned by perceptions of its brutality at home while seeking to expand its influence in Europe. This coincided with a rapid expansion of Germany's exports to Russia as the Russian economy started to move out of recession. It was also not the first time in history that growth in trade had occurred at the same time as increased internal repression in Russia. In the early 1930s, despite its struggle against the Comintern, the Weimar government avoided criticism of collectivisation and the Purges for fear of damaging bilateral trade and cooperation.

Conclusions

Through their close interaction, Germans have formed deep and contradictory impressions of Russia over centuries. At various stages, they have found themselves both repelled by Russia's 'barbarity' and entranced by visions of its ordinary people unspoilt by Western influence. They have thought of it as both highly regressive and progressive, as European and Asian, uncultured and cultured, as an ally and enemy, and as a natural economic partner but never an economic competitor. Of course, Germans are not alone among foreigners in identifying Russia's contradictory features. What makes their experience exceptional is the length and intensity of their exposure to Russia and its absorption into the collective memory, whether through their family backgrounds or the study of history or simply growing up in the GDR. Russia is inescapably present in the German consciousness, making Germans more like Poles in this respect than British or French people. The subject of relations with Russia creates discomfort not only because there are so many irreconcilable contradictions but also because a conversation about Russia is a conversation about Germany's place and purpose in Europe.

This opens up the deeper issue of Germany's own centre of gravity and its sense of its balance and weight in Europe, the tension between its integration into Western institutions (*Westbindung*) and Germany's vocation as a country in the centre of Europe (*Mittellage*). The period from 1900 to 1945 exemplifies how revolutionary change in Russia unbalanced Germany to such an extent that, in under twenty years, it lurched from alliance with Moscow to a war of annihilation. The rebalancing of Germany's relations with the USA, a process that has been underway at least since the start of the Iraq War in 2003 when Berlin turned away from Washington, has inevitably raised questions in Germany about whether a reunified Germany remains committed to 'the West' as it did during FRG times, not least because of the erosion of 'the West' as a political concept and the advance of anti-liberal forces in western societies, including Germany. As Ralf Fücks, a leading Green thinker, has noted, 'Russia is positioning itself as the last bastion of Christian values against a decadent 'Gayropa' colonised by America.'[64] To a country with a confused sense of identity and some pronounced anti-American tendencies, as well as an emotional vulnerability to Russian messaging that plays on its fears, the current realignments taking place in Europe and far beyond represent a disturbing challenge.

Against this background, it is understandably difficult for Germans to approach Russia dispassionately and to analyse soberly Germany's policy options. For this reason, the issue of how to handle Russia also sharply divides opinion not just between the main political parties but also within them. In addition, over the past thirty years, much of elite opinion has moved from naive enthusiasm about Russia to deep disappointment with it. As it has been for centuries, Russia remains a subject for Germans that defies balanced discussion.

3

The miracle of reunification

The extraordinary achievement of German reunification in 1990 merits a separate discussion because of its continuing impact on German thinking about Russia. The dramatic events of 1989–90 offered hope to Germans who had been on the front line of the Cold War of a new peaceful era in a unified country in an undivided Europe. Gorbachev's acquiescence to reunification and post-Soviet Russia's acceptance of it pointed to an era of stability and harmony in Germany's relations with Russia, and an unprecedented opportunity for Germany to feel at peace with itself. This in turn encouraged a sense of deep gratitude to Moscow for making such an unexpected outcome possible. Yet the neat conclusion of the Cold War with its quixotic vision of an all-European cooperative security framework stretching from Lisbon to Vladivostok was only a flicker before the sobering realities of the break-up of Yugoslavia and the disintegration of the USSR intruded. Three decades later, there is still nostalgia in Germany for this seductive moment when it finally seemed possible to square the circle and for the country to be fully reconciled with both its western and eastern neighbourhoods.

Coincidence of favourable factors

The reunification experience is also a reference point today for those arguing that Germany and its allies need to defuse the current confrontational relationship with Russia by re-enacting the policies that helped end the Cold War.[1] Again, this reflects a tendency to oversimplify and ignore the larger picture. For German reunification to take place peacefully at such speed required a remarkable coincidence of events, beginning with Moscow's decision to move away from confrontation with the West and view the FRG as its most promising western partner, a move that inadvertently destabilised the GDR. Statesman-like leadership on the part of the main actors also played a major role in containing the process that briefly ran out of control when the Berlin Wall unexpectedly opened. There was considerable improvisation under pressure since Bonn did not have a master plan for reunification. The FRG's operational planning for reunification had stopped in 1960.[2] Fortunately, Helmut Kohl, George Bush and Mikhail Gorbachev together proved equal to the task. The process could easily have gone wrong in several ways: conservative forces could have ousted Gorbachev earlier; the East German authorities could have deployed force to disperse demonstrations. Thankfully, the protests remained peaceful, in large measure due to the influence of the Protestant church.[3] Soviet forces in the GDR and other Warsaw Pact countries might not have stayed in barracks, and as Kohl later pointed out many times, the situation might have been entirely different if Iraq had invaded Kuwait six months earlier and distracted Washington's attention from supporting Germany's delicate negotiations with Moscow on the security arrangements for a united Germany.

Understandably, Germans view Gorbachev as a major historical figure who single-handedly democratised the USSR and changed its worldview. After all, they proved to be the greatest beneficiaries of his policies. However, they tend to conflate Gorbachev's benevolence towards Germany with the idea that 'Russia' bestowed the gift of reunification and deserves gratitude. In fact, with his enhanced presidential powers, Gorbachev imposed his policies on a reluctant Politburo. Defence Minister

Yazov was reportedly outraged at Gorbachev's concession that allowed a united Germany to be a member of NATO, and later called his actions 'treachery'.[4] Moscow's German experts spoke of 'political masochism' and 'a summer sale'.[5] Lamenting the surrender of Russia's territorial gains, the nationalist writer Alexander Prokhanov wrote that 'the bones of Russians soldiers have turned in their countless graves'.[6] Valentin Falin, the Central Committee's top German expert, described the Soviet Foreign Minister Eduard Shevardnadze who negotiated the terms of reunification with Gorbachev as 'America's most valuable agent of influence'.[7] The disjunction between Gorbachev's reputation in Russia and Germany 30 years after reunification has not diminished. Germany's hero is Russia's traitor.

However, this does not stop today's Russian leadership from trying to exploit Germany's sense of debt to it. President Putin noted in 2009 in an interview to mark the twentieth anniversary of the fall of the Berlin Wall that reunification had led to a new quality of relations between Germany and Russia based on trust and gratitude.[8] He was implying that the relationship with Berlin that he inherited after he came to power in 1999 was special because Germany chose to treat it as such in recognition of Gorbachev's agreement to reunification on Western terms. Not surprisingly, Moscow has cultivated this reflex over the last twenty years as part of its efforts to influence German policy towards Russia. It not only encourages Germans to feel grateful for what Moscow allowed to happen at the time but also tries to make them feel guilty about the opportunities missed afterwards to integrate Russia into an all-European security system.

The generosity argument is exaggerated. The peaceful implosion of the GDR and its rapid absorption by the FRG did not come about simply because of altruism on the part of Gorbachev. Rather his consent to these processes reflected the fact that he knew he could not stop them and did not see them as a threat. In this sense, agreeing to the FRG's incorporation into

NATO was not an extravagant concession; it was the best of a series of bad options available to Moscow. Gorbachev yielded to the argument that it was safer to have a united Germany firmly anchored in NATO than not. Seen in this light, Moscow's actions take on a different significance, reflecting facts that Russians understand very well and that Germans and are reluctant to admit openly: the USSR lost the Cold War; defeat brings territorial losses; strong nations pick themselves up and return to action. For Russian policymakers, West Germans after the Second World War demonstrated exactly these qualities, albeit with strong support from their allies. Russia sees itself engaged in a similar process even if it lacks close friends. Nevertheless, it feels that it enjoys respect and understanding in Germany. Up to 2014, Moscow's approach towards Germany was logical. It built close relations with the strongest economic power in the EU and, as part of the process, tried to exploit its sense of obligation to Russia.

Gorbachev's 'new thinking' in foreign policy and his renunciation of the Brezhnev doctrine pulled the rug from under the feet of Moscow's Warsaw Pact allies. Both were responses to the USSR's underlying economic weakness and signalled retrenchment by Moscow. Bloc cohesion was no longer a priority. The USSR was falling behind the West technologically, living standards were stagnant and public health provision atrocious. In other words, Gorbachev concluded correctly that the USSR was no longer able to maintain superpower rivalry at the same level. By putting him in charge, the Politburo calculated that the risks of energetic reforms under a young leader outweighed the dangers of more conservative approaches. Acting in Leninist style, Gorbachev moved quickly to ease international tensions and create a benign external environment that would allow a focus on domestic reform. He came to the realisation that its Central European satellites were more of a liability than an asset because of the costs they imposed on the USSR. In the final analysis, they were expendable even if he hoped that they could pursue a path of independent reformed socialism alongside the USSR.

The GDR beyond rescue

Putin has said that he would have managed the reunification issue differently without specifying exactly how.[9] It is fair to assume that he shares the view of many former Soviet diplomats that Gorbachev committed a serious error by not seeking legally binding agreement that NATO would not enlarge after reunification. Yevgeny Primakov, a member of Gorbachev's Politburo in 1989 and later Russian foreign minister (1996–98), believed that it would have been possible to receive such guarantees.[10] He has also stated that if the USSR had not 'fled' so quickly from Eastern Europe, it could have avoided many problems.[11]

Like Gorbachev, however, Putin has used the standard Soviet arguments to say that dividing Germany was a mistake but that it was the fault of the Western powers when they backed the creation of the FRG. Unlike Gorbachev, however, Putin spent four years in the GDR (1986–90) as a KGB officer. He gained a strong impression of the repressive nature of its system, concluding at the time that the 'strongly totalitarian country' resembled the USSR of the late 1950s.[12] He also experienced the collapse of the GDR at first hand. A decade later, he recalled with bitterness the shock of learning from a Soviet military commander whom he had called for assistance that without orders from Moscow, the army could not help since Moscow was 'keeping quiet'. He concluded that the USSR already no longer existed. 'This was a fatal, incurable disease called paralysis. Paralysis of power.'[13] The latter was a term widely used at the time by Gorbachev's critics in the army and the KGB. Witnessing close up the crumbling of the GDR system appears to have left a strong imprint on the future Russian president who had just turned 37. In addition, his absence from the USSR as it underwent such drastic change during the Gorbachev years possibly made the collapse of the country even more shocking. In his 2005 address to Parliament, describing the human cost of the implosion of the USSR, he called it the 'greatest geopolitical catastrophe of the twentieth century'.[14]

The erosion of Soviet power identified by Putin broke the back of the GDR already weakened by Moscow's refusal to ensure bloc discipline as before. A revealing indicator of the malaise at heart of the Soviet system was Moscow's failure to understand fully the real situation that was developing in the GDR. To keep the star economy of the socialist bloc afloat, the GDR was living beyond its means. Far more so than the Soviet leadership supposed. It was dependent on cheap oil supplies from the USSR, some of which it sold abroad for hard currency[15] as well as increasing numbers of loans from the FRG. By the late 1970s, the GDR's foreign debt was DM 30 billion, six times higher than the limit Moscow had set a few years earlier. Yet Honecker not only kept the truth from Moscow, he did not even inform his own Politburo.[16] Brezhnev had openly warned the GDR leadership of the dangers of financial dependence on the FRG. In 1970, angered by what he perceived as arrogance on the part of the long-serving leader Walter Ulbricht towards Moscow, he starkly reminded Honecker that the GDR depended for its existence on Soviet military power: 'Without us there is no GDR.'[17]

Concern had arisen again in 1984 in Moscow after Honecker ignored further warnings from the Kremlin and signed a DM 950 million credit agreement with the FRG that included as a quid pro quo the GDR allowing larger numbers of its citizens to emigrate. This followed Bonn's provision of a DM 1 billion credit a year earlier. Yet despite East Berlin's intransigence and his personal aversion to Honecker, Gorbachev appears to have believed that the GDR was a model socialist economy with a strong technological base and high standards of labour productivity that could contribute to modernising the Soviet economy.

The miracle of reunification

Right up to the end of Honecker's rule, just weeks before the collapse of the Wall, Gorbachev continued to praise the GDR's performance. Yet already in 1988, the GDR Politburo was discussing the risk of bankruptcy while SED propaganda depicted the GDR as having the tenth-largest industrial economy in the world.[18] In October 1989, the Chairman of the State Planning Commission reported that the country's debt-to-export ratio was 150 per cent, and labour productivity was 40 per cent below the FRG's. To prevent hard currency debt from increasing further would require reducing living standards by 25–30 per cent.[19] In other words, the GDR economy was on the rocks and the key decision-makers in Moscow were apparently oblivious. Gorbachev registered shock when he learned about the report's contents from Honecker's successor Egon Krenz. He had to ask whether the figures were correct. He had not imagined the situation to be so precarious.[20] This backdrop is important because it helps to explain the extent to which the GDR was already in a state of collapse without the actions of Moscow and that the USSR did not in any case have the resources, let alone the will, to prop up a failing system.

Moscow loses control

German commentary on Gorbachev's actions in the run up to the collapse of the GDR tends to ignore his disastrous loss of control of the reform process at home that led to the destruction of the country he set out to strengthen. Growing political and economic problems only increased the urgency to secure financial support from the West, in particular from the FRG. In this respect, Gorbachev was developing a dependency that successive Soviet leaders had explicitly told the GDR to avoid. This would weaken his negotiating hand later when the USA and FRG recognised that financial aid gave them leverage in negotiating the thorny issue of united Germany's relationship with NATO. Robert Gates, the US Deputy National Security Adviser, spoke of a strategy 'to bribe the Soviets out'.[21] As Kohl prepared to fly to Moscow in July 1990 for the meeting with Gorbachev to finalise terms for reunification, his finance minister informed him that the USSR had already fully used a DM 5 billion credit facility opened by the FRG three weeks earlier.[22] This was the largest loan ever made to the USSR. The writing was on the wall for the Soviet economy at a critical moment of negotiation with the West.

If Gorbachev knew history, it was only a Soviet version. He demonstrated fatal ignorance of the USSR's nationalities problem and the foundations on which Soviet rule rested. However, it was understandable that his vision of a Common European Home replacing a continent divided by confrontation did not include a unified Germany. For a man of his generation who as an 11-year-old remembered the German occupation of his home village in southern Russia, he could not have thought otherwise. He had seen the devastation of war in the late 1940s when travelling by train to Moscow to begin his studies. The journey took him through Stalingrad and other cities. The view from the train window of 'harrowing destruction, scenes of fires, and ruins of flattened houses' shocked him and scarred his memory.[23]

During FRG President Richard von Weizsäcker's visit to the USSR in July 1987, Gorbachev pointedly stated that Britain and the USA were responsible for the division of Germany, adding that history would decide the issue 'in a hundred years'.[24] Honecker struck a similar note in January 1989 saying that the Wall would remain for as long as the conditions that led to its construction did not change. It would stand for another 50 or even 100 years.[25] Falin, the International Department's German specialist shared a similar view. Yet the USSR's warming of relations with the FRG beginning in 1987 and Gorbachev's growing hopes that the development of bilateral economic cooperation could help secure his reform effort were also an additional factor destabilising the GDR since it owed its existence to confrontation between the Soviet bloc and the West. It had survived détente in the 1970s because the USSR was committed to keeping its Warsaw Pact allies on a tight leash, as evidenced by the Soviet invasion of Czechoslovakia in 1968. Moscow's reliance on closer relations with Bonn to promote its own internal reforms inevitably called into question the purpose of the GDR. By the summer of 1989, the KGB's best sources were all reporting that the division of Germany was no longer sustainable.[26]

However, there is no indication that policymakers in Moscow had joined the dots and thought about how they could at least delay the momentum towards reunification. An organisational problem contributed to this incapacity. The Ministry of Foreign Affairs was in charge of relations with the FRG while the Communist Party's Central Committee was largely responsible for relations with the GDR via its 'fraternal' ruling party.[27] To make matters worse, Foreign Minister Shevardnadze had divided responsibilities for the FRG and GDR between two departments to the consternation of the Ministry's German specialists.[28] An overall lack of coordination among officials reduced Moscow's capacity to respond to the fast-moving situation that emerged after the collapse of the Wall, leaving the field open to Kohl to set the agenda for fast-track reunification. It was Germany's good fortune to have a federal chancellor with the instinctive understanding of the opportunity on offer and the ruthless determination to pursue it.

The fall of the Berlin Wall – a comedy of errors

The opening of the Wall itself on 9 November 1989 owed more to the bravery of GDR citizens than largesse from Moscow. The Soviet leadership contributed to the process only through its lack of coordination with East Berlin. The regular Monday demonstrations that began in Leipzig in September 1989 and spread across the country, as well as the determination of thousands of East Germans to leave the country illegally via Czechoslovakia and Hungary shook the GDR leadership into announcing a relaxation of travel restrictions. Bureaucratic incompetence and laziness on the part of the GDR authorities made the situation spin out of control. The Interior Ministry officers who drafted the new regulations went beyond their brief and included temporary travel, not just permanent emigration as originally instructed. They did not think the prescribed policy was viable.[29] Public holidays on 7 and 8 November in the USSR and the GDR meant that the leadership could not obtain approval for their new measures from a level higher than a deputy foreign minister, who did not have authorisation power.[30]

However, the GDR Foreign Ministry failed to inform Moscow that the new rules applied to border crossings to West Berlin and not just directly to the FRG, disregarding the authority of the USSR in divided Berlin. With Moscow blindsided, a comedy of errors ensued. Krenz read the new regulation aloud at an improvised meeting of the Politburo with only around half of its full members present. He incorrectly told them that Moscow was happy with the text. The government spokesman Günter Schabowski did not attend.[31] Together, these coincidences would have dramatic consequences later that day. Schabowski then went to give a routine press conference reporting on the results of the day's Central Committee meeting. Despite Krenz telling him that the announcement would make world news, he did not bother to read the document he had received.[32] Reading it for the first time in front of the rolling cameras, he could not grasp its meaning. He wrongly stated that the new regulations would come into effect immediately even though they were only due to do so the next day, prompting thousands of East Germans to head to the border to see if the changes were for real. At 11.30 p.m., a disgruntled Stasi officer in charge at Berlin's Bornholmerstrasse border crossing,[33] fearing for the safety of his men, disregarded orders and opened the gates, while most of the GDR Politburo was unaware of what had been happening. The Soviet Ambassador was tucked up in bed.

The miracle of reunification

Over the next hour and three quarters, 20,000 East Germans rushed through the checkpoint into West Berlin to enjoy their newfound freedom. As Moscow slept, the GDR disintegrated. The next morning, Falin, the Central Committee's German specialist, learned what had happened on from media reports. Gorbachev took the news calmly but it was clear that Moscow had lost control.

Kohl seizes the agenda

Fortunately, the relationship between Gorbachev and Kohl that had begun disastrously had developed into a strong personal bond supported by an excellent rapport between their wives. This was a key factor in keeping the situation in the GDR calm over the coming days, weeks and months. Born less than a year apart, the two leaders were too young to have participated in the war, but old enough to remember it. Although Gorbachev thought himself to be Kohl's intellectual superior,[34] there was strong mutual respect between them. Kohl relates in his memoirs how he took Gorbachev for a walk down the Rhine during his visit to the FRG in June 1989 and compared the river's flow to the sea to the inevitability of German and European unity. Gorbachev offered no reply but Kohl believed that Gorbachev at that point started to re-think his position on the division of Germany.[35]

Even if he had concluded that reunification was inevitable at some point, Kohl's announcement of his ten-point plan in late November 1989 incensed Gorbachev and made him read the riot act to the unwitting Genscher in Moscow shortly afterwards. The Foreign Minister himself did not know about the plan but did not let on. Kohl had kept it from him for political reasons since he worried that Genscher or others could steal the initiative from him.[36] Despite his initial anger, Gorbachev seems to have concluded quickly that sustaining a separate German state was not a viable alternative and genuinely believed that it was for Germans themselves to decide the way forward. The French President François Mitterand was initially highly sceptical of German reunification while the British Prime Minister Margaret Thatcher was resolutely opposed. Mitterand even found a common language with Gorbachev on his opposition to the Ten-Point Plan sparking suspicions in Bonn that France was trying to create a French–Soviet alliance against reunification.[37] However, Kohl's insistence on the need to place reunification in a European framework and his support for deepening European integration eventually won over Mitterand, while strong US support for Kohl's efforts swayed London. Gorbachev clearly felt he was more among friends than enemies.

In the end, Kohl obtained from Gorbachev and Shevardnadze almost everything he asked for. His memoirs list eight key points on which the Soviet side gave ground:

- the agreement to NATO membership
- the renunciation of four-power rights on the signing of the 2+4 Treaty
- the withdrawal only of Soviet forces
- the withdrawal of Soviet forces within three to four years rather than five to seven
- the full integration of former GDR territory into NATO after the departure of Soviet forces
- agreement to the immediate stationing of Bundeswehr units on former GDR territory after reunification
- an upper limit of 370,000 on the size of the Bundeswehr rather than 300,000 as proposed by Moscow
- agreement that allied forces could stay three to four years in Berlin rather than six months.

In return, Kohl conceded only two positions, agreeing that there would be no basing of either foreign forces or nuclear weapons on former GDR territory.[38] Kohl noted the scale of the risk

Gorbachev took in agreeing these terms and the need for Germans to be grateful but he also pointed to the fact that Gorbachev did so with an ulterior motive since 'ultimately he wanted to stabilise his perestroika with our help in return'.[39] Gorbachev's aide Anatoly Chernyaev believed that Gorbachev had concluded that the West had the better arguments about the security arrangements for a unified Germany and that neutrality might prove to be a dangerous option if one day Germany decided it wanted to acquire nuclear weapons.[40]

The final element of luck in the reunification process was the fact that institutions were available to accommodate a unified Germany. The Conference on Security and Cooperation in Europe (CSCE), the European Community and NATO together provided frameworks that reassured both Germany's neighbours and Germans themselves that there was no risk of Germany finding itself once again conducting *Schaukelpolitik* (policy of swinging) between West and East). Germany's agreement to give up the deutschmark in favour of a common European currency signalled its recognition of the need to strengthen Europe to accommodate its greater weight. The USSR's concerns were less about the dangers of German nationalism and more about the strengthening of NATO at the USSR's expense. The Conventional Armed Forces in Europe Treaty signed in November 1990 provided the military reassurance elements for both sides by eliminating the capacity of NATO and the ailing Warsaw Pact to conduct offensive operations with surprise. It also included unprecedented verification mechanisms that were to remain valuable after the dissolution of the Warsaw Pact. In addition, the Bush administration's sensitive handling of relations with Moscow over German reunification deserves particular note. Washington was at pains to play down any sense of triumphalism to avoid weakening Gorbachev at home. Instead, it allowed him to consider the USSR under his leadership as one of the victors of the Cold War. As Bush's 'Chicken Kiev' speech in August 1991 just weeks before the coup against Gorbachev showed, the USA displayed solidarity with him by deliberately not siding with independence-minded republics against Soviet central authority.

Small price paid

Since the collapse of the USSR, Moscow has never expressed regret about Germany's reunification. While it would have been entitled to raise questions about the price paid for Russia's goodwill, it has largely refrained from doing so. Germany paid around DM 60 billion ($57 billion at 1991 exchange rates). By comparison, up to 2015, the total estimated cost of support for integrating the GDR was DM 2000 billion. Kohl fought hard at the G7 Summit in London in July 1991 to secure commitment to back Gorbachev's reforms. He was partially successful, opening the path for IMF support. However, as Yegor Gaidar, the architect of Russia's 'shock therapy' reforms after the collapse of the USSR later wrote, the Soviet side had no concept of how to stabilise the economy if it were to receive western financial support. A serious discussion of a large-scale aid package was out of the question.[41]

Yet after Gaidar and his team came to office and started to implement radical market reforms, no substantial western financial package followed. In 1992, western countries put together a $24 billion aid package but only around $13 billion was delivered.[42] The following year, the G7 increased the financial support on offer to over $40 billion but $15 billion of it alone related to debt rescheduling. The IMF offered financial support worth a paltry $3 billion.[43] There was no offer of a second Marshall Plan as some in the West had called for. Unquestionably, the majority of the Russian population lived through the bleakest of times during the early 1990s as the Soviet economy ground to a halt and GDP shrank by around 50 per cent.[44] During the period 1992–95, there were two million more deaths than births, a demographic decline unmatched in peacetime except during the famine in 1932–33 and Stalin's Terror in 1937–38.[45]

NATO enlargement – Germany not blamed

Despite these human costs, Moscow's dissatisfaction has focused exclusively on one issue linked to German reunification: NATO enlargement. For over twenty-five years, it has tirelessly claimed that NATO member states violated commitments made to Gorbachev not to enlarge NATO beyond the GDR. Western archives offer no evidence to support the Russian position, yet NATO's 'deception' of Russia has also become a well-established fact in many western policy debates, including in Germany. Some commentators choose to extrapolate further. For example, the German journalist and best-selling author Gabriele Krone-Schmalz has criticised enlargement, alleging that by failing 'to treat Russia as a fully-fledged partner', the West hindered 'normalisation processes' there.[46]

To the extent that confusion exists around the NATO issue, it relates to Secretary of State James Baker's initial assurance to Gorbachev in the summer of 1990 that NATO's jurisdiction would not move beyond the inner German border. However, Washington retreated from this position after examining the practicalities of part of Germany being outside the Alliance. Gorbachev then agreed in any case to a united Germany's full inclusion in NATO. He neither asked for nor received any formal guarantees that there would be no further expansion of NATO beyond the territory of a united Germany.[47] The issue was not even under discussion at NATO at the time since the Warsaw Pact and the USSR were both still in existence. Even if the Warsaw Pact's days were clearly numbered, there was no expectation in Western capitals in the autumn of 1990 that the USSR would collapse a year later.

The Russian claim also contains an important additional distortion of fact: while the Russian Federation became the legal continuer of the USSR after its collapse, Russia existed in different borders and its security interests were not synonymous with those of the USSR. Indeed, Russian leaders at the time did not want the West to regard the new Russia as a truncated form of the USSR but rather as a country that had regained its sovereignty and was returning to its European roots after the tragedy of Bolshevism. Furthermore, Russia did not question the USSR's signing of the Charter of Paris in November 1990 with the commitment to 'fully recognize the freedom of States to choose their own security arrangements'. The NATO-Russia Founding Act that it signed in 1997 similarly pledged respect for the 'inherent right' of all states 'to choose the means to ensure their own security'.

Moscow does not point the finger of blame at Germany for NATO enlargement although it could easily do so since the policy originated there. Rather, it identifies Washington as the culprit since Russian military planners view NATO as an organisation run by the USA in the same way that the USSR operated the Warsaw Pact. In fact, Kohl's Defence Minister, Volker Rühe, was the first senior Western official to call for what he called the 'opening of NATO'. He was deeply convinced of the need to integrate Poland into NATO to prevent Poland from establishing a separate regional security mechanism. Genscher was opposed and Kohl was lukewarm, particularly after hearing Yeltsin complain about Rühe during a session together in the sauna. Rühe discussed the issue openly with senior Russian officials and their advisers. Although he was opposed by Kohl's national security adviser and large sections of the Bundeswehr senior leadership, he nevertheless pressed ahead.

In Washington, he met with initial scepticism from President Clinton and his principal Russia adviser, Deputy Secretary of State Strobe Talbott. Both wanted to avoid weakening Yeltsin's position. Rühe shared with the Americans a RAND Study on enlargement that he had commissioned. In late 1993, with the help of the German NATO Secretary General Manfred Wörner and backed by Canada, Denmark and the Netherlands, he was able to persuade the USA to agree to the principle of opening NATO to new members. Rühe relates that up to that point, Washington was pursuing a new initiative known as Partnership for Peace intended as a substitute for NATO enlargement.[48] The US State Department eventually came to support NATO enlargement on the basis that 'when Germany looks east it should see west'.[49] While the USA came to support the initiative to enlarge NATO, the real driving force was the Central Europeans themselves. Rühe was the first senior Western official to understand the justification for their desire to join the Alliance and the need to satisfy it.

Similarly, there has been no vilification of Kohl by Russian officials and no insinuations that he took advantage of Gorbachev's weakness to secure favourable terms for reunification. Responding to his death in 2017, Putin spoke in dignified terms, referring to private visits that Kohl had made to meet with him and how Kohl's deep understanding of international affairs and relations between Russia and Europe had made a strong impression on him, even making him change his view on some issues.[50] This was the highest accolade for a Western leader.

For the Russian Army, the withdrawal within four years of nearly 340,000 soldiers and over 200,000 civilians together with 5,000 tanks, 10,000 combat vehicles, 500 helicopters and accompanying ammunition stocks represented a Herculean challenge. It required the use of 132,000 railway wagons at a time when the railway system of the former USSR was in a chaotic state.[51] Nevertheless, the withdrawal was completed ahead of schedule but without proper arrangements for receiving the returning forces. The acute shortage of military housing, partly offset by German-funded resettlement projects that were part of the aid package agreed with the FRG, became a symbol of the humiliation experienced by the Russian army in the 1990s.

Conclusions

If Russian memories of German reunification are uncomfortable, recalling the weakness of the USSR and the poor strategic judgement of Gorbachev and Shevardnadze, Germans think of the two leaders as having demonstrated bravery and vision by lifting the Stalinist yoke on Central and Eastern Europe and allowing the continent to reunite. As the German historian Heinrich Winkler has noted, reunification settled the German question and the Polish question since Germans accepted without complaint that the borders of a united Germany were those of 1945 and not 1937, a loss of more than a quarter of the territory of the Reich. This was a direct consequence of the forty-five-year division of Germany.[52] Both Germans and Russians tend to underplay the degree of luck involved at the time in avoiding a major confrontation. Equally, both are inclined to view Gorbachev's blessing of reunification on Western terms as generosity when in fact there were no serious alternatives. However, despite their sharp differences of interpretation over the motivations of the Soviet leadership at the time, a polemic on the issue between Moscow and Berlin is conspicuously absent. They are able to agree to disagree.

Reunification continues to influence the bilateral relationship since it remains an emotive issue for many Germans in policymaking positions today who were in their twenties when it occurred and are part of the generation that can remember the Cold War and its spectacularly peaceful end. That outcome appears all the more remarkable in the context of today's confrontation between Russia and Europe and Moscow's efforts to rewrite the security arrangements that enshrined the vision of a Europe 'whole and free'. For today's Russian leadership, it was also a defining event, but a humiliating one. The liberation of Central Europe from the Soviet yoke was not a reason for celebration. On the contrary, it demonstrated the incompetence of Gorbachev and his team. Not surprisingly, while Moscow has encouraged Germans to be grateful for allowing it to unify on such generous terms, it has also appealed to their sense of responsibility for not capitalising on the opportunity to build a Europe from Lisbon to Vladivostok. In this case, cultivating Germany's guilt complex is a valuable tool for encouraging acceptance of the need to revise European security arrangements to 'include' Russia. These efforts occasionally find sympathy at a high level. The former Moscow ambassador, von Fritsch, casually suggests in a recent book that Germany and its partners in the pan-European Organization for Security and Co-operation in Europe (OSCE) should look again at the proposals tabled by President Medvedev in 2009.[53] Germany and its NATO allies showed no interest in them at the time because they were a blatant attempt to put NATO out of business.

The deep sense of shock felt by the German political class in 2014 after Russia's annexation of Crimea and its destabilisation of south-eastern Ukraine once again triggered discussion about how Germany and its allies had failed to embrace the opportunity after 1991 to build a new pan-European security system. If the FRG had been able to transform its relationship with its western neighbours after 1945, surely a united Germany should be able to do the same with the East, the thinking went during the euphoria of reunification. This view ignored the obvious fact that the FRG's integration into the West had been key to achieving reconciliation with its western neighbours and was precisely the reason why such a vision was unrealistic in the case of Russia. It implied that Russia was going to become part of the same western community. Germans, of all peoples, should have known that despite the pro-Western voices in the new Russian leadership, for Russia to follow the same path would have required a revolution in society's cultural attitudes to build democratic institutions and establish rule of law. Neither had ever existed in Russia. Germans after all only succeeded in creating a full-blooded western-style democracy thanks to occupation by the Western powers for a decade after the end of the Second World War. Russia's leaders were not equipped to build them on their own. Although Russia emerged from the end of the Cold War with a sense of catastrophe, it was not prepared to accept that it had suffered defeat. The collapse of the USSR was in no sense a *Stunde Null* (zero hour) as Germany experienced on 8 May 1945.

4

A failure to read Russia correctly

From the collapse of the USSR in 1991 up to Russia's annexation of Crimea in 2014, Germany's Russia policy was remarkably consistent. It rested on the principle of seeking wide-ranging cooperation with Moscow bilaterally as well as through the EU and NATO with the aim of integrating a democratising Russia into Europe. Its underlying assumption was that Russia could be an economic and a security partner for both Germany and Europe. Common interests would outweigh differences. Germany was not alone among European countries in harbouring hopes that Russia could establish a democratic political system, but it believed in them more deeply and held on to them for longer because of its own experience of successful integration into western structures after 1945.

Unification had reinforced Germany's sense of its own transformation since 1945 and persuaded its political class of the need for further European integration to accommodate its increased weight. German policymakers saw this as a broader process that would embrace Russia and the countries in between. Germany's reconciliation with France, in particular, provided an example of how to overcome the past through a shared vision of embedding Germany economically and politically in a community of European states while developing strong ties between its peoples. Why should it not be possible for Russia to do the same? After all, there was a deep historical affinity between the two countries rather than a tradition of enmity despite the tragedies of the First World War and the Nazi invasion. The practice of town twinning and other forms of civic partnership developed between the FRG and France in the 1950s provided a template for developing ties between Germans and Russians that would come to play an important role in bilateral relations. The collapse of Soviet power, the democratic election of a Russian president and Russia's recognition of the independence of the former Soviet republics suggested not just to Germans that Russians had chosen to turn the page on the tragedies of the twentieth century and re-establish their country on a different basis just as Germans themselves had done after 1945. Germany was understandably keen to help Russia along this road as part of the final process of overcoming its past and finding peace with itself.

The problem that confronted German policymakers was the increasing divergence between the Russia they wished to see and the Russia they were dealing with. Their solution was to persuade themselves that it was easier to live with the idea that Russia was generally moving in the right direction albeit more slowly than hoped, than to concede that Russia's leaders did not share the values and interests underlying Germany's optimistic vision for its development. By the end of the 1990s, Moscow had shown that it had other ideas. It did not want to integrate with western structures since this required surrendering sovereignty. It recognised the independence of the former Soviet republics but questioned their sovereignty. In Moldova and Georgia it was sustaining separatist entities that it had helped to create. In foreign relations, it hankered after nineteenth-century 'great power' diplomacy while at home it preferred the tradition of strong centralised rule with limited accountability. It showed concern for the human rights of the Russia diaspora in the former Soviet republics but much less so for those of its citizens at home. Its behaviour demonstrated that it had no interest in creating a culture of rule of law, tolerating not just high levels of corruption but extreme criminalisation of the economy. Instead of relishing the opportunities available to reconnect Russia with Europe, its elites retreated into resentment, increasingly blaming the West for failing to treat Russia properly while themselves showing casual disregard for the welfare of their own citizens.

All these trends were visible by the end of the 1990s and in some cases became magnified as Russia became wealthier and more confident in line with rising commodity prices. Despite promises to establish a 'dictatorship of the law', the system established under Vladimir Putin centralised the distribution of economic rents to a new group of insiders and protected itself by bringing prosecutors and judges under its direct control. Its enforcement of rules of the game based on 'understandings' from the criminal world became Russia's version of rule of law.

In fairness, policymakers do not have the luxury of hindsight to inform their judgements. The revolutions of 1989 had consequences that required the German government to react simultaneously at different levels. While it was privatising the GDR's economic assets, it was negotiating the Maastricht Treaty and creating a path towards a single currency while worrying about refugee flows from the former Yugoslavia and, potentially, from the former USSR. In the aftermath of the break-up of the USSR, it had to consider not just how to mitigate the collapse of the Soviet economy but also how to secure the parts of the Soviet nuclear arsenal now located beyond Moscow's direct control in Kazakhstan and Ukraine. Preventing the smuggling of nuclear materials was another urgent challenge, while the reliability of Russia's Chernobyl-style nuclear power plants was a serious additional concern. These were dangerous times and Kohl later noted, thinking back to 1989 and afterwards that 'with God's help we reached the other side of the bank'.[1]

Nevertheless, after 1991 official German thinking on Russia settled comfortably into a groove and proved hard to shift because of its insistence that Russia had chosen a new path of development and was making progress despite obvious problems. It did not ask enough questions about the feasibility of the change that it wished to see in Russia, the type of system that was emerging and the effects of Germany's support for it as a stepping-stone towards democracy. Germany was not alone in trying to do the right thing but inadvertently strengthening trends that it wished to discourage. For example, supporting Yeltsin because he was a democrat was problematic when his actions were undermining democracy. Equally, buying into the Kremlin's version of the rule of law in the Schröder years reinforced the emergence of a legal culture that undermined the investment environment that Germany wished to improve. In different ways, Britain, France and the USA also persisted with outdated frameworks for dealing with Russia up to at least 2005 when Moscow's different positions on Iraq and Ukraine as well its domestic political agenda had made it plain that there was an increasing disparity of values between Russia and Europe and rapidly decreasing opportunities for partnership. However, Paris, London and Washington had nothing approaching the intensity of Germany's overall relationship with Russia nor its distinct form of cultural, economic influence and even moral influence there. They also did not pursue policies with the same underlying belief and determination.

The importance of relations with Russia is such that since 1990, aside from the early days of Merkel's rule when Foreign Minister Frank-Walter Steinmeier was in the lead on Russia policy, they have been *Chefsache*, the preserve of the Federal Chancellery rather than the Foreign Ministry. However, up to 2014, this did not lead to diminished influence of the Foreign Ministry's traditional *Ostpolitik* thinking on policy towards Russia. During this time, there was no influential figure in the Chancellery of the stature of Horst Teltschik, Kohl's long-term foreign policy adviser to act as a counterweight. Teltschik did not have a Foreign Ministry background and did not subscribe to Foreign Ministry orthodoxies. Instead, the Foreign Ministry transferred its own to the Chancellery. For example, Hans-Dieter Lucas, the Chancellery official responsible for Russia policy in the latter years of Gerhard Schröder's rule, was a career diplomat who had previously been head of Genscher's private office and had served in Moscow. Similarly, Christoph Heusgen, Angela Merkel's influential foreign policy adviser from 2005 to 2017 came from the Foreign Ministry, although he did not have a Russia background. Heusgen's successor, Jan Hecker, a formal federal judge with no connection to the Foreign Ministry, has been the exception to the rule.

Two elements of diplomacy established in the Genscher era deserve particular attention because of their influence on Germany's overall handling of Russia. First, two generations of diplomats grew up steeped in a culture of doing business with Moscow quietly and consistently and with the goal of avoiding conflict but ready, if necessary, to test the limits of the FRG's obligations to its western allies. There was no need for grand strategy or international leadership. Kohl's dramatic seizure of the unification agenda and his decisive actions that followed ran counter to this approach. In line with Genscher's legacy, German diplomacy towards Russia from 1991 to 2014 was energetic but low-key, investing in relationships rather than actions, and seeking to shape EU policy towards Russia rather than take the lead. However, since German diplomacy was programmed to believe that Russia would increasingly develop democratic institutions and rule of law to regain strength, it lacked the instincts to adjust its policies as Russia changed. Preservation of the process became more important than its effectiveness. Expanding bilateral trade relations created the deceptive impression that the relationship was on track.

The second influence from the Genscher years related to the conduct of *Ostpolitik*. The Foreign Ministry had imbibed the lesson that it was possible to bridge seemingly irreconcilable differences with other countries provided that diplomats pursued solutions through dialogue for long enough. Sustaining détente had required constant effort between individuals to maintain trust.[2] This background explains Germany's determined and highly successful efforts since 1991 to establish mechanisms of dialogue with Russia beyond well-developed government-to-government and business ties to link the cultural and scientific communities and increase broader people-to-people contacts. These currently consist of ninety official town twinning arrangements[3] and over 900 partnerships in higher education.[4] No other European country can compete with the range and depth of connectivity developed by Germany, even if these contacts in some cases have proved harder to maintain since 2014.

Examination of Russia policy under the chancellorships of Kohl, Schröder and Merkel (up to 2014) shows that while Russia changed, the core tenets of Germany's Russia policy did not.

Helmut Kohl (1990–98)

At the time of Germany's unification in October 1990, the USSR was still in existence. Kohl signalled to foreign audiences that integration and cooperation were the 'key concepts' for developing the European architecture of the future[5] and avoiding a return to the unstable interstate relations of the nineteenth century. The post-modern era had begun, and a reunited Germany was the proof. For Kohl as a disciple of Adenauer, German unity and a unified Europe were two sides of the same coin. His message to the Soviet leadership was that people in the West had forgotten the extent of the USSR's links with Europe through culture and history and that this connectivity held political value for the future. Anxious to see Gorbachev's reforms bear fruit so that the process of German unification could continue unhindered, his vision of post-Cold War Europe included the USSR, although he placed less emphasis than Genscher on creating new all-European security arrangements.

However, Kohl quickly found himself having to build a rapport with Gorbachev's nemesis, Yeltsin, as a power struggle between the two intensified. He did so with consummate skill without offending either party just as he was able to build a close and highly effective relationship with Bill Clinton after he came to office in 1992, despite having openly supported Bush's re-election. His coordination of policy with Washington proved vital to stabilising the situation across the former USSR. Together, the USA and Germany led a process to provide emergency humanitarian aid, secure the Soviet nuclear arsenal and reschedule the USSR's Paris Club debt now held by Russia. Germany's supply of foodstuffs from Bundeswehr stocks to St Petersburg and other cities made a deep impact on Russian society in view of the Second World War history. Working in tandem with Clinton, Kohl lobbied successfully for IMF and World Bank financial assistance for the new Russian government and offered German experience in 'the establishment of rule of law with efficient, capable administrations close to citizens and independent courts'.[6] Encouraging Moscow to develop *Rechtsstaatlichkeit* (rule of law) would become a recurrent theme for many years in official German statements about Russia. Against objections from several European countries, Kohl also pushed successfully for Russia's admission to the Council of Europe in 1996. Moscow's brutal intervention in Chechnya and its deficiencies around the rule of law and observance of human rights had shown that it did not meet the standards of membership.[7]

The withdrawal of Russian troops from the former GDR, ahead of schedule, contributed to a relationship of trust between Kohl and Yeltsin and encouraged the view in Germany and other western countries that Yeltsin was a man of his word and, therefore, the best guardian of democratic development in Russia. Kohl later acknowledged that Yeltsin could have legitimately asked for an extension since there had been delays in building accommodation for the returning forces that were not the fault of the Russian side. Kohl also noted that by honouring his commitment, Yeltsin had gone against the recommendations of his advisers. The number of desertions by Russian soldiers and the greater frequency of criminal behaviour by the remaining Russian forces were a growing source of concern for the German government.[8] This perceived act of goodwill towards Germany reinforced an attitude of forgiveness for Yeltsin's actions at home. For Kohl, Yeltsin had proved to be 'a completely reliable partner'.[9] He also kept his word on the extradition of the former GDR leader Erich Honecker who had fled to Moscow after the collapse of the GDR and taken refuge in the Embassy of Chile. The Russian authorities immediately flew Honecker to Berlin after he left the embassy in July 1992.

The shelling of the Russian Parliament building in October 1993 during a constitutional crisis came close to triggering civil war and the subsequent establishment of a super-presidency, raising serious questions about the path of political development that Russia was taking. Yeltsin noted before the escalation of his conflict with the Russian Parliament Kohl's prediction that other western countries would sympathise with his use of 'harsh but necessary measures for the stabilization of Russia'.[10] Yeltsin's ill-fated decision to deploy the Russian Army to bring Chechnya to heel put a strain on relations with western countries, including Germany, as it became clear that tens of thousands of civilians had lost their lives. Volker Rühe, the Defence Minister even disinvited his Russian counterpart from the Munich Security Conference in protest. However, Rühe was an exception. Kohl and his Foreign Minister, Klaus Kinkel, resorted to mild rebukes, arguing that Chechnya was an internal affair for Russia and warning of the domino effect if other national republics in the Russian Federation tried to follow Chechnya's example.[11]

When Kohl visited Moscow in May 1994, he sensed that Germany and Russia already enjoyed relations of partnership. Germany was Russia's largest trade partner; economic and cultural agreements were in place and both sides had committed to addressing the sensitive issue of works of art seized from each other at the end of the war. Since his visit to Russia in 1992, Kohl had met five times with Yeltsin and they spoke regularly every two weeks over a direct phone line. Haunted by the wars in the former Yugoslavia, Kohl expected that Moscow would respond to his efforts to make Russia part of the G7 political process by playing a constructive role in addressing crises in Europe and beyond.[12] The personal chemistry between the two men was remarkable given their different backgrounds and temperaments. They were indebted to each other – Yeltsin to Kohl for his support during the 1991 coup and later for bringing Russia into the G7 process; Kohl to Yeltsin for keeping to all his commitments to Germany. If their joint visits to the sauna were a mystery to Kohl's wife,[13] they showed the strong bond between the two men.

Ahead of the 1996 presidential election that Yeltsin was in severe danger of losing to his Communist Party rival, Gennady Zyuganov, Kohl openly expressed support for Yeltsin. Conscious of the risks of taking sides, he saw it as a stark choice between the forces of old that wished to maintain an isolated Russia or a reformist leadership that felt 'part of the world community'.[14] At the same time, Kohl was both realistic and sensitive in his thinking about Russia. Just as he developed concerns about Gorbachev's ability to deliver his reforms as the unification process reached a critical juncture, he worried about the ability of Yeltsin's government to improve the lives of Russian citizens and retain their support. Like Clinton, he recognised the need to respect Russia's national pride and show understanding for Moscow's sense of its diminished place in the world. For him it was important to avoid behaviour that could reinforce Russia's feeling of humiliation while he was also conscious of Russia's historical fears of isolation and encirclement.[15] This certainly explains his initially lukewarm attitude to the idea of NATO enlargement – a sentiment shared both in the Clinton White House and by the US Secretary of Defense, William Perry.

The highly ambitious EU–Russia Partnership and Co-operation

Agreement signed in June 1994 (and ratified in 1997) with its vision of a free trade zone reflected the German desire to treat Russia with respect and to provide a framework for it to become part of a wider European project. It stressed the 'paramount importance' of the rule of law and respect for human rights and the establishment of a multi-party system with free and democratic elections.[16] The EU saw its role in promoting 'gradual rapprochement between Russia and a wider area of co-operation in Europe and neighbouring regions and Russia's progressive integration into the open international trading system'.[17] To support this vision, the EU offered Russia significant technical assistance but no financial package.

Yeltsin's election victory in 1996 owed much to the biased media reporting of his campaign compared to the Communist leader Zyuganov's as well as violations of campaign financing rules. There were also allegations of voter fraud. However, neither Germany nor the EU rushed to express concern at the conclusions of western observers of the vote. It would later turn out that Yeltsin's victory had come at the cost of 'loans for shares' agreements that sold off valuable state assets to a handful of politically connected businessmen at rock bottom prices and helped fund the re-election campaign. This fateful step distorted the shape of the economy and undermined the prospects for developing democratic governance by establishing rentier capitalism that favoured a chosen few. Yegor Gaidar, architect of the radical reforms of 1992 that deregulated prices and laid the economic foundations for a market economy, noted in a later memoir that the main question after Yeltsin's election victory in July 1996 was whether Russia would have 'civilised capitalism accountable to society' or 'bureaucratic, corrupt (capitalism) where severe social inequality breeds waves of socio-political instability'.[18] He did not foresee at the time that rising commodity prices would allow Russia to sustain the latter through a combination of economic growth and restriction of civic freedoms. As Gaidar and his team moved swiftly to create market conditions in 1992, global oil prices were below

$20 a barrel. By 2004, they had almost doubled, bringing increasing relief to the Russian budget as they continued to climb steeply.

Yeltsin's respect for Kohl was an important factor in persuading the Russian government to negotiate a deeper relationship with NATO to offset the negative consequences of NATO enlargement perceived by Russia's military planners. He never forgot Kohl's role in opening the doors of the G7 for Russia.[19] When Kohl visited Russia in early 1997, he found that Yeltsin looked five to ten years older than when he had last seen him just a few months before.[20] Yeltsin was also feeling sore about NATO's plans to enlarge, believing that Clinton had personally let him down by pursuing the policy. As the former diplomat Andrei Kovalev has noted, when Primakov took over as foreign minister in 1996, 'he poisoned the attitude of the Kremlin, parliament and the previously neutral public attitude toward NATO' that led to Russia adopting 'an irrational and illogical' position on NATO.[21] Yeltsin told Kohl that 'the security of all European countries depends on Russia feeling secure'. This was a pithy summary of the core problem in Russia's relations with Europe, and remains valid today. The traditional security policy thinkers in Moscow believed that others needed to sacrifice a degree of their security for Russia to feel secure. This meant that Russia could not accept its neighbours and former allies choosing their own security arrangements independently of Moscow despite its commitment to observe Helsinki security principles defined in the 1990 Charter of Paris signed by the USSR. The corollary of this was that Russia wished to preserve Central Europe as a 'grey zone', a firebreak between NATO and Russia with no regard for the impact on the countries concerned.[22]

Submerged in this approach were signs of the traditional belief that for Russia to be a great country, others must fear it. Despite this fundamental difference of view, Kohl spoke in July 1997 of German–Russian relations being the best in history.[23] In language that was to set the tone for later German policy towards Russia, he said that it was 'now necessary to tie together (*flechten*) the network of partnership with Russia ever closer'[24] through political and economic development and support for Russia's transition to a market economy.

As Kohl's term ended in October 1998, the gap between Russia's demands for treatment as a 'great power' and its diminished economic power could not have been greater. The Asian currency crisis cruelly exposed Russia's economic weakness, in particular its dependency on oil exports and its very weak ability to collect taxes. The financial meltdown in August that year had led to the Russian state defaulting on $40 billion-worth of short-term treasury bonds. The rouble lost over three times its value to the dollar and inflation soared to over 80 per cent, inflicting renewed suffering on a population that had begun to adjust to the shocks of the economic disruption in 1991–92. German hopes for stable and sustainable economic growth in Russia lay in tatters. Just over a year earlier, the G7 countries had formally added Russia as a member. German hopes that the NATO–Russia Permanent Joint Council could build bridges between the Alliance and Moscow were also under threat as it became clear that the two sides had sharply divergent positions on the escalating conflict in Kosovo.

At this time, Andrei Zagorski, an astute Russian analyst, noted that Germany and Russia had parallel rather than shared interests. Differing views of Europe as well as Germany's firm emphasis on maintaining strong transatlantic ties to support European integration limited the possibilities for developing a genuine partnership between the two countries. Russia was not ready to forgo sovereignty to support collective decision-making in multilateral formats.[25] In addition, he noted the imbalance in the economic relationship: in the mid-1990s raw materials accounted for 90 per cent of Russia's exports to Germany while bilateral trade was far more important for Russia (15–17 per cent of its foreign trade balance) while for Germany trade with Russia was only 2 per cent of its overall foreign trade.[26]

For all the enthusiastic rhetoric from Berlin about the development of democracy, rule of law and market economy in Russia,
and the establishment of closer relations between governments
and peoples, there were clear signs that Russia did not want to
take up the western offer of partnership on the terms offered.
From the Russian perspective, the new institutional arrangements
for developing ties NATO were a damage limitation measure
in response to the Alliance's enlargement and a test of whether
NATO countries would treat Russia as an equal member of the
European security community. Opportunities for cooperation and
joint action with NATO were of less interest than a potential
veto over Alliance decision-making. At the same time, seen from
Moscow, membership of the G8 cost the West little and was clearly
designed as a measure to flatter Russia since its economy was five
times smaller than Germany's. Russia's internal transition was also
moving down an increasingly problematic path as the westernis-
ing reformers found themselves increasingly marginalised and the
influence of the main business owning groups grew. Partnership
with the EU sounded attractive on paper but in reality required
painstaking efforts over many years to adjust regulation and har-
monise legislation that were far beyond the immediate capabilities
of Russia's unreformed bureaucracy.

Gerhard Schröder (1998–2005)

The 1998 Coalition Agreement between the SPD and the Greens
contained just two short sentences on policy towards with Russia.
France and Poland ranked higher. The new government would
place relations with Russia and Ukraine 'on a broad footing' with
the 'aim of securing stability in this area by supporting democratic, rule of law, social and market economy reforms'.[27] The
reference to the broad base for relations implied that Schröder
would distance himself from Kohl's 'sauna friendship' with Yeltsin
and there would be a stronger focus on human rights issues. Born

in 1944, the new chancellor belonged to a different generation from Kohl and did not have the same direct memories of the war even it had affected his upbringing. His father had died in combat in Romania six months after his birth.

When Schröder made his first visit to Moscow as chancellor in late 1998, the Russian government was still reeling from the effects of the August default and hopeful that Germany would provide financial assistance. Schröder was in no position to oblige. The German economy was barely growing, and unemployment was at a post-war high at close to five million. Some of this malaise was attributable to absorbing the cost of an overvalued exchange rate as the political price for integrating the economy of the former GDR while annual financial support worth 5 per cent of GDP for the new eastern regions (*Länder*) remained a heavy burden. With Yeltsin's health declining rapidly, there were limited opportunities for the new chancellor to build a personal relationship. The failure of international diplomacy over Kosovo in 1999 had cast a deep shadow over Russia's relations with NATO and led to the expulsion from Moscow of the Alliance's two representatives based at the German embassy. The participation of the Bundeswehr in NATO's air operation against Yugoslavia without a UN mandate – the first combat deployment of German forces since 1945 – provided a severe test of the new coalition. It succeeded in standing firm during the seventy-eight-day campaign until the combination of Russian and European diplomacy persuaded President Milosevic to change course and accept NATO's demands. The episode revealed the limitations of the NATO-Russia Permanent Joint Council. NATO listened to Moscow's objections to the use of force to stop Milosevic's abuses against the majority Kosovar population, but chose to ignore them after international diplomatic efforts with Russia's participation failed. NATO allies witnessed divisions within the Russian government as Yeltsin desperately tried to end the conflict before the G8 Summit in June and Russian forces dashed to Kosovo ahead of a NATO peacekeeping force, nearly triggering a confrontation between the two. This was a worrying indication that the Russian President had lost his authority and that the country was not under proper control. At the same time, there was an outpouring of anti-western, nationalistic rhetoric in Russia. The Soviet dissident writer, Alexander Zinoviev, who had lived in Munich after expulsion from the USSR in 1978, spoke for many Russians when he branded NATO's intervention in Kosovo 'a rehearsal for Russia'.[28]

Six months later, Yeltsin had left office, ceding the reins of power to Vladimir Putin, a young German-speaking former KGB officer who had made an unspectacular career, spending five years in a bureaucratic backwater in Dresden, where he appeared to have little success in his job of recruiting agents in the FRG and had also appeared slapdash. In one case, the Stasi had to take the unusual step of warning the KGB in Moscow that Lieutenant Colonel Putin was trying to recruit a source whose cover was already blown.[29] Putin also lost the keys to the KGB office.[30] Schröder's personal relationship with Putin offered significant opportunities beyond what Kohl and Yeltsin had established, not least because Putin was a competent German speaker, and had risen to high office from humble origins like Schröder. Together with the British Prime Minister Tony Blair, Schröder thought that Putin was a moderniser who deserved personal support. Putin's early years in office appeared to offer confirmation that he wanted to put Russia on a path of rapid modernisation as he oversaw the implementation of economic reforms designed in the 1990s that sparked economic growth and with it, from the German perspective, a welcome increase in trade with Germany. Compared to the Yeltsin days, it seemed to Berlin and other western capitals that Putin had also brought greater stability and predictability. At the same time, the Russian army's campaign in Chechnya and the Kremlin's efforts to control the media quickly showed that modernisation in Russia might take place at the expense of the values that Russia had committed to uphold as a 'strategic partner' of the EU.

Initially, Schröder saw Germany's relations with Russia in the context of its closer ties with both the EU and NATO in which bilateral relations provided a model for the broader process of establishing a partnership with Russia in Europe.[31] Having established a personal rapport with Putin, he spoke of wanting to establish a 'new normality' in relations: 'without illusions, without sentimentalities; open, trusting and engaged, but without denying at the same time our considerable respective interests of our own (*Eigeninteressen*)'.[32] He also referred to the establishment of 'a community of values' as the first requirement for Europe to continue growing together, citing Russia's accession to the Council of Europe and its signing of the European Human Rights Convention. At the same time, he stressed the economic complementarity between Europe and Russia since Russia had abundant raw materials and human capital while the EU was Russia's most important economic partner. He believed in the idea of an energy alliance between Germany and Russia. Echoing the language of Kohl, he referred to the desirability of an 'ever closer fabric of relations' (*Beziehungsgeflecht*) between societies in Russia and Germany that would help the process of finding a solution to the outstanding issues of works of art stolen from each other during the war that were still a burden on relations.[33] Putin later remarked that Schröder had criticised elements of Kohl's Russia policy when in opposition but continued the same line when he became chancellor.[34]

Putin expected to be dealing with a less cooperative German leader. He noted in 2002 that the information he initially received about Schröder said that he was 'reserved' and 'very cold', so he prepared himself accordingly. One can only assume that, as a former intelligence officer specialist in the art of recruitment,[35] Putin was well equipped for the task. To what extent Schröder knew or cared about the tradecraft Putin had learned is unclear. Putin himself had said that his experience of 'work with people' had been useful to him when he moved from the KGB to work at Leningrad University in 1990.[36] The Russian President realised that the ice had broken when Schröder went out of his way to accommodate a request by Putin and his wife to meet privately with an old female friend from their Dresden days 'from the family of a Stasi employee'. Schröder invited her to a lunch with the Putins followed by an excursion on the Elbe. According to Putin, this was a sign that he had made friends with 'a decent man'.[37] Schröder accompanied by his wife and daughter took up a personal invitation from Putin to join him and his family to celebrate Orthodox Christmas in January 2001.

This was a clear indication that an unusually strong relationship was developing between the two men. No other European leader had this level of connection with the new Russian President. Schröder said that he and Putin chatted long into the night, establishing a relationship that went 'beyond the political – without any doubt'.[38] Their wives became jointly involved in the running of a German-Russian Youth Forum set up by their husbands to promote the learning of Russian and German in both countries. The partnership of the wives proved less durable than what German media described as a 'friendship of men' (*Männerfreundschaft*) since both marriages ended in divorce. Continuing the trend from the Kohl years of the Chancellery leading Russia policy, Schröder did not encounter resistance from the Green Foreign Minister, Joschka Fischer, who had little interest in the East. This made him a peripheral figure in relations with Moscow throughout his seven years in office.

Putin's courting of the German political and business elite began in earnest in September 2001 shortly after 9/11 when he addressed the German Parliament in German in a brilliantly written, well delivered speech that is still regularly quoted today. He played cleverly on German historical and cultural perceptions of Russia. He called for Russia's integration into Europe to secure Europe's position as a 'powerful and independent middle point in global politics' based on unifying its capabilities with 'Russia's human, territorial and natural resources as well as with its economic, cultural and defence potential'.[39] The video footage of the speech shows how effectively Putin was able to communicate with his audience despite his obvious nervousness. Many MPs found themselves moved by a young Russian president addressing them in their own language about the spirit of democracy and freedom in Russia and the depth of its cultural relations with Germany. There was little reference to the war. Instead, Putin made flattering mentions of Berlin's spirit of humanism, the influence of German literature on Russians and the considerable role that Germans, including Catherine the Great, had played in Russia's historical development. The speaker was telling his listeners what they wanted to hear. However, there was also a harsher sub-text. Putin referred to the deficiencies of the NATO–Russia cooperation mechanisms and Russia's inability to participate in NATO's decision-making. He also pointed to the lack of trust in Russia's relations with the West related to NATO enlargement and US plans to deploy a missile defence system. Two weeks after declaring solidarity with the US following the terrorist attacks, he could be both pro-American and anti-American, a dichotomy that sold well to a German audience that also had mixed feelings towards the USA.

A few weeks earlier, Schröder had said in an interview that in the long term, the possibility of Russia joining NATO could not be ruled out.[40] He claimed that he was simply echoing the words of Bush's National Security Adviser, Condoleeza Rice, after Putin had raised the issue at his first summit meeting with Bush. In May 2002, with strong support from Germany and the UK, NATO upgraded the NATO–Russia Permanent Joint Council now called the NATO-Russia Council to make Russia an equal alongside NATO member states. Under the previous arrangements, NATO had spoken haltingly to Russia with a single Alliance voice based on carefully crafted consensus positions. However, the apparent progress in improving NATO's relations with Russia contrasted with the setback in US–Russia relations after the decision by the Bush administration to withdraw from the 1972 Anti-Ballistic Missile Treaty signed with the USSR to allow it to focus on building a missile defence system. Moscow feared that the development of such a system would threaten its second-strike nuclear capability and undermine strategic stability.

Relations with Russia appeared to offer an easy, unexpected 'win' for Schröder both domestically and internationally in an otherwise crowded government agenda that included urgent domestic reform, difficulties related to EU enlargement and tensions in relations with Washington. Russia was not a priority issue yet there was strong public support for friendly ties between the two countries, and Schröder's close personal relations with Putin gave him a competitive advantage over all other leaders of major western countries in terms of access to the Kremlin, except possibly for Italy's prime minister, Silvio Berlusconi. In 2003, he boldly joined forces with Chirac and Putin in opposing military action against Iraq by the USA and the UK, and called instead for UN weapons inspectors to return to Iraq. At the time, Germany had a non-permanent seat in the UN Security Council, and Schröder indicated that Germany would not support a resolution sanctioning use of force. The leader of the opposition CDU, Angela Merkel, accused him of making war in Iraq more likely and of weakening both NATO and the EU.[41]

Putin's successful interaction with the French and German leaders within the 'triangle' originally established by Kohl possibly marked the high point of his influence in Europe when he appeared to symbolise hope that Russia was on a path of modernisation that would bring it closer to Europe and sustain the process of erasing dividing lines of the past. He also showed some deft footwork. By befriending France and Germany, he contributed to divisions within in NATO but he left himself room for manoeuvre with Washington with an offer of relief to

Iraq on its $8 billion debt to Russia. Condoleeza Rice reportedly described US policy in response to the 'triangular' opposition as 'Punish France, Ignore Germany, Forgive Russia'.[42] Putin had outsmarted his two European allies. Schröder may have escaped lightly but he had demonstrated to Putin that he was ready to ally himself with anti-American sentiment in Germany for political benefit.

As liberal economic reforms began to bear fruit in the early years of Putin's rule, boosted by rising oil prices and greater political stability, bilateral trade grew significantly. In 1999, Germany imported €8.4 billion worth of goods (mainly oil and gas) from Russia. In 2003, the figure rose to €14.2 billion. Proportionally, exports rose even more – from €5.1 million in 1999 to €12.1 million in 2003, principally cars, machinery and chemical products.[43] Germany's powerful business lobby was delighted. Not surprisingly, German industry saw considerable attractions in a fast-growing Russian market where it had considerable competitive advantage because of its experience and connections, not to mention its enduring reputation as a supplier of high-quality products. The energy companies E.ON Ruhrgas and BASF/Wintershall were particularly interested in expanding the gas relationship since the government planned to start phasing out nuclear power and because declining gas reserves in Western Europe were raising concerns about security of gas supply. With the Russian economy now expanding quickly – growth was over 7 per cent in 2003 as GDP more than doubled after the collapse in 1998–99 – German diplomats began to speak of Germany having the best relations with Russia for 100 years.

Schröder had now assumed Kohl's mantle of speaking up for Russia's interests abroad while also personally defending Putin's actions to strengthen state authority. This included playing down the arrest of Mikhail Khodorkovsky, CEO of Yukos in late 2003, and the subsequent nationalisation of Russia's largest oil company. Accompanied by a large group of top German business managers on a visit to Moscow in July 2004, three months after Putin's re-election, Schröder claimed not to understand the 'excitement' about the Yukos case. He saw 'no indication that it had not proceeded in line with the law ... I can completely understand that a state also wants to have its taxes.'[44] Instead, he went on to praise Putin's economic reforms, while representatives of E.ON and Wintershall signed a framework agreement with the Russian national gas company Gazprom for the construction of the €6 billion North European Gas Pipeline (later known as Nord Stream) directly connecting Russia and Germany. The head of the German business lobbying association in Moscow, Andrea von Knoop, also soft-pedalled the assault on Yukos, claiming that it was a case of 'equal treatment' before the law for businesspeople who had become rich through 'faked auctions and such like'.[45] The day before Khodorkovsky's arrest, Putin had awarded her Russia's Friendship Medal.

Despite occasionally referring to the difficulties facing German companies operating in the Russian market, Schröder did not seek to influence Russia's internal developments. He consistently stopped short of expressing concern about property rights or rule of law although he said that he discussed difficulties in Russia's trans-formation process in private with Putin.[46] He was indifferent to Russia's continued retreat from democratic norms and practices, including increasing restrictions on media freedoms. He claimed bizarrely in late 2003 that Putin was an 'absolutely pure demo-crat'[47], a statement that has haunted him ever since. Like Blair, he was prepared to accept the Kremlin argument that Russia was fighting international terrorism in Chechnya, but he did so without expressing concern about the tactics used and the extent to which they could be counter-productive by breeding terrorists. However, this was not a consensus position within the coalition. He failed also to identify problems with the presidential election in Chechnya in August 2004 that saw the Kremlin-sponsored can-didate win 74 per cent of the vote amid allegations of fraud and continuing human rights violations committed by Moscow-backed paramilitary forces. 'Own interests' had trumped values.

It was understandable from a German domestic perspective that Schröder wished to boost trade with Russia as he set about reforming the German economy, and that he sensed support in his party and the broader public for developing good relations with Russia. However, Berlin's readiness to take a pragmatic approach without emphasising values suited Moscow well. Schröder's justification was along the Brechtian line of *Erst kommt das Fressen, dann die Moral* (first the grub, then the ethics). He argued that a prosperous Russia would find it easier to guarantee democracy, rule of law and free media, strongly implying that economic development had to come first.[48] He consistently referred to the scale of the task facing Putin but without warning of the scale of the problem that could arise if Russia side-lined civil society and developed unaccountable institutions on a traditional model.

Nevertheless, in 2001, he was instrumental together with Putin in creating the Petersburger Dialog, a mechanism intended to connect civil society in Germany and Russia with the involvement of representatives from the worlds of business, culture, education, media and politics (see Chapter 7). It proved to be a revealing example of the difficulties involved in deepening relations beyond government and business since it ran up against the two sides' different understandings of the term 'civil society' and the criteria for participation. For the Russian side, 'civil society' meant representatives of organisations connected with the state, while the Germans viewed it as a broad range of individuals who form the fabric of a liberal democracy. By this stage, Russia was building what Kremlin political technologists described as 'managed democracy'.

To sustain its 'business-first' approach, Germany shifted the problematic elements in relations into other fora. Difficulties related to European security belonged in NATO while the EU and the Council of Europe were the places to tackle the broader issue of Russia's adherence to European values. In the cases of both NATO and the EU, Berlin sought to widen the opportunities for dialogue and interaction with Russia, pushing hard to deepen NATO's cooperation and consultation mechanisms with Russia, while together with France creating the idea of 'four common spaces' to reinforce the flagging EU–Russia 'strategic partnership'. Frank-Walter Steinmeier, Schröder's Chief of Staff, was an enthusiastic proponent of the 'common spaces' idea. The EU–Russia Summit in May 2003 signed off on the initiative that later struggled to develop substance.

These efforts to deepen cooperation on both the NATO and EU fronts were also logical from Berlin's perspective because of the NATO decision in November 2002 to invite seven countries to begin accession negotiations, as well as the EU decision a month later to admit eight Central European countries. In both cases, Estonia, Latvia and Lithuania with their shared borders with Russia would form part of a neighbourhood that, from Moscow's perspective, had radically changed. It was tempting, therefore, for Berlin to work to keep German–Russian relations trouble free and pass them off as part of the healthy 'growing together' of Europe and Russia. The problem with this approach was that it encouraged Moscow to deal with EU capitals on a bilateral basis, a format that was more direct, less bureaucratic and included business. Not only was it far easier for it to achieve results this way, but Russia could also heavily influence EU policy by concentrating on a few capitals. Naturally, the emphasis on bilateral ties also provided opportunities to play off some EU members against others. As Moscow gradually lost interest in partnership with the EU, decreasingly viewing the organisation's intentions as benign, the temptation to exploit its divisions and prevent the emergence of a unified Russia policy grew.

In Russia, Schröder's relationship served to strengthen Putin's public image and became an increasing source of concern to Russian opposition politicians who were convinced that Germany had de-prioritised democratic values and was conducting a cynical *Realpolitik* consisting of unconditional support for Putin and lobbying the interests of German business in Russia.[49] In Germany too, discomfort was growing. Media coverage of Russia was becoming increasingly negative as civic freedoms came under further attack. However, it is noteworthy that in the run up to the Orange Revolution in Ukraine in 2004, Berlin moved quickly to uphold the principle of fair elections, accepting the conclusions of OSCE election observers that there had been massive falsification of the presidential election results.[50] Schröder played a role in defusing the crisis after speaking with Putin twice by phone to persuade him that that the election needed to be re-run.

The defining features of Schröder's Russia policy were his continuation of Kohl's personalisation of relations with the Russian president and his belief shared with his predecessor that development of trade would promote economic growth, which would in turn encourage democratisation and rule of law. There might have been merit to this view if the exact opposite had not occurred. By 2005, there were ominous signs that Russia was reverting to a neo-feudal system of governance with the associated weakening of property rights and civil society, accompanied by an increasing disregard for the principles of rule of law. German policymakers at the time either did not fully understand the developments taking place in Russia or chose to ignore them. Schröder was boasting that Germans and Russians were 'closely connected as never before' united by 'a strategic partnership for a peaceful, prosperous Europe and a stable world order'. For him this was one of the miracles of European history.[51] His family had also developed a closeness with Russia. Putin helped the Schröders adopt two children from Russia,[52] the first while Schröder was still in office. They were considered too old to adopt in Germany.

It is not hard to believe that the procurement of children created a kinship between the two men that Putin was able to exploit to the maximum. The Chancellor's lobbying of the Nord Stream pipeline and his later acceptance of the role of Chairman of the Shareholder Committee of the company building the pipeline caused outrage in Germany. He and Putin had attended a ceremony to mark the signing of the contract on the construction of the pipeline two weeks before Schröder left office, and the former chancellor confirmed his acceptance of the new role barely three months later. This was a coup for Putin and revealed Germany's lack of regulation to prevent senior government officials from exposing themselves to potential conflicts of interest. It also pointed to a disturbing tendency to disregard the sensitivities of Poland and Lithuania that objected to the project. Visiting Berlin in October 2005, the Lithuanian President castigated Berlin for not consulting with Vilnius on the issue, accusing the Chancellor of 'complete ignorance' of neighbourly relations.[53] Schröder replied that Germany had 'a sovereign right to take steps to make sure it has reliable and sustainable energy resources'.[54] It was symbolic that the Schröder era of relations with Russia should end on this sour note. It showed that for the sake of the 'strategic partnership' Germany was prepared to suspend its moral principles in favour of economic interests.

Angela Merkel (2005–14)

The 2005 CDU/CSU election programme used strong language to distance itself from Schröder's foreign policy, noting the lack of a comprehensive foreign and security policy concept and the damage to Germany's reputation in the world 'through a systematic hollowing out of NATO and through Russia and China policies bereft of principles'. It expressed a desire for good relations with Russia – but not over the heads of its neighbours and it called for Germany not to ignore problematic internal developments in Russia.[55] However, the need for a Grand Coalition produced a policy vision that differed less significantly from the previous SPD–Green version. It noted that Germany had a particular interest in supporting Russia's modernisation and that its aim was a prosperous Russia 'orientated to values to which Europe is committed' that 'with consideration of its traditions successfully overcomes the transition to a stable democracy'.[56] The divisions over the emphasis of policy were clearly visible in the handling of Russia by the new chancellor, Angela Merkel, and foreign minister, Frank-Walter Steinmeier. Merkel brought a new coolness to the personal relationship with Putin. With her East German background and command of Russian, she was far better placed than her predecessor to read Putin's intentions. She spoke pointedly of partnership between Germany and Russia rather than friendship, and unlike Schröder, she made a point of meeting with NGO representatives when she visited Moscow, and speaking publicly about democratic values. She clearly felt a degree of empathy with Russia. She recalled in a speech in 2006 how aged 14 she visited Moscow and Yaroslavl and went to a disco for the first time where, to her amazement, some young Russians told her that Germany could not be divided permanently. Conversations of this kind did not take place in the GDR.[57]

Meanwhile, Steinmeier was promoting a neo-*Ostpolitik* policy of *Annäherung durch Verflechtung* (Growing Closer Through Tying Together), focused on promoting closer relations between the EU and Russia while de-emphasising the broader goal of supporting political and social modernisation in Russia. This was a significant narrowing of the cooperation field. In language that must have pleased Moscow, the German Foreign Ministry had concluded in a strategy paper that despite Russia developing along a different path from the EU, it remained an important partner that was vital for preserving peace in Europe and resolving conflict in the Balkans and the Middle East.[58] Germany was making itself the *demandeur* in the relationship. It spoke vaguely of promoting 'Russia's constructive engagement through new offers of co-operation and integration' and 'anchoring it irreversibly in Europe through close political, economic and cultural relations'.[59]

The preparation of the paper before the start of Germany's EU presidency in January 2007 was significant. Steinmeier was trying to lay the foundations for negotiating an updated EU–Russia Partnership and Co-operation Agreement by demonstrating that Russia was still welcome in Europe despite increasing frictions over the EU's relations with the former Soviet republics and EU concerns about Russia's back-sliding on its commitments to uphold democratic values. Steinmeier reportedly feared that failure to tie Russia to Europe could lead to it forming an anti-western axis with China.[60] In the view of the Foreign Ministry, an updated EU–Russia agreement should include a free trade area and discussion about closer cooperation with Russia as part of European security and defence policy, including possible joint peacekeeping. The strategy paper placed strong emphasis on the energy relationship and the advantage of putting energy security on to a reciprocal legal basis, including acceptance of EU competition rules.

By 2006, there were growing doubts in Europe about Gazprom's ability to supply both its domestic and international customers. However, there was little sign of concern in Berlin about the evolution of Russia's energy diplomacy and the use of energy relations to seek political advantage in relations with neighbours, even if it was alert to problems related to allowing Russian energy companies to acquire downstream assets in Germany.[61] Nevertheless, Merkel was keen to calm nerves in Poland about its susceptibility to Russian blackmail after the construction of the new Baltic gas pipeline linking Germany and Russia, promising that the German EU presidency would push for Poland to have access to the EU's common energy market. In a departure from her usual realistic approach to Russia, she expressed the hope that Moscow would ratify the Energy Charter Treaty that would protect European investments in the Russian energy sector. Putin had signalled shortly before that there would be no ratification.[62]

Like other western capitals, Berlin appeared to disregard the danger signs in Putin's speech at the Munich Security Conference in February 2007. For the first time, its tone and content revealed the depth of Moscow's frustration with what it viewed as western efforts led by the USA to marginalise Russia in international affairs by bypassing the authority of the UN as it had done in Iraq and trying to replace it with decisions made by NATO and the EU. It was a veiled warning that Russia and the West were on a collision course. Putin also spoke directly about Russia's unhappiness with US plans for missile defence and the refusal by NATO countries to ratify the Conventional Forces in Europe Treaty. He picked up too the theme of how NATO had deceived Moscow over enlargement, asking what had happened to the guarantees it had given to the USSR.[63] This was a reminder that Russia viewed itself as the inheritor of security 'assurances' given to Gorbachev and that it was losing patience over NATO's continued enlargement. The Baltic states had joined the Alliance in 2004 and both Georgia and Ukraine were now seeking membership. A further trend that Berlin had failed to consider, together with most other NATO members, was the rebuilding of the Russian armed forces. The military budget received substantial annual increases from the end of the 1990s after a period of neglect when the army suffered a calamitous loss of discipline and prestige culminating in its humiliation in Chechnya. It was not just the former KGB that was making a comeback.

The Russo-Georgian war in the summer of 2008 set alarm bells ringing in Berlin and exposed a lack of realism in policy thinking. Just three months earlier, Steinmeier had outlined his concept of a 'modernisation partnership' between Germany and Russia, describing Russia as 'Germany and the EU's indispensable partner in shaping tomorrow's political world' and in providing 'security and stability in Europe and far beyond'.[64] Georgia was the first unmistakable indication that Moscow had chosen to break with the West, and that beyond technological modernisation it was not interested in the 'historically unique transformation process'[65] that Germany saw open to it. While Merkel called Russian actions in

Georgia 'disproportionate',[66] Steinmeier favoured not pointing the finger of blame although he echoed the Chancellor's position. He knew the issue well because, earlier in the summer, he had been part of a failed diplomatic effort to avert the conflict.

Berlin's reaction was partly explicable in terms of its reluctance to spoil relations with Russia's new president, Dmitri Medvedev. His election in March had inspired optimism in Berlin and other western capitals about the likelihood of Russia moving back on to a reform track even if Putin, now Prime Minister, was still in over-all charge. In June, Medvedev visited Berlin and delivered a long speech that pressed many of the right buttons with his German audience. He claimed that Russia was building a state that was 'completely compatible' with the rest of Europe and that it had 'come in from the cold'. It was prioritising innovation and aiming to transform the social structure of society to create the conditions for developing democracy and sustainable growth.[67] Steinmeier spoke gushingly about Medvedev's and Putin's purported inter-est in improving rule of law as if they were intending to undo the reforms beginning in 2001 that had stamped out judicial inde-pendence and made the Prosecutor General's Office a tool of the Kremlin to pursue its enemies.

Steinmeier's optimism about the Medvedev presidency may have persuaded him of the need to avoid sanctions against Russia over Georgia when he argued that it was in Germany's 'own interest to return to a normal relationship'.[68] He repeated the cliché that security and stability in Europe were only possible with, rather than against, Russia, warning that Europe would damage itself if, under the influence of emotions, it slammed shut doors to the rooms it would want to enter again later.[69] With Berlin's support, the EU quickly resumed negotiations with Russia on the new partnership and cooperation agreement as if the invasion of Georgia and Moscow's subsequent recognition of the independ-ence of the Georgian provinces of Abkhazia and South Ossetia were minor blips on the bilateral agenda.

While there was considerable evidence that the Georgian President Mikheil Saakashvili had responded unwisely to Russian provocations that led to a five-day war by shelling a Russian 'peace-keeping' force in South Ossetia in violation of international law, the fact-finding report commissioned by the EU concluded that Russia also carried blame for its actions in response. Its extended military action beyond South Ossetia was not even 'remotely commensurate with the threat' to its forces in South Ossetia and was a violation of international law.[70] Nevertheless, Berlin and Paris were keen to keep relations in place and turn the page. Analysing Russia's actions in Georgia in October 2008, Merkel astutely identified the emergence of a deeper problem related to Russian grievances from the 1990s onwards stemming from its alleged treatment by the West. Presciently, she referred to the danger of Russia and Germany coming to entirely different conclusions about what had led to German unification and the expansion of NATO and the EU after the collapse of the USSR.[71] She appealed for open discussion of the issues to avoid the German and Russian publics forming their own opinions 'from which frictions could arise'. Putin's victory speech five and a half years later marking the annexation of Crimea demonstrated that Merkel had been correct in anticipating that Russia would develop its own historical narrative.

A dispute over gas prices between Russia and Ukraine in January 2009 was another revealing indicator of how Russia's relations with Europe were changing. Brinkmanship in the complicated gas relationship between the two countries had become an annual ritual and had led to a brief interruption of supplies to Ukraine in 2006. This time it was different. As part of its effort to punish Ukraine for allegedly siphoning gas intended for Europe, Gazprom turned off supplies to Europe through Ukraine. Ukraine's national gas company Naftogaz said that it had closed down the transportation system because Gazprom had stopped supplying, while Gazprom claimed the problem was with Naftogaz. Whoever may have been to blame was irrelevant for European consumers. Gazprom had enjoyed an unblemished reputation with its Western European (primarily German) customers for reliability of supply, but on this occasion caused several countries in south-eastern Europe that were 100 per cent dependent on Russian gas to suffer gas shortages. The cut-off lasted thirteen days. It was the first time since the construction of the pipelines in Soviet days that supplies had stopped altogether.[72] Several other countries were partially affected, but there was sufficient gas in storage in Germany and elsewhere in Western Europe to cope. The experience reinforced the case in Germany for building the new Baltic gas pipeline to deliver gas directly to Germany and finally forced the EU to think seriously about security of supply.

The ten-year gas contract that Ukrainian Prime Minister Yulia Tymoshenko agreed with Putin turned out to be highly unfavourable for Ukraine and pointed to Russia's willingness to exploit Ukraine's gas dependency for broader foreign policy goals. Led by Poland and Sweden, the EU was already considering how to respond to Russia's actions in the 'shared neighbourhood' that led to the Eastern Partnership, launched in 2010, which aimed to support closer relations with the EU in Armenia, Azerbaijan, Belarus, Georgia, Moldova and Ukraine. Moscow labelled this the 'Poltava Coalition', a historical reference that betrayed its concerns about the future of Ukraine. In 1709, Russia had defeated Swedish and Polish forces in the Battle of Poltava – today a city in eastern Ukraine. Direct competition between the EU and Russia in the new *Zwischeneuropa* was just beginning as Russia moved to establish a direct southern gas transportation route via Bulgaria to bypass Ukraine.

After viewing the EU in the early Putin years as a useful counterweight to US influence in Europe and a benign entity in its own right towards Russia, policymakers in Moscow had woken up to the EU's transformative power. Its 2004 'big bang' enlargement to Central Europe followed by the accession of Bulgaria and Romania in 2007 was a powerful indicator of its attraction that Russia could not counter. However, enlargement had also brought divisions on key issues, notably policy towards Russia. Nevertheless, Moscow had also started to feel the EU's regulatory muscle as it prepared to introduce its Third Energy Package, which had significant consequences for the conduct of Gazprom's business in the European market (see Chapter 6).

Despite the lessons of the Georgia experience and abundant evidence that Medvedev was not the ultimate decision-maker, Berlin decided to court him. It hoped that President Obama's 'reset' policy would improve US–Russia relations with positive consequences for EU–Russia relations, as well as bilateral ties, but there were increasing references to inadequate levels of trust between Russia and its western partners, including Germany. Medvedev's poorly presented idea of a European security treaty was initially outlined in Berlin shortly before Russia's intervention in Georgia. It gained no traction because of it. German policymakers also viewed it as a blatant attempt to put NATO out of business.

The 2009 coalition agreement between the CDU/CSU and the Free Democratic Party (FDP) stated that the German government viewed Russia as 'an important partner in overcoming regional and global challenges', including Afghanistan, the Middle East, international terrorism, climate change and global epidemics.[73] It also declared optimistically that it would 'support Russia in consistently continuing the course of modernisation and, in the process, reducing the shortcomings related to human rights, rule of law and democracy'. The appalling death of the 37-year-old lawyer, Sergey Magnitsky, tortured in a Moscow prison barely three weeks after the new government was sworn in spoke volumes about how German policy had become divorced from reality. Nevertheless, Merkel occasionally showed flashes of realism when describing Russia's broader development. In a speech to German business in 2010, she spoke of the main problem facing Russia in the future as one of over-centralisation. This was subtle criticism of Putin's construction of a 'vertical of power'. One of Putin's first actions as President in 2000 had been to rein in the power of regional governors and remove them from the Federation Council, the upper legislative chamber. The abolition of direct elections for governors in 2004 strengthened the trend towards hyper-centralisation.

The appointment of Guido Westerwelle as foreign minister in 2009 created expectations in Moscow of a new dynamic in relations. The change was only limited. Germany's first openly gay foreign minister did not shy away from addressing human rights issues in Russia, including homophobia. He pointedly visited Poland before travelling to Moscow and initially avoided using the term 'modernisation partnership',[74] although the term later crept into his vocabulary. He also sharply criticised Russia's protection of Syria in the UN Security Council and consistently raised with Moscow the issues of freedom of expression for artists and journalists. However, while his readiness to speak publicly about differences of this kind was in contrast to Steinmeier, he nevertheless placed them in the traditional context of a thriving economic relationship between Germany and Russia, and common interests in the area of international terrorism and non-proliferation of nuclear weapons.[75] Steinmeier's return as Foreign Minister in 2013 restored the traditional SPD diplomacy towards Russia of avoiding open confrontation and always signalling a path to dialogue in cases of disagreement. Unlike some forces in his party, Steinmeier did not subscribe to the philosophy of 'equidistance' for Germany between the USA and Russia. He was a transatlanticist who strongly believed that there was a way for Russia to play a constructive role in Europe without the need to replace existing European security arrangements.

A test of this assumption was Germany's effort in 2010 to encourage Russia to cooperate in solving the long-standing Transnistrian conflict in Moldova under an EU–Russia security council. Germany had acquired a taste for conflict resolution after it contributed forces in 1996 to the NATO-led peacekeeping operation in Bosnia-Herzegovina in which Russia also participated, albeit with separate command arrangements. Germany had gone further in Kosovo in 1999, commanding a multinational brigade as part of the NATO peacekeeping force deployed there. These deployments to the Balkans were significant in view of Germany's history in the region during the Second World War since they symbolised its confidence in its transformation since then. However, the initiative on Transnistria proved to be an embarrassing failure. Conceived as a response to Medvedev's proposals for a European security treaty, it was poorly coordinated with other EU members and aroused suspicion that Germany was trying to conduct EU policy 'in a secretive way'.[76] The Russian side lacked assurances that the issue was a top priority for the Chancellery and did not see the benefits of making compromises.[77]

Merkel clearly preferred dealing with Medvedev rather than Putin. He did not have a KGB background, and even if he had loyally served Putin for fifteen years, he seemed to have a more modern outlook and continued to speak of an agenda for change based on economic and social renewal that was appealing to parts of Russia's growing middle class. He also did not try to intimidate her as Putin notably did in 2007 when he deliberately brought his Labrador to a meeting, fully aware of her fear of dogs. Yet it was clear at the time that only a small group in the ruling elite shared this vision and that it lacked influence. Putin's *siloviki* associates could not take Medvedev seriously and in foreign policy, his hands were tied. Putin had warned Merkel in March 2008 that the West should not expect the new president to change course and that it was a mistake to view Medvedev as a 'man of the West'. There was little doubt that Putin remained in overall charge of both domestic policy and foreign policy during his time as prime minister. The only public sign of dissent between Medvedev and Putin was over Libya when Russia abstained together with Germany in a UN vote endorsing a no-fly zone over the country. Medvedev criticised Putin's use of the word 'crusades' to describe the subsequent air strikes. However, Berlin, like Obama and his advisers, was deceiving itself by thinking that it was dealing with even a semi-empowered decision-maker.

Medvedev's humiliating announcement in September 2011 that he supported Putin's candidacy to replace him in the 2012 presidential election dashed German hopes that a second Medvedev term would usher in a period of genuine modernisation. The stand-in president had clearly wanted to stay. By this stage, the US–Russia 'reset' was over, and Russia's relations with the EU and NATO were stagnating. Moscow was becoming increasingly frustrated by the impact of the EU's Third Energy Package on Gazprom's business model in Europe and EU efforts to diversify its gas supply away from Russia. However, German–Russian business ties continued to develop, symbolised by the opening of the Nord Stream pipeline in November 2011, for the first time connecting Germany directly to Russian gas supplies. This again pointed to contradictions in German policy. Its stated aims of supporting the EU's energy security strategy based on diversifying energy sources and the commitment to consider the legitimate interests of its neighbours in building relations with Russia were in clear conflict. Ignoring warnings from Lithuania, Poland and others that the new pipeline served Russian political objectives, Merkel stated pointedly at the opening ceremony that Nord Stream was a 'commercial project'.

Notwithstanding the absence of structural economic reforms and the deterioration of the human rights situation in Russia during the period after Putin's re-election as president in 2012, the new German government that took office in late 2013 still spoke of pursuing a modernisation partnership with Russia. Clear indications of Russia's demodernisation, with the notable exception of its armed forces, which were still enjoying substantial reinvestment, and its turn away from Europe were not sufficient to deter the Grand Coalition from restating the tired formula that 'security in and for Europe can only be achieved with, not against Russia'.[78]

It ignored the fact that the opportunity for establishing a cooperative security relationship had passed long ago. Moscow was now
digging in for what it saw as inevitable confrontation.

Putin had returned to the Kremlin after unprecedented protests
in late 2011 by middle-class Russians, angered at his decision to
seek re-election, effectively depriving voters of a real choice of a
national leader, and the foreclosing of Medvedev's tentative efforts
to develop a reform agenda. The authorities had to dig deep to
reassert control and reconsolidate support for the regime in what
they appeared to view as a potentially pre-revolutionary situation.
Liberal economic reforms and strengthening rule of law were off
the agenda as the Kremlin moved to establish 'fortress Russia',
requiring the expansion of state ownership in the economy, the
promotion of anti-western conservative values, the defence of the
Kremlin's version of Russia's national interests and the intimida-
tion of opposition forces. The passing of legislation in July 2012
requiring NGOs engaged in 'political activity' to register as foreign
agents if they received foreign funding dealt a serious blow to the
development of Russia's fledgling civil society. The definition of
'political activity' was so loose that it covered any organisation that
criticised government policy. This change in the law and the harsh
sentences handed down to participants in the May 2012 protest on
Bolotnaya Square in Moscow on charges of rioting showed that
Russia's leadership had shelved ideas for societal modernisation.

The 2013 coalition agreement nevertheless spoke of extending
the modernisation partnership into other areas to make progress
at the levels of society, politics and the economy. Its ambition was
to intensify Germany's contacts with the Russian middle class and
civil society. It noted that Russia was 'required to adhere to legal
and democratic standards to which Russia has also committed
itself internationally'.[79] It also spoke of seeking a new partnership
agreement between the EU and Russia. Strikingly, the agreement
was published a day before the start of the Eastern Partnership
Summit in Lithuania at which Ukraine's President Yanukovych

indicated that he could not sign the proposed Association Agreement with the EU because of Russian pressure. For all its good intentions, Germany's Russia policy was about to be cruelly exposed as having misread Russia's development and the calculus of its leadership. The over five-fold increase in German exports to Russia from 2000 to 2011 (in 2011 exports were worth €34 billion)[80] had not contributed to an improvement in the investment environment or promoted the rule of law. In the World Bank's 2008 Ease of Doing Business Index, Russia had ranked in 106th place out of 178 countries. In 2011, it had fallen to 123rd place. In Transparency International's Corruption Perceptions Index it fell from 133rd place out of 181 countries in 2008 to 136th in 2011. The development of trade simply showed that the Russian leadership was correct in believing that western companies would continue to do business in Russia without the far-reaching legal and governance reforms that their governments claimed were necessary.

Despite the weak compromises of the coalition agreement, part of the German political class was becoming anxious about the direction in which Russia was heading. Parliament had unanimously passed a tough and impressively detailed resolution in November 2012 initiated by the Greens[81] that called on the government to observe its international human rights obligations and expressed concern at increasing Russian restrictions on democratic freedoms, including limiting opportunities for protest, discouraging NGOs from receiving foreign funding and broadening the definition of high treason. Andreas Schockenhoff, the government coordinator for civil society links with Russia, played a key role in its drafting. For years, he had been an outspoken advocate of the need for a 'values partnership' with Russia and had earned the wrath of the Russian authorities.[82] Unprecedentedly critical of the Kremlin's retreat from democracy, the resolution expressed concern about Berlin's readiness to put economic interests before values and its de facto acceptance of the Kremlin's concept of modernisation being defined in traditional technological terms. It also sounded the alarm about future relations, correctly predicting that the internal developments in Russia threatened to restrict opportunities for cooperation, and identifying the danger that these 'could lead to a growing alienation between Russia and the rest of Europe'.

It was a significant victory for the *Wertefraktion* (values faction) in Parliament, which saw Russia policy as too focused on economic interests and supporting the Kremlin's narrow interpretation of modernisation to the exclusion of societal development. It argued that rule of law and fair competition were essential for developing the Russian economy and that the Russian government needed to be in dialogue with civil society and the new middle class since they were natural partners in a modernisation process. Small and medium-sized German companies doing business in Russia, sometimes with difficulty because of corruption issues, could hardly disagree about the need to improve the investment environment.

Yet Parliament's warning appeared to go unheeded. Berlin chose not to connect the dots as it viewed Russia increasingly turn away from European norms and the Kremlin's growing attraction to the latest iteration of Russia as a 'cultural nation' with interests, rights and responsibilities on the territory of neighbouring countries. Russia was redefining itself as a nineteenth-century great power with a distinctive identity and the capacity to 'balance' Europe in the interests of long-term stability, as it had done in 1815 and again in 1945.[83] At the same time, the European Commission was in charge of the process of negotiating an EU Association Agreement (including a Deep and Comprehensive Free Trade Agreement) with Ukraine but in the absence of political oversight from Berlin and other capitals when it was needed. In the summer of 2013, Russia placed strong political and economic pressure on the authorities in Kyiv to encourage them to abandon the agreement. Armenia had opted for membership of the Customs Union over an Association Agreement with the EU after Moscow used increased gas prices and arms sales to Azerbaijan as a signal of the measures it could take to weaken Armenia's international position if it chose to leave Moscow's orbit. Russia had also applied pressure to Georgia and Moldova, indicating that Russia's opposition to the EU's initiative was not just restricted to Ukraine. However, there was no *démarche* from Berlin to address Russian concerns about technical aspects of the Agreement, in particular the potential issue of goods from the EU being illegally repackaged and sold in Russia as Ukrainian under free trade arrangements within the Commonwealth of Independent States. However, despite later protestations to the contrary, Moscow did not seek these talks as a matter of priority. It possibly did not believe that the EU was serious about signing such a far-reaching agreement with Ukraine. As a senior Russian source later confirmed, they had been on offer on several occasions at previous EU–Russia summits.[84] For all its desire to manage bilateral relations within an EU framework, Berlin had underestimated the impact of the Eastern Partnership on relations with Russia. If Moscow's initial reaction had been relaxed because it did not see significant political or financial weight behind the initiative, it suddenly changed its position when it saw the risk of Ukraine drawing closer to the EU.

By contrast, Germany's patient role in securing the release from prison of the former Yukos CEO Mikhail Khodorkovsky and his colleague Platon Lebedev in December 2013 was an indication of its reach into the Russian system and its desire not to give up on some human rights issues. The charismatic Green MP Marieluise Beck who had a long-standing interest in human rights issues in Russia and Eastern Europe joined forces with the former minister of justice, Sabine Leutheusser-Schnarrenberger (FDP) in a cross-party effort to raise the profile of the politically motivated prosecution of the two men on charges of tax evasion and theft. Former Foreign Minister, Hans-Dietrich Genscher, was instrumental in the process of negotiating their release, meeting personally with

Putin to discuss the problem and persuade him of the case for freeing the two men on humanitarian grounds. On his release, Khodorkovsky flew to Berlin and held his first press conference there.

Conclusions

Public discussion in Germany about Russia has failed to properly address the central issue of how, over more than twenty-five years, German policy managed to read Russia incorrectly, allowing optimism to override realism. Despite the increasing evidence that policy aspirations were becoming divorced from Russian reality, successive German governments remained in denial about the type of changes taking place in Russia and their effects on Russian behaviour. Of course, they were not alone among western countries but they had reason to know better than most what was happening in Russia, and how the gradual re-emergence of a traditional model of governance in Russia with corresponding views of the West could not be wished away through dialogue, more dialogue and the promise of closer economic links.

As a result, Germany inadvertently ended up supporting a system in Russia that was friendly to Germany but increasingly hostile to German interests as it moved on to a confrontation footing with the EU and NATO, Germany's strategic anchors. Such a policy failure was particularly surprising in the case of a country with such deep knowledge of Russian history and political culture, including Russia's traditional view of its periphery as a buffer for security protection. German policymakers should have been alert to Russia's instinctive need for 'privileged relations'[85] with the newly independent states and how this would create conflict, given Russia's sense that it was entitled to limit their sovereignty for its own benefit. In the early 1990s, liberal policymakers in Moscow and not just Russian nationalists believed that Russia-first policies were necessary to reduce the economic burden on Russia itself, but with the expectation that a reinvigorated Russia would eventually regain influence over the former republics.[86]

Rebuilding an exclusive zone of influence in its neighbourhood became a defining feature of Russia's relationship with Europe during Putin's first term as president (2000–4). Yet Berlin appeared to pay little attention tp the Kremlin's strategy of reconstituting Russia on a traditional authoritarian model that did not require copying western institutions and would preserve Russia's distinctiveness. To protect this system required keeping close neighbours such as Belarus, Georgia and Ukraine on a tight leash. Moscow described these countries simply as being in 'a traditional sphere of interest', one that they could not escape.[87] Similarly, Germany was remarkably insouciant about Russia's reading of NATO enlargement, and did little to counter it. It should have impressed on Russia's leaders that from a German perspective a key driver for enlargement initially to the Czech Republic, Hungary and Poland was the need to conclusively settle the German question to the benefit of Europe and Russia. This message never entered the Russian public discourse during the 1990s when the country was still open to alternative arguments from the West.

The sensitivity of NATO enlargement eventually registered in Berlin. Germany intervened in 2008 together with France to prevent an ill-advised US plan to grant NATO Membership Action Plans to Georgia and Ukraine. This move possibly pre-empted Russian action against Ukraine since the operation conducted in 2014 to seize Crimea was developed years earlier as a response to moves to integrate Ukraine into the Alliance. However, the compromise communiqué language at the NATO Bucharest Summit, fought over by Germany and some Central European countries, was not helpful in reassuring Moscow about NATO's intentions: 'We agreed today that these countries will become members of NATO.'[88] To NATO insiders, the open-ended formulation was vague enough for it not to oblige member states to admit the two countries at any time in the short or medium term, and then only assuming they had no conflicts with Russia. In other words, unable to find a consensus, NATO had kicked the issue in to the long grass and expected Moscow to understand.

Although Russian decision-makers will have known this, thanks to personal assurances and intelligence data, it was not how they chose to view the issue, given their tendency to interpret diplomatic language by the letter and not its spirit. Again, the German system with its sophisticated understanding of Russian sensitivities should have identified the problem and gone the extra mile to communicate the message to both the Russian elites and the broader public. However, this did not happen, and the response came quickly as Russia increased its pressure on Georgia and succeeded in goading the Georgian president into attacking Russian 'peacekeepers' in South Ossetia just four months later. This was a signal to Ukraine and NATO of the limits that Moscow felt obliged to set on the Alliance's enlargement.

At the same time, there were also signs of prescience. Reluctant to take Russia to task over its actions in Georgia, part of the German establishment was nevertheless thinking about what Russia might do next. The Foreign Ministry chose to open a general consulate in the eastern Ukrainian city of Donetsk in 2009. Its purpose was to learn more about a region that Germany did not understand well in anticipation of further possible disputes on Russia's borders. By contrast, later signs that Russia was seeking to mobilise its diaspora in other countries through a 'Russian World' concept did not receive the attention they deserved. Berlin missed the opportunity to intervene in 2013 to prevent the issue of Ukraine's Association Agreement being used as a pretext by Moscow to exert control over Ukraine's foreign and security policy. While the European Commission had the negotiating mandate, there was still space for Germany and others to provide the political cover required. Berlin appeared more concerned about the well-being of Yanukovych's enemy, former Prime Minister, Yulia Tymoshenko, who had received a politically motivated jail sentence and claimed to be suffering from a serious health problem. The government even arranged for a group of German doctors to travel to Ukraine to examine her. The argument that Germany was in an election campaign in the summer and early autumn of 2013 (federal elections took place on 22 September) and could not react in time to address the problem in time is hardly persuasive. The issue had been on the agenda for several months beforehand and it was clear that the Russian leadership had changed its view of EU enlargement from Putin's statement in 2004 that Russia had no objection to Ukraine joining the EU.[89] At that time, Moscow still saw NATO as the threat to its interests rather than the EU.

Similarly, Germany failed to spot that the re-establishment of the Russian armed forces was taking place under a High Command that regarded NATO not just as an enemy that had taken advantage of Russia's weakness in the 1990s but as an alliance that had aggressive intent in Russia's neighbourhood. The proof was Kosovo. The military leadership's ability to find a common language with Putin and his KGB associates who were running both the government and the country's strategic industries brought a crucial unity of views about the threats facing Russia and the ways to respond to them. This built on a strong sense in both quarters of resentment towards the West, albeit without pinning blame directly on Germany. As Putin claimed in 2002, having always defeated Germany in war, Russians do not feel wounded or aggrieved towards Germans.[90]

Seen in a historical context, the settlement of the German question in 1990 opened the Russia question: how should Russia, an expanding EU and the Europe in between (*Zwischeneuropa*) relate to each other and what institutional arrangements should support these relationships? It is understandable that Germany could not demonstrate a clear vision in the early 1990s of how Russia and its neighbourhood were likely to develop. The collapse of Europe's last empire had come at a dizzying pace on top of rapid German unification, and had effects that spread far beyond the borders of the USSR. The scale and pace of change were over-whelming and policymakers focused on managing the situation day by day. However, in the years that followed, German policy towards Russia and the other newly independent former Soviet republics was hostage to the post-modern thinking that prevailed in the West rather than Russia. Moscow went back instead to nineteenth-century concepts of great power relations in Europe. Even the Yeltsin reformers saw Russia as destined to play an unre-strained leadership role on the territory of the former USSR to the advantage of the West.

Remarkably, German policymakers recognised these trends but comforted themselves with the thought that they had succeeded in deepening relations and bilateral trade was booming. They contin-ued to believe that since Germany 'needed' Russia in Iran, Syria and on other international issues, it was, therefore, a 'partner'. As they saw it, the only alternative policies were 'containment' or 'benign neglect'.[91] The concept of conditionality and opportuni-ties to incentivise Russian behaviour were conspicuously absent. There was no consideration of how Germany and the EU could deploy their economic and 'soft' power to encourage Russian policymakers to change course. Berlin was unwilling to accept that its romantic view that Russia was on a path to democracy was at least fifteen years out of date and that Germany's policies had become counter-productive as Russia refashioned its instru-ments of power to make itself a competitor of the West. It called this policy 'strategy' and noted that it had no means to influence events in Russia directly. The absence of serious debate about the increasingly obvious shortcomings of Russia policy reflected the lower place of Russia on the German policy agenda. The Arab Spring, and the euro crisis, for example, were the new priority issues. Governments understandably move to more urgent issues or areas where there are greater opportunities to achieve results.

By 2013, Russia fitted into neither category. As it began to stagnate, so did the German policy focus on Russia. There was another more serious underlying reason for the increasing disconnection between Russian reality and German policy goals. There was a shortage of Russia expertise at senior levels in the Foreign Ministry, and Parliament no longer had the same number of qualified foreign policy specialists. The Federal Chancellery too lacked Russia specialists and it had limited connectivity with the German 'Russia Community'.[92] Disagreement about Russia within the coalition made it an issue that few were willing to air because there was such polarisation of views on Russia not just between the parties but also within them. The closure of the well-regarded Federal Institute for Russian, East European and International Studies (BIOst) in Cologne and its fusion with the Berlin-based German Institute for International and Security Affairs (Stiftung Wissenschaft und Politik) in 2000 was symptomatic of a trend visible in other countries, such as Britain and France, with a strong tradition of scholarship on Russia. Governments no longer had the appetite to support stand-alone research institutes that had their roots in the Cold War when the traditional Russia problem apparently belonged to the past. A generation of specialists on Russia and the region left the scene without replacements. Expertise within the defence sector withered away too as the Bundeswehr underwent a savage round of cuts to expenditure on personnel and armaments that reduced its manpower by two-thirds in the twenty-five years that followed unification.[93]

Media coverage had also contributed to the loss of nuanced discussion because of its extreme focus on Putin, a reflection of the Kremlin's media strategy of creating a Putin personality cult for domestic purposes. In common with media coverage of Russia in other western countries, the focus on Putin provided a simple framework for viewing Russia and encouraged a divergence of views that hardened positions within the *Russlandversteher* and *Russlandkritiker* camps. This was a result of both editorial policy and a loss of openness in Russia itself that restricted journalists' access and made their reporting less informative. In any case, the

Russia 'story' no longer carried the excitement of the 1990s for the German public as Russia appeared more stable, better governed and less unpredictable. The numbers of German journalists in Moscow declined in the 2000s, and in 2013, the business newspaper *Handelsblatt* closed its office in Moscow that it had operated for twenty years.[94]

For all its connectivity at government level as well as through the Petersburger Dialog and myriad partnerships in education, science and between communities, not to mention business relationships, Germany had become disconnected from Russia and lost the feel for its complexity and contradictions. This became dramatically apparent in early 2014 when Russia once again found itself taken by surprise in Ukraine.

2014: abandonment of illusions

When Steinmeier returned as foreign minister in December 2013, revolution was brewing in Ukraine. Two weeks earlier at the EU's Eastern Partnership Summit in Vilnius, Ukraine's President Viktor Yanukovych had opted late in the day not to sign the proposed EU–Ukraine Association Agreement. Video footage showed Merkel sternly telling the Ukrainian president that EU leaders had expected more from him. He sheepishly explained that since coming to power in 2010, he had found himself 'one on one in very unequal relations with a strong Russia' and was facing 'very big threats'.[1] He was not bluffing. Over the summer, Moscow had placed severe economic pressure on Kyiv, reducing bilateral trade by 25 per cent and threatening further sanctions.[2] At one point, it stopped all imports from Ukraine for five days.[3] Resorting to personal diplomacy, Putin had then tried to persuade Yanukovych to sign up to the Customs Union between Russia, Belarus and Kazakhstan but Yanukovych still dug his heels in.

End of the 'modernisation partnership'

Yanukovych's decision not to proceed with the Association Agreement triggered protests in central Kyiv. In freezing temperatures, these seemed likely to peter out until the Ukrainian authorities used force to disperse them. Their heavy-handed response simply inflamed public anger and brought out more protestors. A hard-core group set up camp on Kyiv's Independence Square determined to oust Yanukovych and his government. EU countries, including Germany in particular, had failed to recognise the broader processes at work in Ukraine and the dangers that they posed because Russia had changed more than they realised or were prepared to admit.

Nevertheless, when he addressed Foreign Ministry staff on his first day back as minister, Steinmeier used uncharacteristically strong language to condemn Russia for taking advantage of Ukraine's economic plight to prevent it signing the Association Agreement. The same day, Putin granted Kyiv major financial assistance, including a $15 billion credit and a discounted gas price to ward off economic crisis. Steinmeier also castigated Ukrainian security forces for using violence against peaceful demonstrators. At the same time, he asked whether the EU had underestimated Ukraine's weakness and divisions and not seen that it was too much for the country to choose between Europe and Russia.[4] This was ironic since Steinmeier had been one of the EU foreign ministers who, back in 2007, had given the green light to the European Commission to begin negotiations with Ukraine on an Association Agreement when Germany held the EU presidency. Back then, Berlin still believed that Russia was on a genuine path of economic and societal modernisation at a time when its relations with the EU were less fractious.

Steinmeier now came close to admitting that his pet project, the Modernisation Partnership, had failed. He attributed its unfulfilled potential not to the Russian leadership turning its back on Europe and its rejection of reform in general but to a lack of 'courage, creativity and readiness' on both sides. Even if he was now wary of using the term 'modernisation partnership', he still spoke of the need for 'Russia and the West to be connected not just economically but through common basic convictions'. He also warned of competition for spheres of influence in the Pacific and elsewhere in the world that could have consequences for Europe. His assessment was correct. There was indeed no longer agreement with Russia on basic principles since Russia now no longer spoke of the Helsinki Final Act as the foundation of European security. Its reference points instead were Yalta and Potsdam. However, Steinmeier did not mention Russia's claim to a sphere of influence in Ukraine and other post-Soviet countries. This reluctance to see the security implications of Russian security policy thinking reflected a long-established tendency in the German system to view relations with the East through a Russian prism, including its historical view of the region. It suited Moscow for Germans to continue to feel guilt predominantly towards Russia even if Belarusians and Ukrainians had disproportionately suffered at the hands of the German invaders in the Second World War since this form of guilt projection reinforced the place of other Soviet peoples in a 'Russian world' beyond Russia's borders.

However, Berlin was now waking up to a rapidly changing global environment. In a prescient speech at the Munich Security Conference in late January 2014, President Joachim Gauck spoke thoughtfully of Germans moving to 'a form of responsibility' in the world that was unfamiliar. He described how Germany profited disproportionately from an open world order that allowed it to combine interests with values and that its core interest in the twenty-first century was to preserve this 'structure of order' (*Ordnungsgefüge*). He noted that the world was in political and economic flux with the danger of widespread conflict in the Middle East just as the USA was re-thinking its global engagement.[5] Gauck called for Germany to avoid the temptation of navel-gazing by hiding behind historical guilt, and to play a more active role as a guarantor of the international order from which Germans had benefited so handsomely for decades. He did not refer specifically to China or Russia but spoke of respect for human rights as the basic condition for security and a peaceful, cooperative world order. He was directly challenging SPD thinking embodied by former Chancellor Schmidt that *Ostpolitik* should place greater emphasis on non-interference in international affairs than on human rights.

Revolution in Ukraine and the annexation of Crimea

The visionary speech was well timed. Within two months, as Ukraine's 'Revolution of Dignity' gathered pace, Germany was shouldering the responsibility that Gauck had described. The USA and Britain were more preoccupied with events in the Middle East, leaving it to Germany to fashion a western response. The Obama administration's efforts to 'reset' relations with Moscow had ended in acrimony in 2012 after Putin's return to the Kremlin, limiting its appetite for further engagement with Russia. Steinmeier led the 'Weimar Triangle' effort together with the Polish and French foreign ministers to broker an agreement between the Ukrainian government and opposition leaders to end the political crisis that turned bloody as police fired on demonstrators in Kyiv. Putin's representative at the negotiations did not witness the agreement that pledged to form a new government and hold fresh elections under an earlier Constitution. Moscow seemingly had little faith that the deal would stick. Having signed the agreement, Yanukovych immediately fled the country with his ministers, abandoning its institutions to the political opposition.

Ukraine's constitution contained no provision for the head of state and the government deserting their posts. However, Putin accused western countries of not supporting implementation of the agreement, describing the takeover of government buildings and Parliament's decision to impeach Yanukovych and appoint a temporary administration as an 'anti-constitutional coup and an armed seizure of power'.[6] He suggested that this outcome had destabilised eastern Ukraine. Meanwhile, he had authorised a military operation prepared years earlier to bring about the secession of Crimea through a local referendum held in violation of the

Ukrainian constitution. To seek legitimacy at home and abroad for Russia's actions, the Kremlin's communications machine went into overdrive branding the temporary leaders in Kyiv 'fascists'. This message reportedly caused initial confusion in the upper echelons of the Foreign Ministry in Berlin as diplomats on the ground scrambled to assemble the facts. Günter Verheugen, the former European Commissioner for Enlargement, who had also served as State Secretary for European Affairs under Schröder, claimed that 'proper fascists' were in government in Kyiv. He was referring to representatives of the right-wing populist party, Svoboda. Andreas Umland, a Kyiv-based German political scientist pointed out that there was no evidence to support this view. He cited a British expert on fascism who had concluded in 2013 that the party could not be considered 'fascist'.[7]

Russia's seizure of Crimea caused a mixture of dismay, disbelief and fear in Berlin. For Germans, in view of their history, Moscow's behaviour was deeply disturbing. Its violation of international law was offensive to their legalistic culture and their acute sensitivity to the inviolability of borders. Inevitably, the annexation of Crimea evoked memories of the Nazi past and the tragedies associated with mobilising diaspora populations and using them to justify territorial expansion in the cases of Hitler's seizure of the Sudetenland and the Austrian Anschluss. Russia had shown that it was prepared to ride roughshod over Helsinki principles and disregard its bilateral treaty obligations to Ukraine. It also ignored its security assurances given to Ukraine in 1994 after it renounced control of the Soviet nuclear weapons on its territory. These explicitly included an 'obligation to refrain from the threat or use of force against the territorial integrity … of Ukraine' and not to engage in economic coercion against it. Yet not only had Moscow annexed Crimea, it was also backing a series of revolts as part of an attempted counter-revolution in the south-east of Ukraine in a region known in Russian history as 'Novorossiya'. Its support led to the establishment of rebel administrations in the cities of Donetsk and Luhansk. A proposal by Vladimir Zhirinovsky, the leader of Russia's so-called Liberal-Democratic Party, a flamboyant figure used by the Kremlin to float ideas publicly, underlined the seriousness of Moscow's ambitions. He suggested dividing the territories of western Ukraine added after the Second World War between Hungary, Poland and Romania as part of a break-up of Ukraine.[8] Not for the first time, Moscow was seriously out of touch with the realities of post-Soviet Ukraine. Its aggression galvanised Ukrainian society, reinforcing its sense of identity and determination to protect its sovereignty. Putin's repeated claims that Russians and Ukrainians were one people rang hollow.

Many commentators in Germany and elsewhere in Europe claimed that the EU's decision to offer Ukraine a closer relationship unnecessarily placed Ukraine in a situation where it had to choose between Russia and the EU. This argument ignores the fact that Russia's growing alienation from Europe after 2004 coincided with its sense that the EU was a strategic competitor rather than an ally and made it impossible for Ukraine to continue balancing between Europe and Russia. By this time, Ukraine was in any case developing a stronger sense of national identity that was starting to change its relationship with both the EU and Russia. In other words, Russia's alienation from Europe magnified regional differences in Ukraine and brought it face to face with strongly contrasting development paths between Europe and Russia. This was far more than simply a question of which economic bloc Ukraine should join.

Those who criticise the EU for offering an Association Agreement to Ukraine tend to disregard the fact that Russia forced Ukraine to choose between the Association Agreement and membership of its new regional integration project, the Eurasian Economic Union (EAEU). The two were incompatible. But there was a halfway house had Russia chosen to accept it. Under the Association Agreement, Ukraine could have retained its free trade arrangements with the Commonwealth of Independent States (CIS), the integration framework originally established in 1991 to cushion the collapse of the USSR. However, Moscow ruled out this possibility by suspending application of the CIS free trade agreement with Ukraine unless it joined the EAEU.

Merkel takes charge

Merkel's statement to the German Parliament on 13 March 2014 signalled a dramatic change in German policy towards Russia. The Chancellor was unequivocal about Russia's disregard for Ukrainian and international law in Crimea, its violation of Ukraine's territorial integrity and its exploitation of Ukraine's weakness. Unlike in the case of Georgia in 2008, there could be no return to business as usual.[9] Summarising her incredulity at Russia's behaviour, she noted that just as in 2008 in Georgia, Europe was now experiencing in Ukraine 'a conflict about spheres of influence and territorial claims as we know it from the nineteenth or twentieth centuries, a conflict that we believed we had overcome'.

She said that from the German perspective, the Association Agreement was an invitation to Ukraine to modernise just as Germany and the EU had proposed a modernisation partnership with Russia. She warned in a phrase that she would later repeat frequently that 'a long breath' would be necessary to solve the conflict. She pointed to the central challenge for Europe of upholding the territorial integrity of a European neighbour and respecting UN principles for balancing interests. She forcefully rejected the parallels drawn with NATO's intervention in Kosovo. Merkel also noted that Russia was part of the globalised world in which countries that only considered their own interests did themselves harm. As she saw it, Russia was clearly tied into this broader community through different mechanisms, including its annual government consultations with Germany, civil society interaction via the Petersburger Dialog mechanism, the German–Russian Raw Materials Forum and more than twenty bilateral agreements with the EU. To back up her point, she referred to Russia's membership of the Council of the Baltic Sea States, the G8, G20 and the NATO-Russia Council, in addition to its negotiating mandates in the Middle East peace process and the nuclear talks with Iran and 'much, much more'.

Merkel's crystal clear logic continued: 'Russia's behaviour in Ukraine clearly represents a violation of basic principles of international law … In this tense and dangerous situation we have to find ways out of the crisis. There is no military solution to the conflict.' She was adamant that Ukraine's territorial integrity was not up for discussion and pointed to three practical steps to support the country: first, Germany would support the creation of an international observer mission and a 'contact group' to seek a political-diplomatic path out of the crisis. Second, EU countries had given political support for an $11 billion economic rescue package from the International Monetary Fund (IMF) and had agreed to sign the political part of the EU–Ukraine Association Agreement to stimulate the process of developing rule of law. Third, the EU would accelerate negotiations on removing visa restrictions for Ukrainians to travel to Europe. It would also stand ready to strengthen Ukraine's energy security. With an eye on Moscow, Merkel referred to the EU's offer of modernisation as part of its neighbourhood policy and not geopolitics. It was directed at no one. Leaving a door open for Russia, she referred to the possibility of discussing a new EU–Russia economic agreement. This would take into account the EU's support for economic modernisation in countries in the shared EU–Russia neighbourhood. Moldova and Georgia also deserved support, she added. Finally, she threatened that the EU would move beyond the suspension of negotiations with Russia on a new Partnership and Cooperation Agreement, including visa liberalisation much coveted by Moscow. It would apply further punitive measures if

Russia continued to be uncooperative in talks to address the situation in Ukraine. She also pledged to help Ukraine strengthen its energy security.

Merkel concluded with a warning to Moscow:

> If Russia continues its course of the last weeks, this would not just be a catastrophe for Ukraine. We would then sense that ... as a threat. This would then change not only the relationship of the EU as a whole with Russia. No, that would damage ... Russia massively, both economically and politically. For – I cannot say it often enough or with enough emphasis – the clock cannot be turned back. Conflicts of interest in the middle of Europe in the twenty-first century can only be successfully overcome when we do not resort to the examples of the nineteenth and twentieth centuries. They can only be overcome, when we act with the principles and means of our time, the twenty-first century.[10]

No official German statement has since expressed so clearly the depth of differences between Moscow and Berlin over Russia's actions in Ukraine and the extent to which their interests and security cultures had collided. Merkel's cold interpretation of the facts and her prescription for action turned Germany's established Russia policy on its head. Abandoning the usual clichés about the essential role of Russia as a security partner in Europe, she set out a clear position and policy, conspicuously distancing herself from the SPD tendency under Schröder to explain away Russian bad behaviour by calling for 'understanding' or the need for dialogue. Russia was no longer a security partner in Europe since it had severely undermined European security. Gone was the mantra that there could be no security in Europe without Russia. Merkel showed no fear in cutting to pieces Moscow's justification for its actions and exposing its faulty logic. At the same time, she placed German policy in an EU framework and called for Europe to speak with a single voice. There would be no *Alleingang* (going alone) by Germany. Such an approach would be dangerous, as Gauck had pointed out just weeks before.

Despite the calm tone of the address and its clear argumentation, the underlying frustration was palpable. Russia's actions made no sense to Germans who had made such efforts themselves to overcome their tragic past only to see Russia wish to rediscover its supposed past glories, including a new cult of admiration for Stalin. Germany had also gone out of its way to accommodate Russia, showing sensitivity for its wounded pride and its impoverishment after the collapse of the USSR. It had tried to embrace Russia only to find its advances increasingly rejected – and now violently so. Nevertheless, despite this disappointment, Germany was also leaving room for dialogue and the possibility for Russia to re-think the logic of its policies. This was the key to maintaining a political consensus in Germany and the EU on the new approach to Russia. Christoph Heusgen, Merkel's foreign policy adviser, was reportedly the architect of the new unsentimental German approach, perhaps helped rather than hindered by his lack of Russia background as a diplomat.

To a country that had so successfully rejected and overcome its totalitarian past and abandoned geopolitical thinking, it was hard for Germans to understand why Russia would not want to follow a similar process, avoiding conflict with its neighbours and focusing national development around strengthening rule of law and democratic institutions. To a German mind shaped by the success of the EU as a peace project, territorial expansion and balance of power politics were simply passé and flew in the face of the consensus-based international politics of a globalised world in which countries no longer act simply out of self-interest but demonstrate collective responsibility in finding solutions to common problems. This post-modern outlook had blinded Berlin to the fact that for some years Moscow had been signalling that it understood the idea of collective responsibility more as a zero-sum game than an exercise based on satisfying mutual interests. This was logical from its perspective since it saw its interests increasingly in conflict with the West's and did not in any case believe in 'win-win' outcomes. Events in Ukraine had finally made Germany wake up to the Russia that it was really dealing with rather than the country it wanted to see. With the annexation of Crimea, the gulf between the two versions of Russia had become unbridgeable.

The main political parties closed ranks around Merkel's policy. Only Die Linke, the fourth largest parliamentary party, voiced disagreement. Its leader Gregor Gysi condemned the government for recognising the new authorities in Kyiv that included 'fascists' from the Svoboda party, arguing that sanctions would have no impact on Putin and would only escalate the situation. In a speech that echoed all Moscow's talking points, he concluded that Russia must receive a guarantee that Ukraine would not join NATO and that its future lay as a bridge between Russia and the EU. He even suggested that Ukraine might need two presidents in a federal or confederal state structure to achieve reconciliation between its eastern and western parts.[11]

There was no disguising the abruptness of the policy change. Just a few weeks earlier in an article published ahead of the Munich Security Conference, Steinmeier had written that, in the long term, a European security architecture without Russia was 'unthinkable'.[12] Russia was seeking its place in the changing world order and it was still not clear which way it would go 'strategically and internally'. The article laid bare confusion about how to pursue relations with Russia when it was, as he put it, 'switching between economic modernisation and setbacks in the political modernisation and opening of the country'. This was a disingenuous assertion, to say the least, because it was clear that the lack of political competition in Russia had bred a predatory investment environment that was constraining growth. Steinmeier spoke about the goal of supporting the modernisation of Russian society but without explaining how to do this beyond 'making western interests count in such a way that they open space and opportunities' for this to happen. Germany's old Russia policy had lost its bearings because it demonstrably no longer fitted with Russian reality.

If Merkel hoped that after her feat of fashioning a European response the USA would help carry the burden of crisis management, she was mistaken. Although Washington set the tone early by sanctioning Russian individuals and entities responsible for the annexation of Crimea, it still left the EU to manage the process of preventing the conflict over Ukraine from escalating further. However, the problem was that Moscow had thrown caution to the wind and was intent on escalating the situation. It had shifted its attention from Crimea to south-eastern Ukraine and was busy encouraging protests in several cities to spark a counter-revolution. The establishment of 'People's Republics' in Donetsk and Luhansk with Russian financial, technical and military assistance led to military conflict as Kyiv sought to reassert control in the rebel-held areas.

EU sanctions

Ukraine had now become a war stoked by Moscow and it was costing lives, including those of civilians. The situation escalated dramatically on 17 July 2014, Merkel's 60th birthday, when a Russian-supplied Buk missile launched from rebel-held territory shot down a Malaysian Airliner (MH17) killing all 298 persons aboard, four Germans among them. Merkel was reportedly deeply shocked by the news and infuriated at reports that separatist fighters were looting bodies of the dead and denying access to accident investigators. In late April, Berlin had also been angered by the separatists' abduction of a team of OSCE observers in Donbas, which included four Germans who were held for a week. In response, with strong support from the UK and others, Germany pushed hard to fashion EU consensus to adopt 'tier three' sanctions against Russia in parallel with the USA. The EU imposed financial sanctions on five Russian state banks and placed an embargo on the arms trade with Russia and the export of dual-use technologies.[13] By contrast, EU sanctions covered equipment for deep-water exploration in the Arctic by the Russian oil and gas industry. Unlike the US sanctions, however, they did not target specific Russian energy producers, such as Gazprom. To keep the sanctions aligned and maintain unity with the EU, Washington did not impose sanctions on the planned expansion of the Nord Stream pipeline, although it left space to do so.[14]

For their part, G7 countries suspended their participation in the G8 until Russia changed its course in Ukraine. This meant pulling out of the G8 Sochi Summit planned for June, which was to be the icing on the cake for the Kremlin after its impressive organisation of the Sochi Winter Olympics. However, Russia kept its place in the G20 and Putin attended the Brisbane Summit in November, despite a war of words beforehand with Australia when the Australian Prime Minister vowed to 'shirt-front' Putin.

If the exact meaning of his words was unclear, the same could not be said of Merkel's when she addressed a think-tank audience in Sydney. Drawing parallels with the events that led to the First World War, she used icy language to depict Russia as an outlier in Europe. It did not engage in mutual respect with other countries and refused to use 'democratic and rule of law means' to resolve conflicts and resort instead to 'the supposed right of the stronger one and disregard the strength of law'. She accused Russia of calling the 'European peace order as a whole into question' by viewing Ukraine as a sphere of its influence, and expressed the resolve that Russia's 'old thinking' and disregard for international law would not prevail even if this would be difficult and there would be setbacks along the way. Answering questions, she created headlines in Germany by saying that one of history's lessons was not to be 'too ready for peace'.[15] She also rubbished the idea that countries in the shared neighbourhood between Russia and the EU needed to seek Moscow's consent to sign a trade agreement.

To Merkel's amazement, Putin told her in Brisbane that the solution to the problem in eastern Ukraine was for Kyiv to buy off the so-called rebels as he had done in Chechnya.[16] The meeting ended on a sour note, with Merkel concluding that Putin did not have a strategy and that there would no quick resolution to the crisis.[17] One upshot though was Putin's agreement to meet with Steinmeier in Moscow. According to one account, Merkel requested the meeting to rid her foreign minister of his illusions about the possibility of reaching a deal with Putin on Ukraine.[18] Even if his subsequent encounter with Putin left Steinmeier pessimistic about the short-term prospects for progress with Moscow on Ukraine, he spoke to a student audience in December in Yekaterinburg about establishing a closer dialogue between the EU and the Eurasian Economic Union to expand trade relations and to address 'concerns about conflicts of interest'. This could be a first step towards establishing an 'economic-political' framework from Lisbon to Vladivostok, he said. With a war of attrition underway in eastern Ukraine fuelled by Russia that had already killed over 4,000, wounded 10,000 and displaced half a million people,[19] this was a bizarrely timed proposal and evidence of the still deeply rooted SPD view that expanded economic relations were the essential tool for managing problems with Russia.[20] It picked up directly on an earlier Putin proposal to develop an all-European economic zone and ignored the geopolitical dimension of the EAEU project that required on the part of its non-Russian members a non-reciprocal surrender of sovereignty to Moscow.

For some of Germany's elder statesmen, the shift in policy went firmly against the grain. Schmidt, the 95-year-old former chancellor, called the initial US and EU sanctions 'stupidity' and expressed understanding for Putin's behaviour. He questioned whether the annexation of Crimea was a violation of international law while claiming that Germany's actions in the Second World War required it to exercise restraint in relations with Russia.[21] The ailing former chancellor Kohl pitched in too, expressing disappointment at the decision to suspend the G8 and warning the West and Russia that they risked throwing away what they had achieved by bringing the Cold War to an end.[22] After all, he had brought Russia into the G8. Former Foreign Minister Genscher admitted that Moscow's actions were not 'free of errors' but implied that the West was also to blame.[23] He expressed nostalgia for the days of Gorbachev and the Charter of Paris, seemingly oblivious to the fact that the new Russian leadership regarded both with disdain. In trademark-coded language, he suggested that the West had acted as a victor at the end of the Cold War and created a revisionist Russia. Yet he praised Merkel and Steinmeier for their efforts to continue dialogue with Moscow – a feat that both would continue over the coming years. Even if the Poroshenko administration had doubts about Steinmeier's sympathies towards Russia, he nevertheless worked hard to maintain a personal dialogue with the Ukrainian government and was a frequent visitor to Kyiv in contrast to the EU's High Representative for Foreign and Security Policy, Catherine Ashton, and her successor Federica Mogherini. Neither was keen to displace Germany as the EU's crisis management leader over Ukraine.

Predictably, former Chancellor Schröder was a harsh critic of Merkel's sanctions policy and warned against the dangers of isolating Russia. Stating only that the annexation of Crimea was 'controversial' and that he regarded it as a fait accompli, he argued along Russian lines that the EU was responsible for the situation in Ukraine because it had not consulted Russia and forced Ukraine to choose between the two. He saw the solution to the crisis in the federalisation of Ukraine without Ukraine becoming a member of NATO. He claimed that Russia wanted to see a 'constructive' solution and had no interest in the situation becoming more acute. Germany needed to consider Russia's security interests and treat it as an equal.[24]

If Schröder sounded as if he was reading a script written in Moscow, there was a reason. A fortnight earlier, he had visited St Petersburg for a 70th birthday celebration arranged by the shareholders in the Nord Stream pipeline company of which he was Chairman. Putin was among the invitees and Schröder spoke with him separately. The attendance of the Russian President at a social function of this kind at a time of great tension in relations with the West and a volatile situation in Ukraine was striking. He clearly viewed the Schröder channel as important for his communication with Germany.

The response of German business

Not surprisingly, German business expressed concern at the potential loss of trade from sanctions as some immediately found their earnings in Russia hit by the devaluation of the ruble. At the height of the crisis, some German companies even feared expropriation.[25] The German Committee on Eastern European Economic Relations (Ost-Ausschuss) was vocal in its criticism of the sanctions policy, warning that 25,000 jobs were at stake. Significantly, the influential Federation of German Industry (BDI) expressed strong support for the government's line. Its chairman, Ulrich Grillo, published an op-ed in *Handelsblatt*, the leading business daily, in late July entitled 'Sanctions are needed'. He argued that Russia's behaviour made a 'business as usual policy' impossible and noted philosophically that while German business was already feeling the effects of sanctions, the economic damage suffered by Germany and EU countries would be more than compensated if they were 'successful in upholding international law in Europe and validating legal principles in general'.[26] In this case, politics came first.[27] The BDI's unequivocal position was a further sign of how Germany's overall approach to Russia had dramatically changed. Never had German business found itself obliged to stand up for principles of international law in the context of Russia. However,

Grillo also counselled against stigmatising German companies for maintaining their relationships in Russia. There was the future to think of as well.

Even before the revolution in Ukraine, the Russian market was looking less attractive for German companies. GDP was already sharply down on the boom years after Putin came to power, registering just 1.3 per cent in 2013 with weak growth forecast for 2014. This suggested that there would be fewer rich pickings compared to previous years. Nevertheless, some major companies were still hungry for business. The CEO of Siemens, Joe Kaeser, provoked controversy in Germany when he travelled to Moscow barely a week after the formal incorporation of Crimea into the Russian Federation and met with Putin and the head of Russian Railways, Vladimir Yakunin, who was on the US sanctions list. He described events in Ukraine as 'short term turbulence' that should not over-influence the company's long-term planning.[28] He referred to the company's 160-years' experience of doing business in Russia and stressed the value of maintaining dialogue. Merkel declined to criticise him.

Germany leads peace negotiations

For all Germany's boldness in reconfiguring its Russia policy and leading the EU's response to Russia's actions in Ukraine, its limitations as a diplomatic player were evident in the peace negotiations that it helped to establish. These took place under the aegis of the so-called Normandy Four group comprising France, Germany, Russia and Ukraine. In a sign of its loss of interest in the region, the British government had made only half-hearted efforts to insert itself into this group, quickly finding that Russia did not want it involved even though the UK, along with France and Russia, was a signatory of the 1994 Budapest Memorandum. This document had provided security assurances to Ukraine after it relinquished control of the part of the Soviet nuclear arsenal located on its territory when it became independent. The four leaders of the Normandy group agreed to establish a contact group consisting of Russia, Ukraine and the OSCE to de-escalate the intensifying conflict in Donbas and seek a resolution. Moscow insisted on representatives of the self-proclaimed separatist entities in Donetsk and Luhansk joining the group. At this stage, Ukrainian regular and volunteer forces were making surprising advances against the rebels and Poroshenko was ready to negotiate for peace with Moscow from a position of strength. In response, Moscow decided to move beyond supply of military advisers, money and arms and to commit regular forces equipped with the latest weaponry. Three operational battle groups totalling nearly 4,000 soldiers crossed the border in unmarked tanks and armoured personnel carriers together with precision-guided munitions.[29]

Their intervention proved decisive in the battle for the town of Ilovaisk in late August 2014, which cost the lives of 366 Ukrainian soldiers and wounded over 400.[30] This was a disastrous military setback for Ukrainian forces and transformed the negotiation process. Ukraine now sued for peace and sought an immediate ceasefire. Moscow's intervention had turned the tables. Forensic examination of video evidence showed the presence of Russian T72-B3 tanks moving towards Ilovaisk before the battle and back towards the Russian border afterwards.[31] German military attachés were also watching carefully in the border areas and had photographic evidence to show military units crossing the border from Ukraine into Russia and being escorted by Russian military police to a rest area.[32] Yet Russia continued to deny that it was providing military support to the rebels.

With firm German support, the NATO summit in September 2014 returned the Alliance to its traditional collective defence role. For nearly twenty-five years, NATO's focus had been on managing security in Europe through partnership and crisis management, including a range of 'out of area' operations in Afghanistan, the Balkans, Iraq and Libya. Member states, notably Germany, had in most cases sharply reduced the size of their armed forces and cut defence spending as part of a 'peace dividend'. Now NATO was returning to the task of shoring up the territorial defences of its easternmost member states that it had never seriously believed it would need to defend, while pledging to keep political communication channels open with Moscow.

Reflecting the changing situation on the battlefield, the peace negotiations that took place in Minsk now included the separatist 'republics' in Donetsk and Luhansk as part of a future political settlement, prolonging the abnormal situation in the east of the country.[33] Nerves were jangling in several European capitals after the President of the European Commission José Manuel Barroso told EU leaders how Putin had casually said during a phone conversation that he could take Kyiv in two weeks if he wanted to. The Kremlin confirmed media reports about Putin's statement but said that it had been taken out of context.[34] The agreement that emerged from the talks (known as Minsk-1) called for an immediate ceasefire and its monitoring by the OSCE as well as a set of other steps aimed at stabilising the situation, including holding elections in both separatist-held areas in line with Ukrainian law. Illegal armed groups and equipment were to be withdrawn and the OSCE was to monitor the Ukrainian–Russian border. The parties would also address the rapidly deteriorating humanitarian situation in Donbas that included interruption of power and water supplies. Over the coming months, the situation worsened as the fighting continued and Russia reinforced the separatist entities organisationally to ensure there would be no repeat of the advances by Ukrainian forces in the summer. Elections took place in the two entities in November without Kyiv's consent and in violation of the agreement reached in Minsk.

As Kyiv began cutting economic links with the two territories, fighting continued and flared up again in early January when insurgents supported by Russian forces attacked the Ukrainian-held town of Debaltseve, a critical transportation link between the two separatist-held areas. There were indications that the rebels had deployed Russian-supplied TOS-1 multiple rocket launcher systems that used fuel-air explosives,[35] a highly dangerous weapon when used near population centres. Fearing a serious escalation of the conflict and mindful that calls in Washington to supply lethal arms to Ukraine could grow louder, Merkel rushed to Kyiv and Moscow with President Hollande in a frantic new diplomatic effort. If this was a Franco-German tandem, there was no doubting who was in charge. Hollande was a peripheral figure throughout the process.

However, on this occasion, the Chancellor conspicuously failed to show her customary sangfroid amid clear signs that Moscow was deliberately stoking the situation to bring the EU to the table to negotiate better terms for a peace deal. Putin had called Ukraine's volunteer battalions fighting in the east 'NATO's foreign legion' claiming they were aimed at Russia. Dmitri Trenin, a Moscow-based analyst well known in the West, told the *Financial Times* that the statement indicated Moscow could feel provoked to 'formally enter the war, taking the conflict to a whole new level'.[36] Some western commentators saw the escalation of the information war as evidence of the Kremlin applying 'reflexive control', the practice of influencing an adversary's perception of a situation to gain advantage.[37] As part of this process of conditioning the psychological atmosphere, Russia had reportedly deployed Iskander short-range missile systems to Kaliningrad Region in December 2014.[38] The missile can carry either conventional or nuclear warheads and with a range of 500 km is just capable of reaching beyond Germany's north-eastern border from Kaliningrad.

An influential older generation of former German officials, senior businesspeople and politicians responded to this rising pressure with an emotional appeal to the government to restore dialogue with Moscow and for Europe to embark on a new policy of détente.[39] To the doubtless delight of readers in Moscow and the horror of those in Warsaw, it referred to the danger of excluding

Russia from Europe, arguing that since 1814 it had been among the 'recognised' powers that had shaped Europe. It noted Russia's legitimate need for security. The signatories of the appeal appeared oblivious to the fact that the Congress of Vienna in 1815 had granted Poland to Russia and was a less than perfect analogy for addressing the problem of conflict in Ukraine, and that from 1919 onwards, Europe had been trying to establish a security system that prevented large countries swallowing up smaller ones. The text strongly implied that Russia's actions in Ukraine were understandable. Schröder was among the sixty signatories, together with the Chairman of the Ost-Ausschuss and other prominent members of the *Russlandversteher* community. Horst Teltschik, Kohl's foreign policy adviser, also signed.

Within days, 100 Eastern Europe specialists from academia, journalism and politics, including the eminent historian Karl Schlögl, struck back with a sharply worded critique that noted the large amount of half-truths circulating about Ukraine in German media, including those based on statements by Kremlin spokesmen. It called for German Eastern Europe policy to be based on 'experience, factual knowledge and analysis' rather than on 'pathos, forgetting of history and sweeping judgements'.[40] Schlögl had also refused to accept a Pushkin Medal awarded to him by Putin in November 2013 for contributions in the area of culture and science.[41]

German diplomacy reaches its limits

Despite this injection of common sense into the German debate, the Kremlin's strategy appeared to work. As intense fighting continued in Donbas, Merkel and Hollande together with Poroshenko negotiated with Putin through the night. The Minsk-2 Agreement concluded on 12 February 2015 was disadvantageous for Ukraine because it conceded ground to Russia on widening the special status for the two separatist entities as part of an amended constitution.

This was a key component of the Russian plan to 'federalise' Ukraine and use the two 'republics' as Trojan horses to prevent Ukraine from ever joining the EU or NATO. According to the British analyst Duncan Allan, Merkel and Hollande were so keen for a ceasefire that they agreed to political provisions at odds with Ukraine's existence as a sovereign entity.[42] However, the many contradictions in the Agreement and its unclear sequencing made it open to different interpretations and allowed Ukraine to take a position largely supported by its western allies. This prioritised addressing the security situation in the two entities before holding elections there. Nevertheless, Steinmeier later tried to fudge the issue with his proposal of a 'formula' to encourage step-by-step implementation of the provisions for holding elections. Not surprisingly, it went down better with Moscow than with Kyiv.

German diplomats had hoped that it would be possible to implement most of Minsk-2 by the end of 2015, ahead of Germany's chairmanship of the OSCE in 2016. The Russia expert Stefan Meister had noted in the run-up to the OSCE chairmanship that Germany's desire to see progress in relations with Moscow was leading it to put more pressure on Ukraine to implement its Minsk commitments than on Russia.[43] Ernst Reichel, the German ambassador in Kyiv caused a furore by unwisely suggesting that there was no problem holding elections in Donbas with Russian forces present since this was what had happened in the former GDR in 1990 before Soviet forces had left. While this statement was highly insensitive towards the Ukrainian authorities in view of the illegal referendum held in Crimea after the deployment of Russian forces, this was the first time a German official had acknowledged the presence of Russian forces in Donbas.[44] Berlin distanced itself from the ambassador's words but did not disavow them.

Steinmeier's pitch to Parliament on upcoming Germany's OSCE chairmanship heavily invoked the spirit of *Ostpolitik* and its achievements, but without any discussion of why the problems in relations with Russia were different from those of détente times and how Russia now had different motivations. These included the establishment of a set of security principles pre-dating those of Helsinki. Gernot Erler (SPD), the Government Commissioner for Cooperation with Russia and Steinmeier's chief Russia adviser, was an *Ostpolitik* disciple wedded to the possibilities of resolving differences with Moscow through dialogue. Through the OSCE chairmanship, he saw the opportunity to reconnect with the traditions of détente that would allow Germany to put in place 'confidence-building steps'. While Germany's efforts kept the Minsk process going and helped alleviate some aspects of the humanitarian crisis in Donbas, it did not lead to any diplomatic breakthrough in resolving the conflict. This in turn meant that the EU's sanctions tied to Russian action to support implementation of the Minsk Agreements stayed in place. European diplomacy led by Germany could only go so far. Without the USA at the table, there was insufficient influence and a lack of potentially attractive trade-offs to encourage Russia to change its policy.

German diplomats described the policy of managing the new security challenge posed by Russia as *Geschlossenheit und Entschlossenheit* (unity and resolve), language reminiscent of the Cold War. Despite the difficulty of agreeing a policy among 28 EU members and 29 NATO member states, western countries succeeded in doing so, a feat made possible by Merkel's ability to exercise leadership in the EU together with her strong atlanticist instincts. She did not lose her faith in the USA despite the damage to her relationship with President Obama after revelations in late 2013 that the US National Security Agency had tapped her phone calls for years.

Perhaps the most potent symbol of Germany's changed position towards Russia and its new approach to European security was its agreement at the 2016 NATO summit in Warsaw to lead one of the four multinational battalion-sized battlegroups deployed in the Baltic states and Poland to strengthen the Alliance's defence and deterrence posture. It took up this role in February 2017 and sent a 2,500-strong force to Lithuania. The issue of deploying German forces in central Europe was sensitive not just for German public opinion, given the actions of the Wehrmacht there during the war. Germany had occupied Lithuania from June 1941 to January 1945. However, even though Lithuania borders on the Russian exclave of Kaliningrad, the deployment did not prove politically controversial in Germany, nor did it cause resentment in Lithuania. Although Moscow criticised NATO's forward deployments, it did not single out Germany or other European force contributors for special attention, choosing instead to focus on holding snap exercises and unveiling a new armaments programme, including upgraded nuclear weapons systems.

Inconsistencies in policy

Despite the dramatic shift in policy, there were inevitable inconsistencies and occasional deviations. In 2016, Horst Seehofer, leader of the CSU and Minister President of Bavaria, travelled to Moscow for a meeting arranged with Putin by his predecessor Edmund Stoiber. The visit earned him strong criticism in Berlin. Observers saw it as part of a self-promotion campaign by the Bavarian leader ahead of federal elections in 2017. For the government, he delivered an unhelpful message to the Kremlin by emphasising his opposition to sanctions. He even earned a rebuke from the Russia Commissioner Erler who accused him of helping Russia undermine European unity on sanctions.[45] Bavaria, home to Siemens and other companies with long-established trade links with Russia, had started to feel the effects of reduced bilateral trade even if Russia was only in ninth place among Bavaria's foreign trade partners in 2014.[46]

In the run-up to the election and ahead of NATO's Warsaw summit, Steinmeier played to the SPD audience, condemning military manoeuvres in Poland and the Baltic states, including a Polish-led military exercise with the participation of Germany and nine other NATO member states as 'sabre-rattling and howling for war'.[47] In September 2016, Sigmar Gabriel (SPD), the Economics Minister, led a business delegation to Moscow to meet with Putin and other members of the Russian government. Discussions included the construction of a second Nord Stream pipeline and possible German financing for the proposed rail link between Moscow and Kazan. By this stage, parts of the German business community were concerned that continuing sanctions could lead to a long-term loss of markets in Russia to Chinese competitors.[48] The value of its exports to Russia had nearly halved from their 2012 level of €38 billion.[49] Symbolically, the news of the destruction of a UN aid convoy bound for the Syrian city of Aleppo cast a cloud over the visit amid strong suspicions that Russian aircraft were responsible. It was a reminder that the range of problems in relations with Russia had expanded well beyond Ukraine. Indeed, Russia's intervention in Syria beginning in 2015 had contributed to the dramatic exodus of the Syrian population to Europe and created severe dissension within the EU on how to deal with the problem. Merkel's decision to welcome close to 900,000 Syrian asylum seekers in 2015 placed her and her government under great pressure.

In a sign of changing times in the SPD, Heiko Maas, the new foreign minister from March 2018, struck a sharper tone in his dealings with Moscow. He noted after just a month in office that Germany's Russia policy should be guided by 'realities' and that 'Russia had always defined itself more as separate from the West and partly in opposition to it'. Russia was 'acting in an increasingly hostile way', he said.[50]

The Nord Stream 2 debacle

For all the new realism and clarity of thought about Russia, there was a major contradiction in German policy: the initiative to double the capacity of the Nord Stream pipeline directly linking

Russia and Germany under the Baltic Sea. Heavily lobbied by Schröder and Gabriel – the latter in his capacities as economics minister and later as foreign minister – the controversial project has angered Ukraine and several EU countries because of its geopolitical implications and its undermining of the spirit of EU sanctions against Russia. Its purpose is to reduce still further the volumes of Russian gas transiting Belarus, Poland and Ukraine. It also incurred the wrath of the Trump administration, provoking US sanctions against it. The genesis of the pipeline consortium in 2015 and its rapid construction to the point of near completion in early 2020 is a symbol of Germany's inability to shake off two sets of traditional reflexes. German industry views Russia as a source of raw materials and a market for German finished goods while large sections of the political establishment continue to believe in the stabilising role of energy trade in the *Ostpolitik* tradition. For industry, there was an additional argument. The new pipeline would further reduce the risk of gas supplies transiting Ukraine to the benefit of German and European consumers. Germany would still have to cope with the supply risk from Russia, but it would be easier to do this directly and without the issue of Ukraine complicating matters.

The pipeline drama is also evidence of the enduring influence of former Chancellor Schröder and the old SPD lobby. In 2005, Schröder became Chairman of the Shareholders' Committee of Nord Stream AG, the Swiss-registered company that owns and operates the original Nord Stream pipeline and was still in the role fifteen years later. Built at a cost of €7.4 billion, it became operational in 2011–12 with an annual capacity of 55 billion cubic metres. Matthias Warnig, Putin's Stasi friend was appointed CEO of the company, an indication of the project's importance for Putin personally. At this time, Germany was importing 34 billion cubic metres of gas annually from Russia.[51] With 51 per cent owned by the Russian state gas company Gazprom, it has two German shareholders that each own 15.5 per cent stakes, Wintershall Dea and a subsidiary of E.ON. Nord Stream was part of an effort by Gazprom to achieve direct access to the Western European market and reduce its dependence on transit infrastructure.

In the summer of 2015 as fighting continued in Donbas, five major European energy companies, including BASF and E.ON, agreed to join a consortium to double the capacity of the existing pipeline. It was unclear what incentives Moscow had offered the European investors. Schröder became chairman of the Nord Stream 2 AG consortium in October 2016. The agreement between the companies was remarkable, given the controversy around the first project and the strategy adopted by EU member states to diversify gas imports and with EU sanctions in place against Ukraine. One of the aims of the project was to reduce further transit dependence on Ukraine, a step that would increase Gazprom's influence as a supplier of gas to Ukraine since Ukraine could no longer exercise leverage through its control of the gas transportation infrastructure on its territory. Its loss of transit would also reduce Ukraine's strategic importance to the EU as well as depriving it of revenues. This was hardly a way to strengthen Ukraine's energy security as Merkel had vowed to do. In addition, Poland, the Baltic States and several other central European countries were bitterly opposed to the project, but this was not enough to prevent Berlin pursuing a Germany-first policy. However, the government was clearly split on the issue with the Economics Ministry led by Gabriel enthusiastic and actively lobbying in support, the Foreign Ministry sympathetic and passive, and the Chancellor's Office unenthusiastic but hopeful that the European Commission would find the project incompatible with the rules of the Third Energy Package and stop it. Gabriel saw the danger. In a meeting with Putin in October 2015, he spoke of placing the project under German rather than EU rules to overcome potential legal obstacles.[52] This clumsy statement damaged his reputation at home.

In public, German diplomats stuck faithfully to the public message that this was a 'purely commercial project' and that it was not the government's business to interfere. Yet privately, they often admitted this was nonsense. It was impossible to argue that the project was purely commercial when the majority shareholder was Gazprom, a state company and agent of Russian energy diplomacy, and the source of gas was Russia. However, the project enjoyed not just high-level patronage from Schröder and Gabriel, it was also popular with the federal states of Mecklenburg-Pomerania, Brandenburg and Saxony, which stood to benefit from the creation of new infrastructure to transport the increased volumes of gas to the south. However, Merkel woke up late to the project's significance, accepting only in April 2018 that there were 'political elements'[53] to it and making a more forceful case for continuing gas transit through Ukraine. Moscow showed little interest in accommodating Berlin. It proposed a mere 15 billion cubic metres per annum (bcma) when the Ukrainian transit system carried 93.5 bcma in 2017 down from 137 bcma in 2004.[54] This coincided with an initiative by thirty-nine Republican senators in Washington to persuade President Trump to force Germany to stop the project. Shortly afterwards ahead of the NATO Summit, Trump accused Germany of being 'totally controlled by Russia', angrily stating that Germany received '60–70 per cent of its energy from Russia' and referring to the construction of Nord Stream 2. The real data told a different story. In 2018, Germany was importing around 40 per cent of its natural gas from Russia and gas was 23.5 per cent of primary energy consumption,[55] in contrast to 35 per cent in the UK.[56] In 2018, 36.3 per cent of Germany's crude oil imports came from Russia[57] with oil making up 34.3 per cent of primary energy consumption.[58]

A week before Trump's attack on Germany, the respected DIW economic research institute in Berlin published a devastating critique of the rationale for Nord Stream 2. It concluded that the significance of natural gas in Germany's primary energy consumption was declining, there was no economic or security need for the pipeline and that it was bad for the environment. It also pointed to the project's lack of commercial viability and cited a report by an analyst at the Russian state bank Sberbank who calculated that the pipeline would operate at only 60 per cent capacity and that its net present value would be negative at €5 billion. The same report stated that 'the project would primarily serve geopolitical interests and strengthen the pipeline industry.'[59] The company was run in the interests of contractors and not out of concern for profits, the analyst said.[60] Sberbank terminated his employment after the report appeared. Mikhail Korchemkin, a respected Russian energy specialist, has argued that the project is attractive for Gazprom's European partners since Gazprom is covering €31 billion out of the total project cost of €40 billion, a cost that may simply be passed on to gas consumers in Russia. In his view, the only beneficiaries in Russia will be the contractors engaged to build the pipeline who are run by Putin's close associates.[61] Little discussion has taken place in Germany about this aspect of the project and the likelihood that it is reinforcing the very type of corrupt practices that Germany theoretically wishes to discourage as part of its desire to see improved rule of law in Russia.

German support for Russia in the Council of Europe

Nord Stream 2 was not the only inconsistency in Berlin's new Russia policy. Together with Paris, Berlin brokered a compromise allowing the restoration of Russia's voting rights in the Council of Europe's parliamentary assembly, five years after their suspension in 2014 in response to the annexation of Crimea. Russia had threatened to leave the human rights organisation unless its delegation regained the vote. It had also stopped paying its membership contributions, placing the organisation's finances under strain. The problem with Berlin's position was that Russia had not met any of the conditions for restoring its voting rights set out at the time of their suspension. Critics argued with justification that allowing Russia back as a voting member undermined the credibility of the Council of Europe. Moreover, there was substantial evidence of human rights violations in Russian-occupied Crimea. Berlin justified its position saying that if Russia left the Council, this would adversely affect human rights protection in Russia since Russian citizens would no longer be able to take their grievances to the European Court of Human Rights. The Ukrainian government reacted with fury to the decision, claiming that the Council of Europe had given up its role as a protector of human rights.[62]

Conclusions

Germany surprised itself, its European allies and Russia with its forceful response to Moscow's behaviour in Ukraine. With the annexation of Crimea, Moscow crossed a Rubicon, provoking a qualitatively different German response from the one it had seen in 2008 after it invaded Georgia. At that time, Germany together with the USA, France and several other EU member states had pursued a policy of appeasement by rushing to mend relations. Russia was not even required to observe its ceasefire commitments. The naive hope was that Medvedev's presidency that had just begun would bring Russia closer to the West and place Russia on a more promising trajectory at home. By 2014, Russia had shown it had lost interest in seeking a cooperative relationship with western countries and would pursue its interests independently, guided by its own values. Russia's actions in Ukraine brought these differences into sharp relief and gave Merkel the political space to change the basis of Russia policy. Germany was now prepared to confront Russia on the issue of security principles, and its convictions were strong enough to take the EU with it. German policymakers cleverly designed this response as an EU policy to insulate Germany from Russian attack while at the same time achieving the broadest possible impact. They succeeded in creating a durable political consensus in the EU by stressing the need to keep communication channels open with Moscow while trying against the odds to push forward a process to achieve a peace settlement in Donbas. EU foreign ministers formally adopted a policy of five principles along these lines in March 2016, which made any substantial change in the EU's position on Russia contingent on implementation of the 'Minsk Agreement' while keeping open space for 'selective engagement' with Russia on issues of interest to the EU.[63]

There was also an impressive degree of coordination of policy with Washington, even if the USA appeared at times only semi-engaged and insensitive to the strain that Germany's crisis management was placing on the coalition and public opinion, particularly when the Syrian refugee crisis peaked in 2015–16. Merkel saw the issues with admirable clarity and despite underlying differences of emphasis, the coalition partners were able to pursue a generally well-coordinated policy. Despite the obvious imperfections of the Minsk agreements, German diplomats can argue with justification that they at least created a process and made it possible to address some aspects of the humanitarian crisis in the region. In diplomacy, a process sometimes serves to slow down events and seek compromises as calculations change.

The common denominator that brought about the cross-party consensus was Russia's violation of international law and its open disregard for Ukraine's sovereignty and its treaty-based commitments to Ukraine. The shooting down of MH17 provided the additional shock that brought EU countries together and emboldened them to follow the German lead. As in other countries, German business quickly adapted to the sanctions regime. Despite opposition to sanctions in some circles and the efforts by Steinmeier and Gabriel to water down the terms for lifting them by offering Russia a phased timetable dependent on gradual implementation of the Minsk-2 Agreement, they have held firm. This partly reflects the fact that they were relatively mild and only capable of inflicting real damage over a longer period. They were designed to hurt the Russian economy rather than causing it unacceptable harm. Germany, in particular, would never have supported such a radical policy. As such, the sanctions have left a modest impact on Russia's economy, perhaps costing it 1–1.5 per cent of GDP per year in the short term but rising to as much as 9 per cent over the medium term.[64] However, sanctions have hurt Russia in another way. Deprived of private western capital, Russia has been forced to seek Chinese state capital as a replacement, a quite different proposition and one that is uncomfortable for Russia, particularly in the strategically sensitive energy sector. Putin himself has admitted that sanctions are a hindrance in the energy sector but has downplayed their significance.[65] Yet sanctions have served an important symbolic function by showing both Kyiv and Moscow that western countries regard Russia's behaviour in Ukraine as unacceptable and are committed to the principle of preserving Ukraine's sovereignty and independence.

NATO's return to the Harmel doctrine of deterrence and dialogue was uncontroversial for Germany because of its positive connotations as an analogue of *Ostpolitik* and its role in ending the Cold War. The offer to play a leading role in NATO's enhanced forward presence on its eastern periphery, in a country bordering with Russia, asked much more of Germany and was strong evidence of its readiness to contribute in full measure to Alliance efforts to deter further Russian violations of the European security order. Germany deserved more credit than it received from its allies for taking this step. It may not have been spending enough on defence, as Trump tirelessly pointed out, but it showed courage in taking on a sensitive new role.

Moscow's intervention in Syria and the increasing pressure on civil society at home contributed to a rolling negative news cycle about Russia as did the evidence of Russian 'active measures' in Germany. Together, these factors helped to maintain a political consensus around the need for sanctions. The 'active measures' included the hacker attack on the German Parliament in 2015 and the fake news story about the rape of a 13-year-old girl in January 2016 that briefly stirred the Russian community in Germany (see Chapter 7). The attempted assassination in March 2018 of the defector Sergey Skripal in Britain with a chemical weapon by serving Russian military intelligence officers provoked shock in Germany and led to Berlin expelling four Russian diplomats in solidarity with the UK. This was also a response to a second, more extensive hacking operation first identified in December 2017. The attack compromised a range of German government systems, including the Foreign Ministry and Defence Ministry and may have lasted up to a year.[66] The murder of Zelimkhan Khangoshvili, a Georgian citizen wanted by the Russian authorities, in broad daylight in a Berlin park in the summer of 2019 added to the impression in the German government that Moscow had lost its inhibitions and was no longer concerned about damaging relations with Germany. The victim was a Chechen who had applied for political asylum in Germany. Moscow said he posed an Islamic terrorist threat.[67] Federal prosecutors belatedly concluded that the Russian state was connected to the murder only after investigative journalists pointed to his connection with the Russian Security Service. As a result, Berlin expelled two Russian diplomats claiming that Moscow had failed to support the investigation.[68]

Evidence of Russian malfeasance on these multiple fronts helped to preserve public support for the government's Russia policy. Nevertheless, some commentators swam against the tide. Gabriele Krone-Schmalz, the former television journalist based in Moscow in the late 1980s continued to publish popular books condemning the demonisation of Russia and the arrogance of the West. The doyenne of the *Russlandversteher*, she believed the West was responsible for provoking Russia and that the USA was opposed to successful cooperation between Russia and Europe. She even argued that Russia had not violated international law in Crimea.[69] She unquestioningly accepted Russian grievances about western behaviour and, like others of her generation who identified with the Gorbachev years and the promise of a different Russia, had no feel for the development of Ukraine since the collapse of the USSR. Nor did she show any understanding of Russia's culture of strategic thinking.

Another member of this group with an outdated understanding of Russia, but in his case with foreign policy expertise, was Horst Teltschik who expressed nostalgia for the Paris Charter and the vision of a peaceful order stretching from Vancouver to Vladivostok. He criticised NATO's 'inflexible' strategy towards Russia claiming that it was unrealistic to tie the prospect of reducing tensions and rebuilding trust to Russia making concessions[70] and that it would only escalate the conflict with Russia.[71] On Ukraine, he argued that to prevent the escalation of the conflict, Ukraine needed inter alia to end its 'terrifyingly high corruption'.[72] There was no reference to the problem of corrupted state institutions in Russia as a security problem. Instead, there were respectful words about Putin and a photograph of Teltschik with him in his Sochi residence in 2007[73] together with the black Labrador that he famously allowed to wander into a meeting with Merkel.

General Harald Kujat, formerly Inspector General of the Bundeswehr and Chairman of NATO's Military Committee, was another vocal critic of the government's policy on Ukraine. He regularly took to the airwaves to criticise western policy towards Russia over Ukraine. The former SPD Minister President of Brandenburg, Matthias Platzeck, an enthusiastic Russophile who had grown up in the GDR, also frequently appeared in the media calling for dialogue instead of confrontation. However, these dissenting voices and those heard from the left and right of the political spectrum did not shake the basic consensus that Russia had changed and that Germany must resist the dangers it posed.

There are strong grounds to believe that Putin had either not given sufficient thought to Germany's response to Russia's actions in Ukraine or had simply miscalculated what it would be. After the EU's half-hearted reaction to Russia's invasion of Georgia in 2008, he could hardly have expected Germany to shape such a comparatively strong and determined position. In all probability, he had expected Ukraine to collapse in 2014 and to re-group under Moscow's wing in the absence of western support. It quickly became known in Berlin that the Chancellor's Office believed Putin had lied to Merkel after he denied that the 'little green men' who took control of Crimea were Russian soldiers. Apparently, this was a turning point for her.[74] She had, in any case, concluded during her telephone calls with Putin that he was 'living in another world'.[75] Before this, Russia had enjoyed from its perspective a politically valuable and economically lucrative relationship with Europe's most influential country knowing that Berlin was reluctant to stand up to Russia. However, by the summer of 2019, Putin clearly did not believe that he had burnt all his bridges to Berlin. He received the outgoing German ambassador for a farewell visit and described Merkel in flattering terms, referring to her as the 'Iron Chancellor'.[76]

If Merkel's moment of weakness in early 2015 when she rushed to Moscow fearing an escalation of conflict in Ukraine was explicable, given Germany's extreme sensitivity to the danger of war, the German establishment's acquiescence in Nord Stream 2 was not. Not only has the project undermined the credibility of western policy of resistance to Russian aggression in Europe and the pursuit of a single EU energy policy aimed at diversifying sources of supply, it has also openly disregarded the concerns of Germany's Central European neighbours. Worse still, it will damage Ukraine. The project plays into Russian hands by depriving Ukraine of an important asset in its asymmetrical relationship with Russia. The loss of transit takes away its ability to protect itself from Russian blackmail over energy supplies and diminishes its strategic importance for the EU. This is far more consequential that the loss of transit revenues. In short, Nord Stream 2 represents a policy failure that owes much to the residual influence of parts of the Schröder lobby and sections of industry that believe in prioritising

Germany's commercial interests over the security interests of Ukraine and allies in the region. The inability of the CDU/CSU and other parties to build a common position against the project also suggests that Germany instinctively wishes to keep a card in play to show to Russia that Germany wants to overcome the current estrangement between the two countries. The absence of opposition to the project on the grounds of its corrupting effect in Russia reflects a remarkable level of denial about the true nature of the system that has emerged in Russia since 2001. In April 2018, Merkel belatedly conceded that Nord Stream 2 was not an exclusively economic project and that its 'political factors' required consideration. For the first time, she referred to the need to ensure that the project did not displace Ukraine as a transit country for the export of Russian gas.[77] However, she did not mention the fact that the deep reforms in the Ukrainian gas sector after 2014 had made Ukraine a reliable transit partner and effectively undermined one of the main arguments of German business in favour of the pipeline.

The poisoning of the Russian opposition politician Alexey Navalny in August 2020 caused an unexpected crisis in German–Russian relations after a specialist German military laboratory first identified that the substance used was a Novichok nerve agent banned under the Chemical Weapons Convention. Foreign Minister Maas hinted that if the Russian authorities did not investigate properly, they could force Germany to change its position on Nord Stream 2. Merkel appeared to share his view. Two Christian Democrat candidates for the chancellorship called for a stop to the pipeline together with representatives from the Greens. However, when the Greens tabled a motion in Parliament to halt the pipeline's construction, the coalition parties roundly rejected it with support from Die Linke and the AfD.[78] Ultimately, although the government wanted to send a strong European signal to condemn Russia's violation of the Chemical Weapons Convention and the use of Novichok to try to assassinate Navalny, it did not have the courage of its convictions. It appeared concerned about the legal ramifications of sanctioning the project. Some German analysts also believe that an additional argument against stopping the project was that it would hand victory to the Trump administration and that continuing with it was the lesser evil.[79] In October 2020, Berlin-based US energy specialist Thomas O'Donnell concluded that the project appeared dead because of US sanctions pressure that enjoyed bipartisan support in Congress.[80]

The Nord Stream blot on Germany's generally impressive leadership of the EU response to Russia's behaviour in Ukraine shows that there has so far been only a radical shift in policy thinking on Russia rather than a revolution. This reflects the fact that for over twenty years, Germany displayed a blindness to developments in Russia, wishing them to be something other than they were, even if to observers elsewhere, the trends were perfectly clear. Deeply held views take time to wash away. The British analyst James Sherr had written in 2009:

> Today Russia is pursuing a number of classically nineteenth century aims – great power status, diminution of the rights of small powers and the formation of 'regions of privileged interest' – and it is doing so with a mixture of classical and twenty-first century tools – intelligence and covert penetration, commerce and joint ventures, 'lobbying structures' and litigation, energy and downstream investment and, in the former USSR, Russian diasporas and other 'civilisational' forms of soft power.[81]

It is hard to believe that the German security policy community had not come to similar conclusions. Yet before 2014, there was no adjustment of policy to reflect these realities, instead there was a deepening of traditional mechanisms of cooperation. At the same time, German policymakers failed to read the obvious signals from Moscow to Ukraine in the summer of 2013 and missed a vital opportunity to intervene to clarify the purpose of the Association Agreement and ways to address alleged Russian concerns about EU goods entering Russia re-packaged as Ukrainian products. For years after the imposition of EU sanctions and Russian counter-sanctions, Moscow tolerated Belarusian re-exports of food products to the Russian market that had originated outside Belarus.[82]

Despite its impressive range of contacts in Russia and its extensive, well-maintained machinery of dialogue, Germany listened to the music from Moscow without hearing the tune. Merkel's reconfiguration of Russia policy was dramatic because of the extent to which it was out of date. With its contradictions and limitations, her new approach was the art of the possible.

6

An unfulfilled economic relationship

Wishful thinking about Russia has extended to the economy too. German officials, politicians and commentators tend to overstate the economic value of Germany's trade relationship with Russia based on its potential rather than its reality. Admittedly, Germany currently imports from Russia around 50 per cent of its coal, nearly 40 per cent of its natural gas and just over a third of its crude oil while it has a significant share in the Russian market for its machinery and cars. Nevertheless, its overall trade with Russia is surprisingly small given the size of Russia's economy, its population of 143 million and its close location. However, these links are of considerable political importance for German policy-makers. The long-standing gas bridge between the two countries, in particular, embodies Germany's concept of a close relationship based on mutual dependence that ties Russia to Europe. The trade figures tell a story. In 2019, German exports to Poland were 2.5 times higher than to Russia and imports nearly twice as high[1] even though Russia's GDP that year was over 2.5 times larger than Poland's.[2] Admittedly, this data does not capture the value of German investments in Russia. Nevertheless, for German companies, the allure of the Russian market is limited in practice by Russia's inability to move its economy away from dependence on raw materials exports and establish a reliable investment environment. Since 2000, when Putin came to power, the place of raw materials in Russia's GDP has increased rather than decreased[3] despite repeated commitments by its leaders to diversify the economy. In 2018, oil and gas accounted for 46 per cent of Russia's budget revenues.[4] Ironically, Germany's relatively stable imports of Russian oil and gas over this period have reinforced Russia's 'resource curse'. Germany has consistently been Russia's largest market for energy exports.

For policymakers brought up in the *Ostpolitik* tradition, trade and particularly energy relations are a stabilising force locking the two countries in a relationship of interdependence. After the collapse of the USSR, economic ties were central to Berlin's vision of partnership in which Germany and other EU members would bring high-value skills and goods to Russia and participate in Russia's transformation process. German companies large and small were enthusiastic about the Russian market owing to its proximity and potential size. Among major industrial companies, Ruhrgas had the deepest Russia experience. Starting in the early 1970s, it had established the personal relations in the Soviet gas industry and government that were the foundation of a large and highly successful business for both sides. Its competitor Wintershall built a strong relationship with Gazprom in the 1990s, and the two contributed to making Germany Gazprom's largest export market and its biggest source of revenues.

German commercial banks took advantage of their experience from Soviet days to seek new business in capitalist Russia alongside major companies such as AEG, Mannesmann, Siemens, Thyssenkrupp and others that had also done business with the USSR. The car manufacturers BMW, Daimler-Benz, Opel and Volkswagen all quickly found demand for their products in Russia and some of them later established local manufacturing capacity. Major retailers such as Metro and Rewe opened stores in Russia as Russians' purchasing power grew. Large numbers of *Mittelstand* companies (those with up to 500 employees) saw attractive opportunities in Russia and began to establish a presence there. Russia's financial collapse of 1998 hit German investors hard, but those that stayed in many cases cashed in on the boom years of the Russian economy from 2003 to 2007. By 2014, there were 6,200 German companies registered in Russia.

Thirty years after its transition to a market economy, Russia still exports raw materials to Germany in exchange for finished goods. In 2018, oil, gas, petrochemicals, coal and steel were Russia's top exports to Germany, while its five top imports from Germany were machinery, chemical products, cars, car parts and measuring equipment. These made up over 10 per cent of Russia's total imports.[5] At the same time, Germany was Russia's most important trading partner in Europe and second overall globally only to China[6] with 7.6 per cent of its exports going to Germany. Remarkably, despite the industrialisation policies of the USSR, the pattern of trade today between Germany and Russia is fundamentally unchanged from more than a century ago. In 1913, Germany accounted for around 48 per cent of Russia's imports and 30 per cent of its exports.[7] It was Germany's second largest trading partner after Britain. At that time, Russia's main export to Germany was grain rather than hydrocarbons, but Germany's main exports to Russia were advanced machines, chemicals and electrical goods.[8] In other words, the traditional complementarity in economic relations persists, reflecting Germany's continued engineering pre-eminence and its need for raw materials set against Russia's richness in natural resources and relative technological backwardness. The interdependence in this relationship is currently limited to the mutual benefits of the gas trade in which Germany needs the gas and Russia needs the market. In 2018, Germany accounted for 37 per cent of Gazprom's gas sales to Western Europe.[9] In 2019, Gazprom sold slightly less gas to Europe than it did on the Russian domestic market, but it earned over twice as much from European sales[10] because of its obligation to sell its gas at regulated prices in Russia.

Against a backdrop of increasing oil and gas sales to Europe since 2015 despite EU sanctions, Russia has de-emphasised Europe as a source of modernisation because of the current collision of political interests and values. This overall picture makes it hard to subscribe to the view of US analysts such as Stephen Szabo who depict Germany's relationship with Russia as an example of its geo-economic power.[11] Russia is clearly not responding as this theory suggests it should, since it no longer sees Germany as an essential partner for reshaping its economy. If anything, the relationship illustrates better Russia's geo-economic influence through its ability to condition German behaviour using German industry's interest in accessing cheap Russian gas. The Nord Stream 1 and 2 pipelines are a monument to this form of Russian 'soft' power.

Even in 2012 when German exports to Russia reached a historic peak of €38 billion (up from €5.9 billion in 1996), Russia ranked only eleventh among Germany's export markets, just behind Poland.[12] At that time, Russia was Germany's seventh most important source of imports (€42 billion), slightly behind the UK.[13] In 2019, German exports to Russia had dropped to €26.5 billion, putting Russia in fourteenth place behind Hungary. The value of exports to Russia was one third of those to the UK and less than a quarter of those to the USA.[14] The proportion of imports from Russia, predominantly oil and gas, was higher at €31 billion but under half the value of imports from France and less than a third of those from the Netherlands. The story is the same with German investment in Russia. Germany's stock of accumulated direct investments stands at around $20 billion, a surprisingly small share, and not much larger than the investments of France and the UK, which have smaller economies and fewer links with the Russian market.[15]

This context is important because it also underlines the underdeveloped non-oil and gas economy in Russia. This situation reflects the spectacular growth of the state-controlled sector of the Russian economy from 2003 and the sharp deceleration of GDP growth since 2012 when it was still over 4 per cent.[16] According to Russia's Federal Anti-Monopoly Service (FAS), the state's share of the economy in 1998 was around 25 per cent. By 2018, several estimates suggest that it was probably around 60–70 per cent and accounted for 7–10 per cent of GDP. FAS noted that the state's role as an economic player beyond its regulatory functions made it 'capable of substantially distorting competition'.[17] One of the side effects of the 'statisation' of the economy has been the restricted development of small and medium-sized enterprises (SMEs). Aleksey Kudrin, Chairman of the Accounts Chamber and former Minister of Finance (2000–11), has repeatedly argued that to boost growth and reduce dependence on oil exports, Russia must invest more in healthcare, education, science and innovation, as well as improving the quality of public administration while also giving more power to the country's regions.[18] Yet despite its very large reserves, the Russian government seemingly has no serious intention, for now, of investing in education and healthcare to improve human capital or in alleviating the problem of poverty. In the first half of 2019, nearly 20 million Russians were living below the government-defined poverty line.[19] These general trends explain why for the world's top exporter nation, Russia remains a disproportionately small market with limited growth prospects. In 2019, it accounted for a mere 2 per cent of Germany's overall exports and 3 per cent of its imports.[20]

However, the energy relationship between Germany and Russia is significant and provides the crucial underpinning of their political relationship. Gas imports from Russia are strategically important to Germany because of its increasing reliance on gas for power generation in addition to traditional industrial and heating needs. Gas sales to Germany are a vital source of revenues for Gazprom that allow it to absorb subsidised prices in Russia. To this extent, there is interdependence in the gas relationship. Crude oil is in a different category since it is an easily traded global commodity and is more easily transportable than gas, which relies on fixed infrastructure. Germany can currently only cover 7 per cent of its gas consumption from indigenous reserves and these are in decline.[21] In 2017, Russia accounted for 51 per cent of its gas imports, Norway 27 per cent and the Netherlands 21 per cent.[22] Like Norway and the Netherlands, Russia delivers gas to Germany by pipeline. Germany imports only negligible amounts of liquefied natural gas[23] although the government is backing plans to build three new small-scale LNG import terminals to fuel ships and heavy trucks.

The radical *Energiewende* (energy transition) reforms that began a decade ago mean that the importance of gas as a bridging fuel is set to grow as Germany aims to meet its 2050 Paris commitments. To do so, Germany plans to close its coal-fired power plants, which still generate over a third of its electricity, by 2038. The decision after the Fukushima disaster to bring forward the closure of Germany's nuclear power plants to 2022 has also significantly increased Germany's gas market in the short to medium term. Not surprisingly, state-owned Gazprom is keen to capitalise on an opportunity that brings commercial as well as political benefits for Russia. German industry's positive experience of working with Gazprom and its Soviet predecessor over decades has conditioned the view of the government and encouraged it to see gas relations with Russia through a commercial prism. This downplays the role of gas exports as part of Russia's diplomacy and helps explains why different parts of the German government insisted for so long that the Nord Stream pipeline was an 'economic' project. They were simply echoing the belief of German industry that Gazprom was a capable and reliable commercial partner. The government's reliance on industry goes further since German energy companies rather than the government are primarily responsible for security of supply. Despite the origins of the German–Russian gas trade being in the Cold War, the security of gas deliveries in Germany is a commercial and technical issue rather than a political one.

The continuing prevalence of this view, despite serious deterioration of Germany's relationship with Russia since 2014, is testimony to the stability of the gas trade. This is all the more impressive given the transformation of the European gas market since 2010. In the early days, there was a basic symmetry in the gas relationship: a Soviet monopolist supplier sold its gas to West German regional monopolies on oil-indexed, long-term contracts with take-or-pay obligations. There was an equitable share of risk: the producer carried the price risk while the importer faced the risk of not selling the contracted gas volumes in full. The arrangement suited both sides and governed the gas trade for decades.[24] The Third Energy Package adopted in 2008 challenged the business model enjoyed by Gazprom and the German utility companies in several ways, including a requirement for integrated energy companies to sell off their gas and electricity networks to prevent them from gaining market advantage by blocking access to networks for competitors. The establishment of a national energy regulator to oversee the market was another revolutionary step. The consequences were devastating for the business models of Gazprom's partners.[25]

The provisions of the Third Energy Package also had direct implications for the economics of Nord Stream 1 since the issue arose of third-party access to the OPAL pipeline that transports gas from its entry point in Germany to the Czech Republic. Without an exemption, the pipeline could only operate at 50 per cent capacity. The issue enraged Putin. Speaking to a German business audience in Berlin in late 2010 when he was prime minister, Putin denounced the Third Energy Package for infringing the rights of the investors in Nord Stream, branding the EU's approach 'uncivilised'. He described as 'robbery' the requirement for Gazprom and its German partners in Lithuania to sell assets.[26] Ahead of the same event, he signed an article justifying Nord Stream 1 and South Stream, its planned analogue under the Black Sea, on the basis that the efforts of transit countries to exploit their monopoly position as carriers of Russian gas did not correspond to the interests of either Russia or the buyers of Russian gas.[27] At the same time, he served up the vision of a 'harmonious economic community from Lisbon to Vladivostok'. He also expressed Russia's interest in modernisation based on European technologies that were the most compatible with 'Russian production culture and its traditions'. At this time, Europe was still the preferred partner and Putin spoke of possibilities for strategic alliances in shipbuilding, aircraft construction, car manufacturing as well as other areas such as pharmaceuticals, medicine, nuclear energy and even space.[28] The German government's reaction was surprisingly muted. Merkel pointed to the impending creation of the Eurasian Economic Union and its unpredictable policies on import duties, suggesting that Russia was not moving in the right direction.[29] These were clear signs on both sides that all was not well in their trade relationship. Just weeks before, GM had pulled out of the planned sale of its German subsidiary Opel to a consortium of the Canadian car manufacturer Magna and Russia's Sberbank after the EU raised questions about the deal.

For Gazprom and its German partners, the future suddenly started to feel very uncertain. Not only was the Third Energy Package upending the old business model and threatening the commercial viability of the new direct gas link between Russia and Germany, but there were other serious problems. The *Energiewende* introduced uncertainty about future gas demand. It was possible that the renewables industry backed by the government would become more competitive and that technological progress would overcome the deficiencies of solar and wind power to store the electricity they generate and provide a source of supply to consumers not dependent on the sun shining and the wind blowing. This could substantially reduce the window of opportunity for gas as a bridging fuel and affect the financing of upstream development. In addition, the shale gas revolution was turning the USA into an exporter of LNG and creating a gas glut that set spot prices tumbling in the emerging hubs for gas trading.

To make matters worse, the aftermath of the 2008–9 financial crisis led to an unprecedented situation where Gazprom had to accept that long-term contracts were no longer sacred. After a series of legal challenges by its European buyers, including E.ON and RWE, it began to renegotiate prices with its top buyers. The Stockholm Arbitration Institute even ordered Gazprom to pay back €1.5 billion to RWE.[30] Gazprom gradually accepted that it had to change its price formula and relax its take-or-pay requirements to keep market share, albeit at the cost of reduced revenues.

However, there was yet another hammer blow. In late 2011, the EU's competition authorities (DG-COMP) began a three-and-a-half-year investigation into Gazprom's business practices in Europe after complaints by Lithuania. It believed that Gazprom was abusing its dominant position in the EU market and preventing the free flow of gas across member states and that it might have prevented some countries from diversifying their gas supplies. The two sides reached a settlement in March 2017 after more than a year and a half of negotiations against the backdrop of the dramatic deterioration of relations between the EU and Russia over Ukraine. Gazprom bowed to the EU's regulatory powers and avoided a hefty fine and the embarrassing publication of DG-COMP's statement of objections that covered 600 pages. The settlement required Gazprom to accept several legally binding rules aimed at ensuring the free flow of gas in Europe and competitive pricing. These included a commitment not to leverage its dominance in gas supply.

The readiness of the two sides to compromise was all the more remarkable given that tension between the EU and Russia over Ukraine had led to EU sanctions against Russia and Russian counter-sanctions against the EU. There was also no disguising the fact that the EU had forced Gazprom to change its business practices even though it had ridiculed some provisions of the Third

Energy Package just a few years earlier.[31] In addition, there was still no resolution to the issue of the OPAL pipeline. This meant that Gazprom and its partners could only use half its capacity. Throughout this period, gas continued to flow without interruption. German industry could argue with justification that the gas trade between Germany and Russia was a stabilising influence not just on the bilateral relationship but also on the EU's ties with Russia. This was despite the EU's energy strategy adopted in 2015 that emphasised the need to diversify the EU's sources of supply and increase its resilience to energy shocks. Events in Ukraine in 2014 had clearly left a deep mark on EU thinking and made it impossible to separate Europe's gas relationship with Russia from geopolitics.

Crude oil exports to Germany and other EU countries have not traditionally had the same sensitivity as gas since oil has been a globally traded commodity for decades that does not rely on deliveries by pipeline. Transportation by sea and rail provide flexible alternatives. West Germany began importing Soviet crude oil earlier than gas because of its availability. In 1960, the USSR supplied 9 per cent of its total consumption – far less than for Greece (22 per cent), Italy (19 per cent) and Austria (14 per cent).[32] The USSR's sales of crude oil to West Germany and other Western European countries increased through the 1970s after the 1973 OPEC oil embargo and the subsequent rise in prices. The first Druzhba (friendship) pipeline built in 1962 connected the GDR and other Soviet Central European satellites with the oil production centres in West Siberia and delivered crude directly to a newly built refinery at Schwedt in the north of the GDR, close to the Polish border. Today, the Russian state oil giant Rosneft owns a majority stake in the Schwedt refinery and minority stakes in two other smaller German refineries.

The USSR also supplied enriched uranium to the FRG and other Western European countries in return for nuclear reactor components from European manufacturers, including German companies. As the historian Frank Bösch has noted, the Soviet government viewed West German businessmen as political negotiators. He cites the example of how the Soviet Embassy in the FRG contacted Berthold Beitz, the chairman of Krupp and a member of the International Olympic Committee (IOC), to report the withdrawal of 10,000 soldiers from Afghanistan and request that the IOC should reconsider its boycott of the 1980 Moscow Olympics.[33] Krupp was an exporter of large-diameter steel pipes to the USSR for pipeline construction and Beitz was a distinguished public figure in West Germany known for saving up to 800 Jews from the SS in occupied Poland during the Second World War. The Kremlin's use of former Chancellor Schröder in his capacity as politician-turned-businessman to carry out its lobbying work in Germany and Europe builds on this earlier tradition.

Although German industry continues to underline the success of its exclusive gas relationship with Russia over decades, there are signs of its limitations for the companies directly involved. Wintershall has only a 25 per cent stake in two upstream projects in West Siberia while Gazprom has 100 per cent stakes in a number of trading and storage subsidiaries owned through its joint ventures with Wintershall. The different opportunities in the two markets and their contrasting structures – the state dominates gas production and trading in Russia while the state is absent from the sector in Germany – make it hard to balance mutual market access. E.ON's hostile takeover of Ruhrgas in 2002 changed the relationship with Gazprom and led to the sale of its 6.4 per cent stake in the Russian state company in 2010 after relations soured over gas pricing. However, E.ON remains a shareholder in Nord Stream through a subsidiary. It also invested in the Russian electricity sector, boldly acquiring outright control of the OGK-4 power generation company in 2008. Its expectations of industrial growth fuelling increased demand for electricity have not materialised and the Russian power market has remained stagnant. By contrast, RWE tried but failed to secure a position in the

Russian electricity sector. Unlike E.ON and Wintershall, it also became a leading partner in the Nabucco pipeline project that competed with an alternative Gazprom-led project to bring additional gas supplies directly to southern Europe. Nabucco never left the drawing board because it was unable to secure a commitment from Azerbaijan to supply the pipeline. RWE also supplied gas to Ukraine via Poland in 2014[34] as part of the new Ukrainian government's efforts to reduce gas purchases from Russia.

German industry's hopes of exploiting commercial opportunities in energy conservation and renewables in Russia have also not lived up to expectations. Launched amid fanfare in 2009, the Russian–German Energy Agency (RUDEA) aimed to raise energy efficiency levels in Russia through a jointly run business venture. The Russian Energy Ministry had concluded that Russia could double its energy efficiency in a decade.[35] Specialists believed that Russia could save the equivalent of twice the volume of gas it exported to Europe if it adopted the necessary measures and technologies to reduce the waste of energy in industry, household heating and other areas. With their experience of addressing these problems in the former GDR, German companies were in a strong position to assist. At this stage, Germany was still concerned about Gazprom's future ability to supply the Russian market and meet its commitments to Europe since its main fields in West Siberia were in decline and it was still in the process of investing in new production. Yet RUDEA, a prestige project blessed by Merkel and President Medvedev, signally failed. The head of the German Energy Agency, one of its shareholders, noted the difficulty of attracting investment to improve the energy efficiency of apartment blocks where the apartments belonged to private owners and the heating equipment to the state.[36] Poorly insulated apartments built in the 1950s were among the worst sources of wasted energy. Lacking commercially viable projects, the agency quietly faded from the scene in 2013, well before tensions over Ukraine impaired bilateral cooperation.

It is difficult to quantify the effect of EU sanctions on German business in Russia. Exports to Russia fell by 18 per cent (down to €29.2 billion) in 2014 and by a further 26 per cent (down to €21.7 billion) in 2015 before returning to growth in 2017.[37] The devaluation of the ruble played a role in bringing down the headline numbers as did import substitution and localisation of production. The ruble's volatility was a further indication of an economy heavily dependent on raw materials exports. The Ost-Ausschuss noted also that cheaper labour costs in Russia made it more attractive to produce there.[38] For some food producers, the loss of the Russian market because of Russian counter-sanctions meant lower prices for their products in the EU market because of supply gluts. However, from 2017 there were clear signs that German investment in Russia was picking up again, partly in response to the cheaper ruble. The same year saw a rebound of German machinery exports to Russia – up over 22 per cent. This was a significant number since machinery is consistently the largest category of goods exported to Russia. However, globally, German companies increased exports in 2015 by €72 billion (up 6.4 per cent) and by a further 1.1 per cent in 2016.[39] They continued to grow steadily between 2017 and 2019. This almost certainly explains the continuing absence of strong resistance to sanctions against Russia by leading German companies. Either they have managed to diversify markets or they have invested for the longer term at cheap prices in Russia. In 2018, German companies reportedly invested €3 billion in Russia, an amount not seen since before the financial crisis in 2008–9. One example of this is the new Mercedes-Benz assembly plant outside Moscow that opened in 2019. At the same time, localisation requirements in contracts from state companies are making it harder for some German companies than before. The number of German companies currently registered in Russia indicates tougher trading conditions. At the start of 2020, they were down to under 4,300.[40] Nevertheless, the current levels of bilateral trade look set to continue even if they will suffer as elsewhere from the immediate consequence of the coronavirus pandemic.

In a thoughtful paper published in 2019, the Ost-Ausschuss put forward a new agenda for expanding the German–Russian economic relationship.[41] Top of its list was an 'efficiency partnership' to increase Russia's low levels of labour productivity through modern management and production efforts. It noted that German business had an interest in ensuring that Chinese technologies and business models did not displace European versions. Other areas for focus were development of the Russian SME sector, expansion of business education contacts as well as digitalisation. The paper noted that Russia had software and Internet giants there were lacking in Europe and the largest e-commerce market in the world. Alongside other areas of opportunity for partnership, including logistics, climate change, food production and health, it listed civil society. This was an important addition and pointed to the understanding in the *Mittelstand*, in particular, that an innovative market economy and an effective social support system in Russia require a strong civil society to hold officials to account and reduce corruption. *Mittelstand* businesses do not have the same capacity as large companies to access the Kremlin to resolve problems.

On the broader economic and political relations, the paper was weaker. It argued in favour of developing a concept of a 'European prosperity space' with common bodies to establish harmonised standards between the EU and the Eurasian Union, a fanciful suggestion as long as such a gulf continues to exist in governance systems between the two. It offered no view on how or when this might come about. It also criticised EU sanctions for hardening positions between Europe and Russia over Ukraine. The paper demonstrated the continuing gap between German business's vision of the Russian market's potential and its reality, but it did not discuss the reasons for the discrepancy. German companies are not alone among foreign business groups in Russia in not wanting to speak truth to power, but in their case this is a missed opportunity. German business not only has an outstanding reputation in Russia for competence, it also has a long-term approach to investing in the country. Its collective voice could strengthen those constituencies in the Russian system that see the limitations of the current governance model and wish to reform it. In this respect, German business has little to lose and much to gain.

However, it is impossible to ignore the stain of corruption in German business activity in Russia that goes back to the 1990s. Some of the best-known cases relate to major German banks. According to German investigators, Commerzbank executives assisted the telecommunications minister Leonid Reiman, a close associate of Vladimir Putin, in illegally privatising state assets worth $1 billion.[42] After a six-year probe, in 2011 German prosecutors charged four Commerzbank managers with money laundering.[43] They agreed to pay fines to settle the case. Deutsche Bank was later involved in money laundering on a far greater scale. After a group of investigative journalists from the Organized Crime and Corruption Reporting Project published details in 2017 of a scheme involving the laundering of $20 billion out of Russia through Moldova and into the European financial system between 2010 and 2014, Deutsche Bank admitted that its involvement in the so-called 'Global Laundromat' was 'high'.[44] It also conceded that it was 'possible' that it had broken the law or violated regulations on corruption, bribery and money laundering. In a separate case, British and US regulators imposed heavy fines on Deutsche Bank for failing to enforce anti-money laundering controls and facilitating the transfer of $10 billion of unknown origin on behalf of unknown clients to offshore banks between 2012 and 2014. Deutsche Bank in the UK helped transfer $6 billion to overseas bank accounts through 'mirror trades' that allowed the conversion of rubles into dollars and the covert transfer of these funds out of Russia.[45]

For its part, Dresdner Bank, then Dresdner Kleinwort Wasserstein (DKW), played a role in the dismemberment of

Russia's largest oil company Yukos after the arrest of its CEO, Mikhail Khodorkovsky in 2003. It received a mandate without a tender required by law to value Yukos's main producing asset that the Russian authorities had deliberately devalued by issuing tax claims against it that threatened its production licences. Dresdner's involvement gave a veneer of respectability to the auction in which an unknown company with $300 of share capital and an office above a liquor store in a provincial city paid $9.8 billion for the asset. The state company Rosneft then bought the asset and the tax claims melted away. Putin's economics adviser called the sale 'the scam of the year' that showed 'the lack of rules' in Russia[46] and resigned his position. The head of Dresdner Bank's Russia operations at the time was Putin's friend, Matthias Warnig.

It was not only the banks that engaged in questionable practices. The Siemens global bribery scandal that surfaced in 2006 included illegal payments made in Russia. A US court fined the German conglomerate $600 million after it admitted violating the Foreign Corrupt Practices Act. Investigations had uncovered €1.3 billion of suspect payments to officials around the world to secure contracts. US investigators alleged that from 2004 to 2006, a Siemens subsidiary in Russia paid around $740 million to government officials to secure contracts for the design and installation of a $27 million traffic control system in Moscow. In the process, the Siemens company colluded with a competitor to raise its price offer so that Siemens won the tender. It then hired the competitor for the project at an inflated rate. It paid $2.7 million for alleged services, including a sham traffic study. Subcontractors funnelled $600,000 from these amounts to senior officials managing the quasi-governmental entity that ran the project. The US investigators noted that up to 1999, German law did not prohibit foreign bribery and that bribes were tax deductible.[47]

US authorities also fined Daimler $185 million in 2010 as part of a settlement after it admitted committing bribery offences between 1998 and 2008 in twenty-two countries, including Russia, to boost sales. US investigators said that the company's corrupt dealings earned over $90 million in illegal profits and that it classified the bribes internally as 'useful expenditure'. It claimed that Daimler's senior management authorised the bribe payments. In Russia, the company issued invoices inflated 10–30 per cent over the contract price and transferred the difference to the designated accounts of officials. In another case, the company wired DM110,000 to a German bank account held by a Russian official to ensure the sale of four vehicles to a Russian government agency. It later paid 'commissions' worth €488,000 to Latvian bank accounts in the name of individuals related to the same official.[48] The German judicial authorities showed little interest in Daimler's admission that it had violated the Foreign Corrupt Practices Act.

Siemens' business in Russia again made international headlines after it emerged that four gas turbines delivered to Russia during 2015–16 ended up in Crimea in violation of western sanctions. Siemens claimed that the turbines were an order for another power plant project in southern Russia and that its business partner Tekhnopromeksport had deceived it. In an effort to protect its reputation, it sued Tekhnopromeksport for contract violations and asked for an injunction to ensure the return of the turbines and the cancellation of the contract. The courts did not find in Siemens' favour. This was a salutary reminder of the difficulties facing foreign investors, including major German companies, in asserting their rights in Russia. The affair put an end to Siemens' joint venture with Power Machines and severely complicated Siemens' desire to access the lucrative Russian market for gas turbines.

Conclusions

The economic relationship has failed to live up to its promise. Merkel noted drily in March 2014 in a meeting with the leading business associations after Russia's seizure of Crimea that although bilateral trade with Russia was worth €76 billion, 'it did not form Germany's entire economic engagement'.[49] Such comments are rarely heard in Germany in political debate because of the prominence of the energy relationship and the unquestioned *Ostpolitik* orthodoxies around the stabilising influence of trade. As Chancellor Schmidt believed, 'those who trade with each other do not shoot at each other',[50] a questionable assertion in view of Germany's earlier twentieth-century history. To admit to relatively small, underdeveloped economic ties is to puncture the image of a strong and stable basis of relations with Russia that cushions the obvious political problems of today. It is also an admission that Russia's progress along the path of modernisation has so far been disappointing. For this reason, the impact of sanctions on German business and the losses to the economy have been less than spectacular because there was not so much to lose in the first place. If the EU were to find itself in a trade war with the USA, hardly a fantastical hypothesis at the time of writing, the losses would be far greater. The USA is Germany's largest export market in the world. In short, Germany engages in a measure of conscious self-deception about the economic relationship, perhaps to help it worry less about Russia.

For now, it is difficult to see that there will be a qualitative change in the economic relationship at any point soon. The traditional structure of trade will remain in place since Germany will continue to need Russian hydrocarbons in the short to medium term even if crude oil volumes are likely to diminish quickly as the green transportation revolution gathers pace. However, increased gas sales to Germany are unlikely to offset a reduction in crude oil exports for Russia since the gas business is much less lucrative. For now, oil and gas revenues make up 40 per cent of the state budget.[51] Russia has vast potential to decarbonise its energy exports but there are no plans in place to prepare for doing so despite the EU's commitment to achieve net-zero greenhouse gas emissions by 2050. Overall, the Russian economy looks set to experience further low growth over the coming years in the absence of

a major effort to develop competition, increase efficiency and promote the rule of law essential for protecting investments. Russia's
membership of the WTO since 2012 has not so far added the
economic impetus expected. While this is partly due to sanctions
and the relatively weak performance of the world's developed
economies since then, the continuing structural problems of the
Russian economy, including its heavy dependence on raw materials exports, its lack of competition and high level of corruption, are
more to blame. A shrinking labour force will also restrict growth
opportunities over the coming years.

Undoubtedly, if Russia were to have a reformist leadership
committed to developing independent courts and removing bar-
riers to competition, German companies could play a vital role
in developing sectors of the economy that deliver high value-
added products and services. Yet for now, that remains a distant
prospect. In the meantime, both the German government and
German business need to be honest with themselves and Russia
about the opportunity costs of the Russian leadership's current
policies. The Russian economy risks a hard landing if it cannot
replace the revenues currently earned from oil production that are
likely to decrease significantly over the next thirty years.

At the same time, German business and the German government also need to recognise the mistakes made by German
companies in Russia and the damage they have caused. The corrupt practices of some of corporate Germany's proudest names
can only have strengthened views in the Kremlin and in Russian
society generally that western values are a sham. Such behaviour
undermines German efforts to promote rule of law in Russia and
adherence to international law abroad. In addition, Putin's ability
to buy the lobbying services of Gerhard Schröder, who continues to
make the Kremlin's case in Germany, underlines the susceptibility
of western politicians to money. Admittedly, this practice is much
more developed in Austria where several former senior politicians
have gone to work for Russian companies. The Russian leadership

has good reason to conclude that western business and politicians will always be happy to play by other rules behind the façade of democracy and rule of law. The German government's silence on these issues along with other western countries, in particular Britain and the USA, creates the impression that it is indifferent to them. Such passivity sends the unfortunate message to Moscow that countries professing rule of law have flexible principles.

Finally, the Russia debate in Germany has not focused on how Germany's desire to continue buying large volumes of oil and gas from Russia has contributed to preserving the dominant position of hydrocarbons in the Russian economy. It has also ignored the issue of how expansion of energy relations has helped to cement in place a ruling group that has become increasingly hostile to German interests. There is also a disturbing lack of nuanced discussion in Germany about the advantages and disadvantages of expanding imports of Russian gas because of the polarisation of views on Russia and the absence of a strategic framework for thinking about Russia and the challenges it poses. Notably, there is no discussion about possible ways to use the energy relationship to influence Russian thinking, for example by underlining the speed of greening in the transportation sector. This revolutionary development promises to reduce sharply crude oil imports in the medium to long term, and it should serve as a serious wake-up call for Moscow. Future historians will have to decide to what extent German commercial *realpolitik* contributed to prolonging the life of the current Russian system, as some believe the West did with the USSR in the 1970s when it bought Moscow's oil and gas. The difference at that time was that Moscow saw détente rather than confrontation with the West as necessary for its survival. For Germany today, the economic relationship with Russia camouflages the level of confrontation between them.

7

Russian influence in Germany

By virtue of culture, history and its pivotal role in shaping Europe's policy towards Russia, Germany currently finds itself exposed to two forms of Russian influence. One is 'soft' power, including culture, language and co-optation; the other is 'harder' power, including traditional espionage and agent recruitment as well as new forms of disinformation and a novel type of threat in the form of cyber security attacks. Disinformation was widely used against the FRG during the Cold War by both the USSR and the GDR, albeit through much narrower channels than those available today, thanks to the proliferation of electronic and social media. The 'soft' power mechanisms aim to encourage sympathy for Russian positions and acceptance of Russia as a major European power on its terms, while the 'harder' versions seek to exploit Germany's internal political divisions and disrupt its alliances amid broader efforts to undermine the integrity of the EU and NATO. This dual strategy of simultaneously charming and pressurising Germany is logical from a Russian perspective. However, it also carries risks since too much pressure risks alienating Germans and blunting their sensitivity to Russia's needs.

Although the Russian leadership has severely damaged the relationship with Germany, it has not so far broken it. Germany's political consensus on the need for dialogue and cooperation with Russia endures, accompanied now by a measure of deterrence.

Nevertheless, as noted in Chapter 5, there has been a significant change of policy towards Russia since 2014. Russia's reputation has suffered greatly among both the political class and the public, and there have been signs of deterioration in people-to-people contacts with fewer meetings taking place and reduced numbers of Germans learning Russian.

The damage to Russia's position in Germany since 2014 is underlined by the continuing agreement of the governing parties on the need to maintain sanctions over Ukraine. In March 2015, an Allensbach opinion poll pointed to the German public's clear position on who was primarily responsible for the conflict in Ukraine. Fifty-five per cent of respondents blamed Russia while only 20 per cent blamed Ukraine. Only 17 per cent said the USA was responsible – a revealing statistic given the anti-American streak in German public opinion. Sixty-one per cent believed that Russia was seeking to conquer Ukraine. At the same time, only 8 per cent of respondents said they had a positive view of Putin, down from 43 per cent in 2001.[1] More recently, the public's disillusionment with the Trump administration appears to have affected perceptions of Russia. In a YouGov poll in late 2019, 54 per cent of respondents said they favoured cooperation over deterrence in dealing with Russia while 55 per cent wished Europe to be responsible for its defence without the USA.[2] Clemens Wergin, a columnist at the conservative newspaper *Die Welt* noted in exasperation how Russia's continuing aggression in eastern Ukraine had triggered an 'appeasement reflex' among Germans.[3] He also expressed horror at a poll instigated by the Ost-Ausschuss among its members in Russia. Only 3 per cent opposed Nord Stream 2. Yet despite these attitudes, the government's position on sanctions has remained unchallenged.

Prior to 2014, despite increasingly negative news coverage of Russia in German media, the Russian authorities continued to enjoy sympathy and respect for their country in the German political class and the public at large. As discussed in Chapter 5, no other major European country had tried so hard to demonstrate understanding for Russia's historical legacy and the challenges facing its leaders. The major political parties all continued to believe that it was important to view Russia as a partner and unquestioningly accepted the Russian line that there could be no security in Europe without Russia and that Germany and its allies 'needed' Russia to address problems as far afield as Afghanistan, Iran and Syria. The parties had their own networks of contacts with Russia, including through their political foundation offices in Moscow. In the case of the SPD, these dated back to Soviet days. For example, Schröder, the prime illustration of a politician co-opted by Russia, first visited the USSR in the mid-1970s as a board member of the SPD's Young Socialists.[4] Big business too had its political relationships in Russia and shaped German government thinking about the importance of the Russian market. This was not difficult given the *Ostpolitik* legacy, which had bred the view that the development of bilateral trade was essential for keeping Russia close to Europe and avoiding confrontation. At the same time, there was consensus on the need to pursue the maximum possible dialogue and connectivity with Russia through cultural, educational, scientific and sporting links as well as broader people-to-people contacts. This was Germany's 'soft power' strategy. The election in 2000 of a German-speaking president with empathy for Germany put the icing on the cake.

Formats for dialogue

The structures and mechanisms for dialogue had largely taken shape in the 1990s. The key format for government contacts was the *Regierungskonsultationen*, the annual high-level meeting of the two governments attended by the German chancellor and the Russian president together with cabinet ministers and business leaders. Several of the ministries had their own bilateral cooperation programmes. In 2006, Merkel travelled to Tomsk for her first experience of this format. She described it as 'perfect talks in a perfect atmosphere'.[5] She attended with eight members of her cabinet and a twenty-strong business delegation, including Deutsche Bank, Siemens, E.ON, BASF and Deutsche Bahn. The main agenda for the talks was an energy partnership. The dismemberment of Yukos in 2004 and the rising pressure on Shell to cede control of its Sakhalin-2 project clearly did not spoil the mood as BASF agreed terms with Gazprom on an asset swap, giving it access to the Russian upstream and Gazprom an enhanced position in the German downstream market.

The successful Tomsk meeting led to the establishment of a German–Russian Chamber of Commerce spurred by a 25 per cent growth in bilateral trade the previous year. For German business, this complemented the Ost-Ausschuss, originally established in 1952 to support West German business in the USSR. Based in Berlin, it has around 350 members following a merger in 2019 with the Osteuropaverein, a lobbying group representing small business. Although the Ost-Ausschuss appears to have lost some of its influence as trade with Russia has declined in recent years and German business has expanded its presence in other markets, it retains an important voice. Unlike chambers of commerce in some European countries dealing with Russia, it is a serious, properly funded and well-connected organisation. It channels an informed but largely uncritical view of the Russian market without political commentary but gives space for Russian views on specific issues such as sanctions.[6] Representatives of Deutsche Bank, Siemens and the energy company Uniper, an investor in Nord Stream 2, are among its board members.

The Ost-Ausschuss has a Berlin-based analogue for societal contacts, the Deutsch-Russisches Forum. Established in 1993, its mission is to promote dialogue between the societies of Germany and Russia on issues in bilateral relations. Financed by German business and the Foreign Office, it has an energetic leadership that runs an impressive programme of activities, including conferences and seminars in Germany and Russia on a wide range of topics ranging from cultural relations to history and economics. It also supports youth exchanges and town twinning. Since the outspokenly Russophile former SPD prime minister of Brandenburg, Matthias Platzeck, became chairman in 2014, the organisation has acquired greater political visibility.

With trustees and board members such as the journalist Gabriele Krone-Schmalz and the former head of the German–Russian Chamber of Commerce, Andrea von Knoop, both well known for their pro-Moscow positions, the Forum has developed a reputation as a centre of *Russlandversteher* thinking. Former Russian ambassador to Germany, Vladimir Grinin, is among the trustees together with Vladimir Yakunin, a close associate of Putin and former head of Russian Railways who is on the US sanctions list. Alexey Mordashov, the German-speaking chairman of the major Russian steel producer Severstal, is also a trustee. Martin Hoffmann, the Forum's long-standing managing director who grew up in West Germany, is a critic of EU sanctions because of their effect on the societal links so carefully nurtured since the end of the Cold War. In late 2014, he published an article arguing that Germany was losing 'an entire people, a large European-thinking people' and claimed that 'the great majority of the Russian people' felt unheard by the West and misunderstood. He denounced the West's arrogance and double standards as well as its refusal to treat Russia as an equal and its belief that it had 'the better values'.[7] It was ironic that someone who had devoted their career to building civil society links with Russia to such good effect was echoing the Kremlin line to defend their work. After all, over the previous decade, the Russian authorities had taken extensive measures to strangle civil society. Hoffmann had received the Order of Friendship medal from Putin in 2007 for his contribution to friendship and cooperation between Russia and Germany.[8]

As discussed in Chapter 4, the Petersburger Dialog is a key mechanism for high-level interaction between societies in

Germany and Russia. Established in 2001 and funded mainly by the German Foreign Office, this potentially promising initiative has produced limited results because of the different approaches of the two sides, the Germans seeking broad discussion with civil society and the Russian side seeking only a narrow exchange. However, the symbolic importance of the Dialog for both sides has ensured its continuation, not least because the German government believes that Putin takes a personal interest in it. This has meant that the Dialog's full meeting has taken place annually every year since 2001 except for 2014 because of events in Ukraine and 2020 because of COVID-19. The different approaches of each side are reflected in their memberships. The Germans have nearly double the number of Russians and are a curious mixture of *Russlandversteher* and *Russlandkritker* while the Russian side includes a range of academics, members of Parliament, former officials, journalists and others united in their loyalty to the Russian system. The deputy board chair on the German side, Oliver Hermes, chairs the Ost-Ausschuss. Platzeck is a board member while the journalist Krone-Schmalz and the pro-Putin author and Gazprom lobbyist Alexander Rahr are also members. On the Russian side, the former head of the Russian Olympic Committee Vitaly Mutko who was implicated in the Sochi Olympics doping scandal is a member. So is the Agriculture Minister, Dmitri Patrushev, son of Nikolai Patrushev, the Secretary of the Russian Security Council, and one of Putin's closest associates.

The Dialog has ten working groups with equal membership covering a broad range of subjects from politics and the economy to health and environment. They meet twice a year ensuring that a dialogue mechanism operates simultaneously across multiple fronts. German participants report that after 2014, dialogue was especially difficult, but there are indications that in some areas, the tone has improved significantly since then. It is not hard to see how the Russian side can use a format of this kind to its advantage. The German participation includes some prominent individuals with a record of sympathising with Kremlin positions and criticising German government policy while the ability of the German side to communicate with its target audience in Russian civil society is severely limited. Critics of the societal dialogue formats say that organisations such as the Petersburger Dialog and the Deutsch-Russisches Forum were established to project western values eastwards but have ended up working the other way round.[9]

Platforms for 'soft' power influence

Other 'soft' mechanisms of influence with potential for co-optation include the German-Russian Youth Exchange Foundation established in 2005. It aims to promote contacts among schoolchildren and young people at national, regional and local levels, including young politicians and 'representatives of state and communal authorities'.[10] The events of 2014 and their aftermath have had no perceptible impact on the Foundation's work. The Russian House of Science and Culture (originally opened in 1984 as the House of Soviet Science and Culture in East Berlin) considers itself the largest foreign cultural centre in the world[11] and claims to have up to 200,000 visitors a year.[12] Situated in central Berlin, it has extensive facilities, including a concert hall, a film theatre and several exhibition rooms. It serves as the base for the Russian state agency Rossotrudnichestvo, founded in 2008, which promotes the interests of Russians living abroad and is responsible for 'international humanitarian cooperation'. Its Berlin operations give prominence to cultivating the memory of Germany and Russia's joint history and providing access to Russian films, exhibitions, music and other cultural opportunities as well as Russian-language teaching. The Russian House's website refers to 'almost 4.5 million Russian speakers' in Germany and a diaspora that is 'developing its ethno-cultural identity and actively performing its bridging function between Germany and Russia.'[13] It lists North-Rhine Westphalia as having the largest diaspora concentration (750,000), followed by Berlin and Brandenburg (300,000) with Hamburg and Bremen numbering 200,000 each.[14] According to its mission statement, Rossotrudnichestvo helps the Russian diaspora in Germany to preserve the Russian language, and its culture and traditions in Germany. There are regional societies linking Russian speakers in 14 of the 16 regions of Germany as well as a national coordinating council based in Berlin.[15]

Other less visible platforms for 'soft' power influence are the two Russian Centres in Germany operating under the *Russkiy Mir* (Russian World) initiative established by the Russian government in 2007 to strengthen Russia's cultural and ideological presence abroad. The 'Russian World' is part of the ideology of today's Russian state based on the unifying factor of Russian culture and Soviet values among Russians and foreigners in both Russia, the non-Russian former Soviet countries and the world at large who speak Russian and take an interest in Russia's future.[16] Two Russian Centres, one in Nuremberg the other in Dresden support the *Russkiy Mir* initiative and have the role of popularising Russian culture and promoting Russian language and literature. In their day-to-day functioning, they bear clear similarities to the Goethe Institute and the British Council, except that they serve the goals of an organisation committed to encouraging Russians and Russian speakers to serve the Motherland. Neither the Goethe Institute nor the British Council has a programme for encouraging resettlement of German or English speakers to their homelands. Nor do they work with churches to promote culture, as does *Russkiy Mir*.

Russian intelligence activity

Not surprisingly, old KGB and Stasi networks successors have played a role in Russia's influence-building activities in Germany. One outstanding example is the Moscow-based Academy of Security, Defence and Public Order founded in 2000. According to Berlin-based researcher Dmitri Khmelnytsky, the first President of the Academy was Viktor Shevchenko, a retired KGB lieutenant-general. Shevchenko claimed that the idea for the Academy came from Putin and received enthusiastic support from the FSB and other law enforcement agencies.[17] Its goal was to bring together Russian public organisations working in the security area. The Academy prepared reports for a number of Russian law enforcement agencies. It also sought contacts abroad and established an affiliate in Germany headed by Wolf-Olav Paentzer, a car salesman in Greifswald, who had been a long-standing Stasi informant.[18] According to one report, he was active in business circles in Germany and met regularly with high-level delegations from former Soviet countries. The Academy awarded him a Lomonosov medal and promoted him to the role of 'Coordinator for Western Europe'. It also established a network in Bavaria where it awarded seventy-five medals, including to journalists, police officers and civil servants. A local doctor even established a representative office for the Academy in the village of Denkendorf. The Academy awarded him the title of professor.[19]

According to Khmelnytsky, the Brandenburg Minister-President Matthias Platzeck also received a medal, as did Gernot Erler, the SPD's top Russia specialist. In 2006, Shevchenko travelled to Bavaria and personally awarded Günther Beckstein (CSU), Deputy Minister President of Bavaria, the Peter the Great medal for 'services to Russia'.[20] German intelligence agencies reportedly started an investigation into the Academy's activities[21] and the Russian authorities closed it down in 2008 for violations of Russian law.

Other Russian intelligence activity had been taking place undetected for more than two decades, as in the case of Andreas and Heidrun Anschlag, a pair of 'illegals' sent to West Germany in the late 1980s using illegally issued Austrian passports. The couple were detained in October 2011 after a tip-off from the US authorities. According to one account, Andreas Anschlag obtained a technical qualification in Germany and worked for an automotive supplier. He took part in events held by political foundations close to the CDU and FDP and attended lectures at the Clausewitz Society and the Society for Military and Security Policy, in search of targets in the Defence Ministry and military intelligence which he could recommend to his Moscow handlers.[22] When security officers arrested Heidrun Anschlag, they found her communicating with Moscow using a short-wave transmitter. She fell off her chair in surprise.[23] An attempt to exchange the pair for two Russians, including a senior FSB officer, who had spied for the USA failed[24] and the Anschlags went on trial. Andreas Anschlag received a six-and-a-half-year jail sentence, his wife five and a half. The German authorities were unable to establish their real identities. They concluded that there must be other illegals operating in the country. There is no evidence in the public domain to indicate that the couple recruited any German officials, but for over two years, a Dutch diplomat provided them with secret documents related to the EU and NATO in exchange for money. Heidrun Anschlag was released from jail in late 2014 and deported,[25] followed by her husband a few months later.[26] The couple's daughter, who was studying at a German university when they were arrested, did not know her parents were Russian and was unaware of their double lives.

Other traces of Russian intelligence activity in Germany are visible in martial arts clubs that teach the systema discipline used by Russian Special Forces. A media report published in 2014 indicated that German security experts had linked the clubs operating in thirty German cities to Russian military intelligence. They believed that they were a tool for recruiting police and army personnel as well as extremist right-wing forces that could be part of a fifth column for use in public disturbances.[27] Similarly, organisations such as the Russian-founded and generously financed European Academy of Natural Sciences in Hanover and the West–East Institute in Berlin with its links to the Russian Orthodox

Church, appear to be academic organisations but with 'soft' power purposes. The Tolstoi Institut established in Berlin in 2014 aims to promote German–Russian friendship. It has proved controversial because of alleged connections with far-right forces in Germany. The Federal Office for the Protection of the Constitution noted in 2016 that the Institute took 'one-sided and clearly pro-Russian positions'.[28] Similarly, the Berlin-based German Writers' Union For International Understanding raised eyebrows when its name appeared among a list of pro-Moscow organisations that had contributed to a report on alleged human rights abuses in Ukraine between 2014 and 2016.

Influence of Russian media

2014 saw a qualitative change in the range of Russian instruments of influence used in Germany, coinciding with the stand-off between Russia and the EU over Ukraine. The previous year, three new media outlets funded by the Russian state had appeared as part of a 'soft' power media offensive: RT Deutsch, Sputnik Deutschland and the monthly newspaper supplement 'Russia Beyond the Headlines' distributed initially by *Süddeutsche Zeitung* under a different title and later by the business newspaper *Handelsblatt*. This was part of an upgrade of the Russian state's communications operations globally. RT Deutsch was a niche venture that lacked the financing of RT in the UK, USA and South America, operating only as an online portal and with a poor-quality offering.[29] Yet its messages reached some audiences, including those interested in Russia and sympathisers with the peace movement.[30] Sputnik Deutschland, a rebranded version of RIA Novosti, offered a news website and took over the radio station Stimme Russlands (Voice of Russia). It had some success in attracting some senior politicians to give interviews. A video agency, Ruptly TV, a subsidiary of RT, opened a Berlin office in 2012 offering professionally produced video material at competitive prices.

The revolution in February 2014 in Ukraine provided the opportunity to use some of these new channels more forcefully as Moscow tried to impose its narrative around the idea that the West had triggered an anti-constitutional coup in Kyiv and brought fascists to power while its seizure of Crimea was a purely defensive action. The trolling operation based in St Petersburg at the Internet Research Agency also targeted Germany with comments on blogs, social media and websites.[31] The journalist Susanne Spahn is one of the few specialists to have investigated the operations of Russian state media in Germany and Russian trolling operations after the revolution in Ukraine. She has shown how RT Deutsch, for example, cooperated with sympathetic voices in Germany, ranging from the outspoken author and publisher Jürgen Elsässer, who completed the journey from the far left to the far right to become a supporter of the Putin system, to the author and lobbyist Alexander Rahr.[32]

The new Russian propaganda effort coincided with the polarisation of political views in Germany from the far left with its sympathies for the USSR and nostalgia for GDR socialism and the appearance of new right-wing forces in the form of the anti-Islamist movement Pegida and the Alternative for Germany political party (AfD). Both favour the normalisation of relations with Russia and they and their representatives, together with those of Die Linke, have provided mouthpieces for injecting Russian messages into political discourse. Wooing the far left and far right simultaneously in Germany is not new to Moscow. As noted in Chapter 1, this was exactly the approach used in the 1920s and it continued in the FRG after 1945. The deputy head of Die Linke's parliamentary party, Wolfgang Gehrke, and his fellow MP, Andrej Hunko, visited rebel-held Donetsk in February 2015, crossing the border from Russia in violation of Ukrainian law.[33] Their visit was a PR gift to the rebel authorities. Similarly, AfD members of regional parliaments and the Bundestag have repeatedly visited Crimea since 2018.[34] The general view among German commentators is that the Russian investment in media channels in Germany has produced minimal results and that criticism of government policy by Schröder, Krone-Schmalz, Rahr and others, whose line of argument is often close to the Russian government's, is more effective.[35]

However, it is impossible to ignore the appeal of Russia-friendly positions to voters in the Russian German community. The AfD, with its sympathy for 'traditional values', has cleverly built support among the 2.4 million Russian German voters (the largest group among the 6.5 million Germans with a 'migration background'),[36] many of whom emigrated to their ancestral homeland only to find themselves marginalised as foreigners. The AfD saw the opportunity to speak to this alienated group and to try to gain its support. As early as 2013, Alexander Gauland, the co-founder of the AfD, called for reconnecting with the nineteenth-century Prussian tradition of cultivating close relations with Russia. The party reinforced its anti-establishment credentials by voicing Russia-friendly positions in contrast to the government's support for sanctions. Ahead of the federal election in 2017, it was the only party to produce Russian-language campaign materials. However, Die Linke was more successful in attracting votes from the Russian German community – 21 per cent voted for the left-wing party while 15 per cent supported the AfD.[37] Twenty-seven per cent supported the CDU, the traditional party of preference for Russian Germans because of Helmut Kohl's role in making possible their emigration from Russia. However, the Kremlin was watching the AfD closely. Documentary evidence later emerged from the presidential administration in Moscow showing that before the election, its specialists in foreign influence operations had identified Markus Frohnmaier, a young AfD parliamentary candidate, as an individual who could operate in the Bundestag 'under absolute control'. Frohnmaier was elected and, at the time of writing, remains an MP despite a scandal after the revelations. He claimed the documents were fake and denied receiving assistance from Russia.[38]

Recent sociological research suggests that the gap between views of Russia between the West and East of Germany is not as significant as many Germans believe. For example, while East Germans are less inclined than West Germans to say that current relations with Russia are 'too close', both groups have similar lines of argument in their positive evaluations of Moscow's role in the reunification of Germany as well their criticism of one-sided media reporting about Russia and their opposition to sanctions against Russia. For both, the issue of Russia is primarily a platform for criticising the government rather than a problem on its own.[39] This suggests that while the eastern German *Länder* generally have closer cultural, economic and personal links with Russia because of their GDR experience than the western part of the country, the difference does not make them significantly more vulnerable to Russian influence.

Other signs of Russian intelligence activity

The 'Lisa affair' in January 2016 revealed the capability of Russian media to mobilise the Russian German community across the country. Lisa, a 13-year-old Russian German girl living in Berlin, disappeared for over a day and reported that three 'southern' men had abducted and raped her repeatedly. A police investigation indicated that her story was false. There had been no abduction and no rape. Instead, Lisa had spent the night with her boyfriend. In 2015, Germany had accepted over a million asylum seekers, the majority from Syria and Afghanistan, sparking protests in parts of the country and fuelling support for the AfD and other groups opposed to large-scale immigration. Lisa's family had connections with the right-wing National Party of Germany (NPD) and were able to amplify their narrative to a receptive audience on social media. They claimed that the police were covering up crimes committed by Muslims.[40] The NPD held a small demonstration, and the story found its way on to Russian national television news. The Russian coverage led to a demonstration by 700 Pegida supporters outside the Federal Chancellery and to a bitter exchange of words between the two governments, after Foreign Minister Lavrov accused the German authorities of failing to investigate promptly.[41] Bound by child protection regulations, the Berlin police could say little about their investigation, and journalists found themselves weighing up two narratives unsure exactly where the truth lay. Lisa's family later claimed that Russian media and Russian officials had exploited it.[42] The incident quickly blew over but provided the German authorities with an unpleasant taste of what a disinformation attack generated by Russian state media could achieve.

The cyberattacks on the Bundestag that began in 2015 were a further wake-up call for the German government. In January 2015, as the Ukrainian prime minister landed in Berlin on his way to see Chancellor Merkel, a Russian hacking group launched a distributed denial of service (DDoS) attack on federal government computer systems that lasted two days. One of their targets was the Chancellor's webpage.[43] In May 2015, hackers targeted the Bundestag and broke into the computer systems of fourteen MPs, including Merkel's, and stole 16 gigabytes of data, sparking speculation that Russia was preparing to interfere in the autumn federal election. Investigators traced the attack to Fancy Bear, also known as APT 28, a group believed to be linked to Russian military intelligence. After the results of a criminal investigation lasting five years, Merkel described the cyberattack as 'monstrous', pointing to a Russian strategy of hybrid warfare that included 'disorientation' and 'manipulation of facts'.[44] In its 2019 report on constitutional protection, the German Interior Ministry listed Russia and China as the states most active in the area of 'cyber espionage' against Germany,[45] noting that since mid-2017, think tanks and organisations fighting corruption were increasingly targets of APT 28. Even though it had created a National Cyber-Defence Centre in 2011, Germany was seemingly unprepared for the 2015 attacks.

In June 2019, German media reported an extraordinary example of naivety in the face of the Russian cyber threat. Hans-Wilhelm Dünn, President of the Cyber Security Council, an association advising the government and major companies on cybercrime had attended a cyber security conference a few weeks earlier in the alpine resort of Garmisch-Partenkirchen. Most of the participants were Russian, and German security experts believe that the event clearly had an 'intelligence background'.[46] Dünn gave a lecture calling for closer ties with Russia and used the opportunity to sign an agreement with a Russian counterpart organisation. It turned out that he had been an election observer in Russia in 2018, one of 300 invited personally by the chairman of the Russian Parliament together with at least six members of the AfD and representatives of other right-wing parties. Dünn also had close relations with the Head of Germany's Federal Agency for Security in Computer Technology (BSI).[47] Despite the obvious potential dangers from his Russia connections, he remained in position. Apparently, there were no restrictions in place for a person operating in an association of this kind. Similarly, the loophole that allowed Schröder to leave office and start working as a lobbyist applies also to former German officials from the Federal Intelligence Service (BND) as well as the Ministry of Interior. Some have retired and gone to work as consultants for Russian companies or individuals with close Kremlin connections.[48] In Germany too, money is a powerful desensitizer to risk.

There was further evidence of a lackadaisical attitude to risk in 2016 when, despite the dramatic deterioration in the bilateral relationship after the annexation of Crimea, the German authorities registered a new think tank in Berlin with close links to the Kremlin. The Dialogue of Civilizations Research Institute (DOC) positions itself as 'an independent platform for dialogue that brings together diverse perspectives from the developed and the developing worlds in a non-confrontational and constructive spirit'.[49] It is an initiative of Putin's once close KGB associate and friend

Vladimir Yakunin, well known for his anti-western and homophobic views. The Institute has its head office in Berlin and Yakunin chairs the Institute's supervisory board.

Yakunin left his position as head of Russian Railways in 2015 under a cloud after long-standing allegations that during his decade in charge he and his family had built a global offshore business empire based on abuse of his official position.[50] During that time, Siemens, with a well-established record of bribery in its dealings with Russian state companies,[51] had been a major supplier of goods and services to Russian Railways worth billions of euros, including a forty-year contract to maintain regional trains.[52] The late Peter Schulze, the German co-founder of the Institute and former head of the SPD's foundation office in Moscow, was open about the Institute's lobbying goals. He told *Der Spiegel* that the Institute's positions on some issues were close to the Kremlin's and that he hoped that 'if well grounded', they would 'get through to decision-makers in politics, economics and the media'. He stressed the need for a European dialogue about a European future.[53] The DOC boasts that it has partners across the world. According to its 2019 report, the Volkswagen Foundation in Germany[54] provided a grant of €53,000 for a DOC project.[55]

The Institute's efforts to recruit German academic specialists have proved unsuccessful and after Schulze's death in 2020, there were no German representatives on its supervisory board or in its management structure. German academics have given the Institute a wide berth despite its financial capabilities. It spent over €2 million on events around the world in 2019, indicating that it has no shortage of funds.[56] In August 2018, German media reported that the German authorities had renewed Yakunin's visa, giving him the right to seek an unlimited residence and work permits in the Schengen area.[57] It is unclear why the German authorities felt it necessary to issue the visa.

Two further factors of influence cannot be analysed because of a lack of information. First, it is hard to gauge to what extent

Russian organised crime has used Germany to launder money. Accessing property registers and identifying the beneficial owners of companies buying real estate pose major challenges for investigative journalists. The general view is that Germany's supervisory authorities are weak and that there are few obstacles to money laundering. However, the scale of the money-laundering problem clearly does not exist on the same scale as in Britain or France because Germany is not a favoured destination for Russia's super-rich class. Second, there is no possibility of assessing the scale and effectiveness of intelligence activities carried out by Russian diplomats. German security sources apparently believe that up to a third of the 400 Russians with diplomatic passports based at the embassy in Berlin and the general consulate in Bonn are under-cover intelligence operatives.[58] By contrast, Germany has only declared intelligence officers at its embassy in Moscow, a revealing example of the different approaches the two countries take to managing their relations.[59]

The 2019 Report on Constitutional Protection placed Russia ahead of China, Iran and Turkey in its list of the main actors in Germany in the areas of espionage and influence operations.[60] Questions also remain about the functioning of the intelligence system in Germany. Some of Germany's western partners point to how intelligence sharing is sometimes a problem and can inhibit a joined-up government reaction. For example, coordination with the German authorities after the Novichok poisoning of the Russian defector Sergey Skripal and his daughter in Salisbury in 2018 was reportedly a challenge because some parts of the German government system were better informed than others.

Conclusions

German discussion of Russian influence in Germany focuses almost exclusively on disinformation, cyber vulnerabilities and the susceptibility of the Russian German community to the AfD message. Clearly, these should all be factors of concern for German policymakers, but they pale in comparison to the significance of Russia's well-established networks in Germany across the worlds of politics, business, media and NGOs. These make Germany an easy target for Russian influence operations. There has been no in-depth research on the political connections of the CDU/CSU and SPD in Russia. For example, it is surely significant that the East German head of the CDU's political foundation office in Moscow has close personal ties with the Kremlin party, United Russia.[61] Yet, in an article discussing foreign political influence in Germany, the head of counter-intelligence at the domestic intelligence agency did not even refer to these relationships[62] – an indication perhaps of their sensitivity. The registration of the DOC and the lack of restrictions on the professional activities of former officials point to further alarming gaps in Germany's counter-intelligence defences.

In addition, Russia's influence-building activities benefit from another factor in Germany, which is unavailable elsewhere in Europe. Despite tensions in bilateral relations, the combination of trauma about Russia and gratitude for reunification require the political class to think in terms of reconciliation with Moscow and to pursue dialogue and cooperation. This creates multiple opportunities across different fronts to build relationships and project Russian views. Some journalists and businesspeople who have served for long periods in Moscow and have 'gone native' provide valuable channels for projecting pro-Russian views. For example, the *Spiegel* journalist Benjamin Bidder, who spent ten years in Russia, caused controversy in late 2019 after writing a story casting doubt on the veracity of Hermitage Capital's account of the agonising death of its lawyer Sergey Magnitsky in a Moscow jail in 2009. As noted in Chapter 6, Andrea von Knoop, the official representative of Germany business from 1993 to 2007, is another example of an outspoken critic of western policy towards Russia. In 2016, Putin granted her Russian citizenship in recognition of her contribution to building business ties. She has lived in Russia for over thirty years.[63] Germany's deep respect for Russian culture is another significant advantage that facilitates the process of conditioning Germans to a Russian message. Currently, 158 members of Parliament (Die Linke and the AfD combined out of a total of 709) whose parties have clearly pro-Russian positions on sanctions, for example, provide Moscow with a much larger influence platform than it has in any other major European country. Finally, a further benefit for Russia in Germany is that public opinion has marked pacifist tendencies and does not support significant investment in defence. For now, Russia can remain sure that Germany's bark will be worse than its bite.

At the same time, in the face of pressures aimed at societal disruption, Germany has proved resilient thanks to its strong institutions, including its media, and its relatively low levels of inequality compared to the UK and the USA. However, past performance is not necessarily a guide to the future since Russia has so far deployed some of its 'harder' instruments sparingly possibly because it does not want to alienate irreversibly its once strongest advocate in the EU and NATO. For example, Moscow chose not to deploy the data it stole from Parliament and government servers in the run up to the federal 2017 election. This would have risked moving beyond managed disruption and damaging the bilateral relationship beyond repair. In the case of its interference in the US presidential election in 2016, Russia appeared to conclude that it had more to gain than to lose, while in Germany the calculation was possibly the reverse. There is speculation that a high-level German warning beforehand persuaded Putin to refrain from interference in the election.

In addition, it is uncomfortable for Germany to discuss the dangers posed by Russian 'soft' power without calling into question the guiding principle of seeking maximum contact with Russia to prevent conflict and as redemption for the past. To this extent, Russia does not need to use the 'harder' instruments of power as robustly as in many other countries to achieve its desired levels of influence. This situation may change if Germany's Russia policy hardens further. Some of Russia's established influence-building advantages are in any case already starting to erode. The *Ostpolitik* generation is leaving the scene. Their successors, born in the 1980s, have less awareness of the Second World War and the division of Germany. They were still children when the Wall fell and have less instinctive sympathy for Russia. Over time, Moscow will need to find new tools and messages to ensure that Germans remain conditioned to respond to its voice. Yet for now, Russia's influence in Germany remains strong and of a qualitatively different nature to that in other major European countries.

8

The outlook

Over the coming years, the issue of Russia is set to become doubly challenging for Germany as Russia's internal situation becomes more complicated and the international environment more disrupted. While the current Russian system has clear weaknesses, it retains the capacity to manage them although stagnating living standards and problems of the leadership's legitimacy could easily become serious sources of instability. However, for now, Russia's leaders have both the will and the resources to increase their suppression of dissent and, if necessary, to use force to prevent any large-scale mobilisation of society against its rule. The Kremlin has been preparing for such a potential scenario for many years after seeing revolutions from below in Georgia and Ukraine in 2003–4. Since then, its message to the electorate has been that 'colour revolutions' are the work of the US State Department, USAID and other foreign agents, and that they are planning to stage one in Russia.[1] The Russian leadership sincerely believes that the large-scale protests in 2011–12 against Putin's third presidential term were the work of the USA[2] as was the Revolution of Dignity in 2014. According to its logic, the USA had no direct interest in Ukraine. Its purpose was to weaken Russia.[3] The Kremlin also concluded that the CIA and the Pentagon among other US agencies were behind events in Belarus in 2020.[4] If the Russian authorities further restrict civic freedoms and abuse human rights, they will deepen their international isolation.

The pattern of recent years indicates that in this situation, Moscow is more likely to increase activities abroad to make its presence felt. It has playgrounds close to home – in the Balkans, the Caucasus, Moldova and Ukraine as well as further afield in Libya and Syria. Russia may also take another step closer to China at a time when tensions in US–China relations are increasing. In short, the scope for the collision of interests with western countries, including Germany, looks set to increase rather than decrease.

Such an outcome is more likely because the Russian leadership appears undeterred by greater confrontation. There are four reasons for this. First, confrontation helps sustain the narrative at home that 'the West' is working to cut Russian down to size as part of a neo-containment policy, forcing Russia into a 'besieged fortress' posture. This putative external danger to Russia allows the leadership to take measures to protect itself against the real threat to its security – its own people. Second, more confrontation increases the Kremlin's appetite for fishing in troubled waters, whether in areas vacated by the USA such as Syria, or in western countries themselves by interfering in their democratic processes to increase their societal divisions. This is part of the strategy to protect the Russian system by shaping the external environment to its benefit. Third, confrontation offers opportunities to expose the weaknesses of the EU and NATO and deepen estrangement between the USA and its European allies. Divisions within the EU on the issue of Russia offer potentially rich opportunities to Russian diplomacy. Fourth, Moscow recognises that confrontation intimidates European governments, encouraging them to find ways of talking more to Moscow rather than creating the means to deter its aggressive behaviour.

Germany's failure to invest in maintaining adequate defence forces after the end of the Cold War says much about its lack of a strategic mindset. It succumbed to a sense of a new peaceful era reinforced by the enlargement of NATO, which relieved Germans of the burden of being a frontier state as they had been for forty-five years as a divided nation on both sides of the Iron Curtain. In this seemingly benign environment, there was less obvious need for US security guarantees and Germany's armed forces needed to focus primarily on out-of-area crisis management to the detriment of collective defence. This had profound implications for the size, structure, equipment and training of the Bundeswehr. In 2007, a senior British officer likened the Bundeswehr's capabilities to those of 'an aggressive camping organisation'.[5] Since 2014, a defence planning process has been in place to rebuild the armed forces' collective defence and deterrence capabilities. This will reach not completion until 2032, leaving a significant gap during which a key vulnerability is visible.

During the Cold War, the US military had the ability to deploy forces to two major theatres at the same time and had enough reserves to deal with a simultaneous minor crisis. It can now only respond to one major crisis and one smaller emergency. Should the US have to deal with a major crisis in the Asia-Pacific region, European members of NATO at present would struggle alongside a smaller US force to maintain Europe's defences if tested. The German government's strategic assessments after the invasion of Georgia in 2008 and the annexation of Crimea in 2014 were clear about the need to reinvest in defence but its leaders did not want to take this message to the public because it would be unpopular. Policymakers still use coded language to make the point. In a speech in October 2020, Defence Minister Annegret Kramp-Karrenbauer spoke compellingly of Germany needing to be a 'strategic giver' rather than remaining a 'taker'. It meant becoming a 'hard, power-political factor'.[6] However, there was no mention of paying for this capability. Her message instead focused on the importance of pre-serving the transatlantic link significantly weakened over the past two decades, and particularly under the Trump presidency.

The crisis of liberal democracy symbolised by Trump's election in 2016 and the rise of populist forces in several western countries have been grist to the Kremlin's mill. For this reason, Russia's leaders feel that history is on their side. Putin boldly stated in 2019 that liberalism had outlived its purpose.[7] Russia's overconfidence derives partly from the fact that it has worked out how to target western weaknesses without provoking serious retaliation. Western countries have signally failed to study Russia's vulnerabilities in the same way and apply pressure to them as part of a strategy to defend their interests.

Behind its claims that it wishes to adapt the international system to new realities, Moscow has a backward-looking agenda. It seeks refuge in the past with its nostalgia for the Yalta and Potsdam agreements.[8] When it talks of a new security order, it has in mind an old one. Ahead of the 75th anniversary of the end of the Second World War, Putin even proposed a summit of the five permanent members of the UN Security Council to discuss global security issues. This, of course, did not include Germany, the country with the largest population in Europe and the fourth-largest economy in the world. The Russian leadership remains obsessed with the extent of US influence in international affairs as if Russia were an equal, and despite clear signs that Washington is returning to a new form of isolationism, demonstrated by its reduced interest in the Middle East. These paranoias continue to fuel the traditional goal of weakening the transatlantic link and returning Europe to its natural state in which Russia can exert greater political influence over the continent. In this respect, Trump's disregard for NATO, his contempt for the EU and his tendency to treat Germany as an enemy rather than an ally made him Moscow's accomplice in weakening transatlantic relations. His assault on Germany for its low level of defence spending and the hostility of his administration to Nord Stream 2 were a deeply unnerving experience for German policymakers that look set to recede to some extent under the presidency of Joe Biden. However, even if the atmosphere improves, a return to the pre-Trump status quo in Germany's relations with the USA looks unlikely because too much has changed in the meantime.

In the case of NATO, Trump only voiced what several pre-vious US presidents had thought but did not wish to say. As Robert Gates, who served as US Defense Secretary from 2006 to 2011 under two administrations has noted, despite commitments made in 2002 to aim to spend 2 per cent of GDP on defence, only five out of twenty-eight member states met the target in 2007–8. They included Greece and Croatia but not Germany. Gates wrote that telling the Europeans to spend more on defence in the aftermath of the global financial crisis was 'about as useful as shouting down a well'.[9] In 2016, Germany's defence spend-ing was still closer to 1.2 per cent of GDP.[10] However, despite its failure to meet NATO defence spending goals, Germany, unlike France, sees the preservation of NATO as essential to Europe's security, adding to the impression in Washington that Germany continues to 'free ride' at the expense of the USA. Trump's deci-sion in the summer of 2020 to reduce further the US military presence in Germany only added to the angst in Berlin that the USA was increasingly unconcerned about downgrading relations with key allies. This followed Trump's decisions to withdraw from the 2015 Paris Climate Change Agreement and to reimpose sanc-tions on Iran despite fierce opposition from France, Germany and the UK. Germany views the growth of international disorder and the erosion of the US-led global system with understandable alarm, because its economy has profited so greatly from it. To make a difficult situation worse, the coronavirus pandemic could have significant consequences for the future of the globalised econ-omy as well Europe's relations with China as the USA steps up pressure to contain China's global influence. This places Germany in an uncomfortable position because of its high volume of trade with China (10 per cent of imports in 2019 and over 6 per cent of exports).[11] These broader problems look set to consume consid-erable time and attention in Berlin over the coming years, pos-sibly to the detriment of attention paid to Russia and the 'shared neighbourhood'.

Adding to the Kremlin's *Schadenfreude* and Germany's discomfort is the situation within the EU. Britain's departure has deprived it of a strong voice on Russia and the region. Sensing the opportunity to enhance French influence, President Macron has favoured a strategic dialogue with Moscow in the belief that Russia can still make a constructive contribution to European security.[12] Germany has not backed him, arguing that the French position risks splitting the EU on the issue of Russia. At the same time, the Hungarian and Polish governments continue to challenge the EU's own values of rule of law while Austria, Greece, Hungary and Italy are among the EU member states increasingly calling into question the purpose of sanctions against Russia. Finally, Germany itself is still experiencing its own brand of populist politics with Die Linke and the AfD strongly represented in the federal Parliament and several regional parliaments, a testament to the levels of disillusionment in the east of the country. The 'flourishing landscapes' promised to the population of the GDR by Helmut Kohl in 1990 have not materialised.[13] This is the problematic backdrop for German policymaking on Russia as Angela Merkel's era ends.

After Merkel leaves office, Germany will no longer enjoy the benefit of a Russian-speaking chancellor who grew up in the GDR with deep knowledge of both Russia and the region as well as a liking for Russian culture. Her GDR background gave her clear insight into the psychology of Putin and his former KGB associates. She reportedly joked after meeting with Putin for the first time that she had passed the test by successfully holding his 'KGB gaze'.[14] She almost certainly had little idea of how long she would end up dealing with him as her counterpart. She put up with his late arrivals to meetings, his crude behaviour and his inappropriate humour. She listened to his characterisation of the Russian opposition as 'sexually deformed',[15] and after the annexation of Crimea, she still valiantly found the patience to keep the communication going despite Putin's lies about Russia's involvement in the secessionists' seizure of power. The calendar of events on the Kremlin's website is littered with references to telephone calls between Putin and Merkel initiated by the German side. The Kremlin made it clear that it was Merkel's job to phone Putin and not the other way round.[16] In 2018, Putin revealed that the Chancellor occasionally sent him bottles of beer from Saxony where he developed a taste for it during his time in Dresden.[17] Russia matters to Merkel, as her determination to speak to Russian human rights activists and critical journalists has shown. Unlike any other European leader, she has sometimes even invited them home.[18] Her successor will not have the same capacity to interpret Russian behaviour and to anticipate the response to their own actions. The next German chancellor will be more dependent on external advice and will almost certainly take time to build a relationship with the Russian president.

For all Merkel's instinctive understanding of the people who had come to power in Russia and their modus operandi, it still took her over eight years to take a decisive turn away from predecessors' policies, and even after doing so, she did not challenge some of the deeply embedded German orthodoxies about relations with Russia. She tolerated Nord Stream 2 since it had political support both within business as well as parts of her own party and the SPD at both federal and regional level. By perverse coincidence, the pipeline emerges from the Baltic Sea close to Greifswald in her electoral district. Despite her impressive knowledge and understanding of the situation in Donbas, she also continued to believe that it was possible to find compromises with Russia on Ukraine through the Minsk process. In early 2020, she returned to a more pragmatic approach with Putin when she visited Moscow for the first time in over four years. Keen to secure Russia's consent for a German-led peace conference on Libya, she did not publicly raise the issue of the Tiergarten murder the previous summer and, according to one account, she praised Putin for visiting Syria earlier that week.[19] In the joint press conference, she reverted to describing Nord Stream 2 as an economic project.[20] However, her response in September 2020 to a German military laboratory's discovery that the Russian opposition politician was poisoned with the nerve agent Novichok was quite different. It triggered once again her strong moral instincts in dealing with Russia that had come to the fore in 2014. Clearly shocked, she said that the crime committed against Navalny violated the 'basic values and basic rights' that Germany and its allies upheld.[21]

Even though Merkel had bravely stood next to Putin in May 2015 and condemned the annexation of Crimea as 'criminal',[22] it seemed only now that she accepted that a criminal regime was governing Russia. Her readiness to speak out about the Navalny poisoning provoked a furious reaction from Moscow as the Foreign Ministry accused Berlin of trying to discredit Russia internationally. Resorting to Stalinist language, it said that if Germany did not share the laboratory test results with Russian prosecutors, this would be a 'crude, hostile provocation against Russia' with consequences for the bilateral relationship.[23] Moscow had not spoken to a German government in this tone since the Cold War. The Navalny poisoning was further proof that enemies of the Russian leadership live in great danger. Yet the murders of the journalist Yuri Shekhochikhin and the politician Sergei Yushenkov in 2003 caused little concern in Berlin. The same applied to the assassination of the journalist Anna Politkovskaya in 2006, another alarming indicator of the character of the system that had formed under Putin's leadership. Similarly, the fatal shooting of the opposition politician Boris Nemtsov in early 2015 during a period of considerable tension in relations between Russia and the EU did not have the same effect on Merkel as the attempted murder of Navalny. It was probably the accumulation of these crimes, together with Putin's lies, the personal experience of cyberattack and the deterioration of Germany's relations despite Merkel's heroic efforts to protect them that finally made her patience snap.

While the sharp deterioration in relations in 2020 spoke volumes about Russia's behaviour, it was also an indictment of

Germany's Russia handling on Merkel's watch. It is reasonable to ask why it took fifteen years to conclude that the criminalised Russian state posed serious dangers to its citizens, its neighbours and Europe as whole. German policymakers knew enough about the Russian system to understand how it functioned and whose interests it served. The answer is that they were not psychologically ready to translate that understanding into policy responses because it required overcoming the hurdle of Germans, who had committed such terrible crimes against Russians and other Soviet peoples, saying that Russia's leaders were criminals. No German researchers or journalists have produced books on the same theme as the late Karen Dawisha's *Putin's Kleptocracy* or Catherine Belton's recently published *Putin's People*, which trace the emergence of the KGB-led Putin system to its origins in the criminal world of St Petersburg. Germany's elites have simply ignored the issue.[24]

To her credit, Merkel was able to go partway down the difficult path of calling out Russian behaviour. When she spoke of Russia's criminal annexation of Crimea, she did so the day after the seventieth anniversary of Germany's defeat in the Second World War. In the same breath she recalled the Nazis' appalling crimes against the peoples of the USSR, among others. However, this flash of courage was not enough for Germany to establish policies towards Russia that clearly differentiated the Russian leadership and its criminal practices from Russian society. For a country with such deep knowledge of Russia, a genuine attachment to it, and a desire to see it develop healthy democratic institutions, this reflex of accommodation was an abdication of responsibility.

By the time Merkel as chancellor began meeting with human rights activists and other critics of the regime, the die was cast. Led by Germany, EU countries were not prepared to take a strong stance against the Kremlin's roll-back of democratic freedoms and its privatisation of the state. Germany's Russia problem was on full show as its instinctive reflexes clouded its thinking and sapped its confidence to look reality in the eye and draw the consequences. Instead of alerting its EU and NATO allies to the dangerous direction the country was taking, Germany continued to talk up business opportunities with Russia as if these were a guarantee against confrontation. Policymakers had forgotten the history of the Cold War when confrontation and trade relations existed side-by-side, notably in the late 1970s and early 1980s. Even after the annexation of Crimea and the imposition of sanctions, there was no desire among the political parties to have an open debate about Russia to reassess relations and policy options. The issue was too uncomfortable, too emotive and too divisive even within the main parties themselves.

For Germany's future Russia policy to be more effective, the next government will need to conduct a comprehensive review of the approach taken between 1990 and 2014 aimed at understanding the reasons for its failure. The key question to answer is why Germany persisted with the same policies for so long when it was clear that they were not only not working but were also accelerating the emergence of a Russian system hostile to the EU and NATO, and working against Germany's interests. As the British author Keir Giles has noted, western countries have a record of allowing hope to triumph over experience, leading from one reset to another, creating a deeper crisis each time the new reset fails.[25] With its acute sense of the perils of nationalism, Germany should have been among the first to recognise the path that Russia was taking based on a hotchpotch blend of patriotism inspired by figures such as Ivan Ilin and Aleksandr Solzhenitsyn together with the Russian Orthodox Church, and where it would lead. It should have known that a relaxation of tensions with the West after Russia's invasion of Georgia in 2008, for example, would embolden Moscow rather than restrain it. After all, the Kremlin's 'sovereign democracy' contained a clear anti-western, confrontational element. It was ironic that Germany stood by passively watching Russia rediscover its own 'special path' (*особый путь*) when it had found peace and prosperity by renouncing its equivalent path of distinctiveness (*Sonderweg*) and aligning itself with the European mainstream. It saw the risks associated with Russia's drift in this direction, but it instinctively chose not to speak up.

Conclusion

This book has argued that Germany's historically conditioned reflexes have distorted its view of Russia and continue to inhibit its behaviour. Put simply, these reflexes are a complex mixture of several factors: fear, sentimentality, ambivalence, economic complementarity, residual *Ostpolitik* reasoning and a sense of obligation to Moscow for allowing Germany to reunify.

The roots of fear, sentimentality and ambivalence in Germany's relations with Russia go deep into the national psyche and have accumulated over centuries to form a contradictory picture of the Russian state and its people and conflicting senses of how to deal with both. The continuing notion of economic complementarity based on Russia's vast resource base and its potentially huge market for German companies goes back over a century. The guilt factor relates mainly to the Second World War and remains a powerful brake on dispassionate analysis and the development of robust policies. However, four generations later, the consciousness of the war and its aftermath is declining. It will be less of an emotional reference point in future relations as the generation of survivors disappears on both sides and its immediacy recedes.

Inherited *Ostpolitik* orthodoxies about economic relations persist. An SPD position paper produced as late as October 2018 argued that since Germany could not change Russia against its will from outside, economic relations could nevertheless have a

245

'stabilising influence on political relations'.[1] The authors were seemingly oblivious to the fact that the expansion of economic relations had led to the exact opposite. Increased trade had served instead to stabilise the Russian system, constraining the development of civil society, and increasing its ability to confront western interests. Again, they should have known better, since the SPD had its own difficulties, beginning in the late 1970s when it saw the democracy movement in Poland threatening its contacts with the Communist regime and destabilising Europe. The British author Hans Kundnani noted in 2014 in a compelling article published in German that Germany's politicians needed to jettison *Ostpolitik* since it belonged to a previous era. He argued that globalisation had created a fundamentally different relationship between the West and authoritarian countries because of mutual dependencies. He explained that that the situation during the Cold War years had been different since the West had exploited the USSR's need for hard currency to force it to make concessions.[2] Despite these persuasive arguments, the *Ostpolitik* logic still acts as a straitjacket on thinking about relations with Russia.

For today's generation of German policymakers, German reunification was the key event in their lives. It will continue to impact views of Russia because of Gorbachev's role in the process and Moscow's continuing reminders to Germans of the debt that they owe it. A deeper reading of history indicates that Germans' gratitude to Moscow is prone to exaggeration and misplaced. The outcome owed far more to historical circumstances, skilful diplomacy and a large measure of luck than to Russian generosity.

Merkel's abrupt shift of policy in 2014 was significant but it stayed within the framework of an older approach that had led to détente in the late 1960s. In its updated form, it consisted of selective cooperation with Russia and continued societal contacts alongside support for Russia's neighbours, sanctions and increased resilience, including the declaratory restoration of collective defence as NATO's core function. The EU's five principles adopted in 2016 embodied this approach. German defence spending even increased from its exceptionally low base. However, Nord Stream 2 showed that the old instincts of *Wandel durch Handel* (change through trade) were still present – so much so that Berlin chose to override the objections of neighbours and allies. Nevertheless, there was much more realism in policy circles than during the years of the Medvedev honeymoon when German policymakers deceived themselves into thinking that he was the key to Russia's future. In late 2017, Manfred Huterer, one of the Foreign Office's most experienced Russia hands noted that the resilience of the Russian system was much greater than many western observers assumed.[3] In his view, this required Germany and its partners to have strategic patience. Yet to have strategic patience assumes the existence of a strategy that Germany did not have. A growing criticism of the Merkel era among Germany's foreign policy community is that the country failed to define its interests and develop a strategy to advance them. The 2020 report of the influential Munich Security Conference noted with irony that the country of the *Gesamtkonzept* (or 'master plan') does not even have a national security strategy.[4]

While 2014 was certainly no policy revolution, the progress in German thinking became clear in the summer of 2019 when Macron proposed 'clarifying' relations with Russia to prevent its isolation and stop it being a permanent theatre of strategic struggle between the USA and Russia.[5] The French President's words caused irritation in Berlin. A decade earlier, German policymakers would have agreed with many of his arguments, but his naivety now shocked them. They could see that the French position was out of touch with reality and that previous approaches of this kind had yielded nothing. Ironically, they also recognised the danger of France splitting an EU consensus on Russia as if Germany's Nord Stream 2 position had not done exactly that. To make matters worse, Macron had not taken the trouble to agree his proposals with other EU member states. Understandably perhaps, Berlin had reason to feel that it had far more to say about Russia than France because of its deeper historical and cultural links and its far more developed relationships there.

The partial nature of Germany's progress since 2014 was visible in another way. In September 2020, the German analyst Stefan Meister published a competent set of recommendations for developing a more effective Russia policy. These included reducing energy deliveries from Russia, addressing the money-laundering problem, increasing defence capabilities and maintaining societal contacts with the help of relaxed visa restrictions. However, there was little new here because similar proposals made five years earlier had remained on the drawing board. Policy had become stuck in a groove.

The absence of a strategic framework for thinking about Russia and designing policy is part of a much broader issue related to Germany's concept of itself as a country that was re-born after 1945 and firmly integrated into western institutions, yet with limited sovereignty and destined to carry the burden of Nazi Germany's crimes against humanity. Thanks to US leadership, it was possible to integrate *Ostpolitik* into a western strategy for moving beyond the confrontation of the 1950s and 1960s in East–West relations to a form of managed competition with arms control treaties and structured dialogue. This led to the Helsinki Final Act and established a framework that made security risks manageable, ultimately serving as an effective regional safety net when the USSR collapsed.

It is understandable today that the USA no longer has the same level of interest in Russia given Moscow's loss of global influence. This does not mean that it has lost interest in Russia. Moscow's preservation of a strategic nuclear deterrent and its efforts to rebuild pockets of regional influence as well its use of cyberwarfare and disinformation tools, including against the USA, mean that Washington defines Russia together with China as a 'revisionist' power.[6] Yet China poses a significantly more serious threat to US interests because of its growing economic power, its increasing military potential and its efforts to rebalance the Indo-Pacific region to its advantage by displacing the USA. Over the longer term, China poses a threat to the USA's pre-eminent role as a global rule setter. At the same time, the USA clearly has serious domestic problems to address to remain competitive. These challenges are set to grow over the coming years, and perhaps decades. As a result, Europe is likely to be an area of reduced focus and commitment for the USA with the leading EU countries and Britain forced to take greater responsibility for contributing to their own security. To cope with this situation, Germany will need to rediscover the art of strategy and the confidence currently lacking to define national interests and align foreign and security policy with its allies. Mitigating the security challenge posed by Russia will require overcoming traditional reflexes and engaging in clear, unemotional, honest thinking that goes significantly beyond the stage reached under Merkel's leadership in 2014.

If German policymakers were to suspend their reflexes towards Russia and speak openly to themselves, they would probably accept the following propositions:

1 The confrontation of recent years is likely to intensify and Germany and its allies will have to learn to live with it while playing a longer game to encourage Moscow to change its course. The long-term goal is to persuade Russia that its current policies are counter-productive and risk further weakening Russia, especially by making it a junior partner of China. History suggests that Russia will eventually turn back to Europe. In the meantime, Germany and its allies need to defend their interests, demonstrate the superior functioning of their political and economic systems and apply an appropriate level of pressure in the right areas to encourage different policy approaches on the part of Russia. The period since 2015 has shown that Moscow is not interested in the EU's selective

cooperation agenda and it seems hardly likely that this will change if confrontation intensifies. In other words, it is time to speak openly about the fact that Russia is not just a competitor; it is an opponent. It will not cooperate with western countries if doing so risks, on balance, strengthening the structures it wishes to weaken. Its reluctance to participate in meaningful cooperation with NATO over many years before the breakdown of relations over Ukraine tells an important story.

2 Official dialogue for dialogue's sake is counter-productive and shows weakness as do empty cooperation programmes. Quantity is the enemy of quality. Dialogue limited to issues of genuine mutual interest with the right people at the right time is more important than operating multiple dialogue channels addressing secondary questions. The unbalanced membership of the Petersburger Dialog undermines its potential value and serves no clear purpose other than the imitation of dialogue. Germany should seek other means to talk to Russia's civil society and consider suspending the Dialog. At the same time, town twinning arrangements and educational exchanges are valuable ways of maintaining contacts with grassroots Russia. It is essential to differentiate Russian society from its leaders.

3 Germany needs to invest more in creating hard power capability. Commanding a NATO battle group in Lithuania is an important step forward politically given the sensitivity at home to German deployments abroad, and especially in areas that the Wehrmacht previously invaded. However, this is not hard power. The force is tiny in size and lacks military utility beyond acting as a trip wire if Russian forces were ever to invade Lithuania. Germany needs to demonstrate to Russia its intention to rebuild the Bundeswehr as an effective force that can make a greater contribution to NATO's military power. By definition, a deterrent must be credible. Equally, Germany needs to substantially improve its cyber defence capabilities,

which have been found wanting in recent years. Finally, investment in LNG and further capacity to diversify energy supplies is essential. The argument that maintaining a heavy dependence on Russia for gas will help stabilise relations has proved false. Indeed, Russia has exploited Germany's willingness to take more gas from Russia to exert greater pressure on Ukraine. The government needs to challenge the views of German industry. Cheap gas from Russia comes at a price.

4 *Ostpolitik* thinking is unhelpful because of a false parallel. The USSR was a status quo power in Europe, whereas Russia today is not. Germany's goal vis-à-vis Moscow today is stabilisation of the post-unification environment, whereas Russia's goal is to seek concessions by disrupting it. The unpleasant truth is that it will not be possible for Germany and its allies to rebuild trust with Moscow until there is a new Russian leadership with a different foreign policy calculus. In the meantime, the only sensible course is to limit the damage to western interests both at home and in the 'shared neighbourhood' and to maintain pressure on Moscow to change course.

5 Germans should stop saying 'there can be no security in Europe without Russia'. The cliché much-beloved by Russian diplomats is a perfect example of Russian thinking that has become a fixed piece in the German discourse about Russia's place in Europe. It camouflages a wider set of arguments that present Russia's behaviour in an uncritical light, including the notion that NATO is a threat to European security since Russia is not a member.[7] Leaving aside the suitability as a security partner of a country prepared to annex a neighbour's territory, it ignores the fact that Russia's current conceptual approach to building security is incompatible with Germany's. Russia believes that its security needs override those of its neighbours' while arguing that security in Europe is equal and indivisible. Equally, German diplomats, like many of their western colleagues, keep saying to the Russian side 'we need

Russia to solve many problems around the world'. How can Germany 'need' a country that is not prepared to cooperate with it? For example, Foreign Minister Maas stated in July 2020 during a visit to Moscow that 'we need Russia to solve conflicts in Syria, Libya and Ukraine',[8] as if Russia were not a party to these conflicts and could be a constructive partner in resolving them. Moscow cannot interpret this approach as anything other than weakness.

6 Germany must pay much greater attention to the problem of Russian influence in Germany and analyse better the networks and channels that Moscow uses to generate sympathy for its positions. It is essential to develop resilience in these areas. Russia's efforts to co-opt Die Linke and the AfD to expand divisions in the regions of the former GDR require a stronger response, including public education that focuses on the nature of the Russian regime. The German public's current anti-American attitudes are a source of concern because they encourage support for pro-Russian positions.

7 A serious effort is necessary to understand how Russia exploits German psychological vulnerabilities. Jan Techau is one of the few German analysts to have recognised that Putin understands the German psyche and how to exploit it, noting that Moscow is continuing where it left off in Soviet days by perpetuating a myth of Russian victimhood as a way of triggering sentiments of German moral failure vis-à-vis Russia. The goal is to drive a wedge between Germany and its western partners, particularly the USA.[9]

8 Germany needs to prepare for Russia's return to Europe under a new leadership that takes a different view of Russia's needs and priorities. Based on the lessons learned from the 1990s, Germany must evaluate how to develop relations in such new conditions, the expectations it should have and a clear idea of the type of conditionality it would apply to support the next phase of Russia's Europeanisation. This exercise needs to take

place sooner rather than later so that Germany and its allies are not surprised by events in Russia. Germany should not shy away from demonstrating to Russian society the possibilities for change in the relationship if Russia's leaders recalibrate their approach to Europe.

9 Germany must put much more effort into supporting the reform process in Ukraine. This country of 45 million people with a territory half again as large as Germany's is on the new geopolitical fault line in Europe as a divided Germany was during the Cold War. If it can build new institutions and set itself firmly on a path of European integration, creating wealth for the benefit of its citizens, it will exert profound influence on the thinking of reformist forces in Russia. Ukraine is key to resolving Europe's Russia problem, contrary to the established thinking in Berlin and many EU capitals that Russia is key to resolving Europe's Ukraine problem. The underlying problem is Russia, not Ukraine.

10 Germany should not take refuge in process. Dealing with Russia requires space to act quickly. Small well-targeted cooperation programmes stand a much better chance of success than large bureaucratic ones that only give an impression of a stable relationship.

11 Germany needs to invest further in rebuilding Russia and Eastern European expertise. This begins with expanding teaching of Russian and other Eastern European languages in schools and universities. The situation in the think-tank world has improved in recent years with the establishment of the Centre for East European and International Studies but there is still a shortage of experts. Parliament too lacks foreign policy expertise in general but has a striking dearth of Russia specialists.

This exercise suggests that for it to make better policy, Germany needs its allies to recognise its limitations and to challenge its instincts towards Russia. They must recognise that in dealing with Russia, Germany is still a traumatised country afraid of itself. This limits what Germany can achieve as a leader of European policy towards Russia, and for this reason, Germany needs others at its side to help it think through and execute policy towards Russia. Perhaps more than most, the issue of Russia exposes Germans' duality, their sense of belonging to Eastern as well as Western Europe, and their effort to find a balance between the two.

It was inevitable that the settlement of the German question in 1990 would open the Russian question – a far greater challenge not only because of Russia's size but also because of its own deeply conflicted sense of where it belongs. Understandably, Russia's uncertainty about itself is deeply disconcerting for Germans given their history. Today's Germany has a psychological need for Russia to feel part of Europe as a genuinely European country. This is a deeply embedded attitude reflecting the recent *Ostpolitik* tradition and Prussia's recognition after 1815 that Russia must have a seat at the European table. Yet at the same time, today's Germany still feels dependent on the transatlantic link as a force multiplier to secure its place in the world. In view of Russia's current condition and outlook, these aspirations are for now irreconcilable and create discomfort in Berlin. Russia may stay on its current track of alienation from Europe for a while yet. The challenge for German policymakers is to design a range of policies together with their key European allies that will accelerate Russia's return to Europe while also ensuring that Europe is ready and able to support a reforming Russia more effectively than it did after the end of the Cold War. Deployment of experience gained in supporting reforms in Ukraine and, hopefully, Belarus, could be a significant help in providing the right type of assistance to future Russian reformers.

In principle, designing a strategy for managing the Russia challenge should not be difficult for a country that gave birth to Clausewitz. The first requirement is a clear definition of Germany's national interests and an accompanying set of policy goals to guide relations with Russia. As noted, having 'good relations' with Russia does not qualify as a policy goal. It is a possible policy outcome. Similarly, dialogue with Russia is a means to an end and not an end in itself as diplomats not just in Germany are often inclined to think. By contrast, supporting Ukraine's independence to preserve peace in Europe, deterring cyberattacks, protecting the public from disinformation and countering money laundering are clear policy goals.

The next stage requires analysing Russia's strengths and weaknesses relative to those of Germany and its allies and moving beyond the necessary defensive responses, many of which are already underway through NATO, to identify areas that can be targeted in non-confrontational ways. As it has been for centuries, Russia's obvious Achilles heel is its economy. Despite a more than tenfold growth in GDP between 1999 and 2013,[10] output in 2019 was only fractionally above where it had been in in 2008 and the outlook is for stagnation because the measures required to promote growth conflict with the Kremlin's political priorities. While Russia has modernised its armed forces to the point where they can reliably defend the country in case of military conflict for perhaps another three decades, lack of economic growth and a failure to reduce dependency on hydrocarbon exports over the same period could seriously weaken the country internally and externally. As noted in Chapter 6, the decarbonisation of transportation is a significant threat to Russia's current business model. If Germany and its allies were to accelerate the timetable for 'greening' their economies as, for example, Britain has already done, pressure would grow on Moscow to reform. It should be a straightforward task to list other areas in which Russia has clear weaknesses from education and healthcare to innovation to productivity and demonstrate to the Russian leadership that it is losing ground relative to Europe and needs to reconnect with it to avoid falling further behind. A key message to Moscow should be that while it is focused on avoiding the mistakes made by Soviet leaders in the 1980s when they reformed too fast, it is currently overextended and risks repeating the mistakes of the 1970s that led to the Gorbachev reforms.

At the same time, Germany and its allies will need to signal their determination to defend their interests. In Germany's case, it is essential that the government shows political leadership and speaks clearly to the public to explain its policies, especially the need to reinvest in defence. To suspend their reflexes and develop strategy, Germans need to talk more openly about their Russia problem, and their allies must make a greater effort to understand it.

Afterword

Russia's full-scale invasion of Ukraine that began on 24 February 2022 marks a turning point in European history, a *Zeitenwende*.

Moscow's use of military force to remove Ukraine's leadership from power and extinguish the country's independence has brought to a spectacular end the 'post-Cold War era' that began with the promise of a democratic Russia and a European continent at peace with itself. A label has yet to appear to describe the new reality in which Germany is one of several western countries that have imposed unprecedented economic sanctions on Russia while also providing economic and military support to Ukraine to help it continue fighting a war of national survival. Russia sees its military campaign in Ukraine as part of a war with the West to define the limits of western influence in global affairs and restrict the weight of the USA in Europe's balance of power. By contrast, Germany and its allies regard their response as defence of the Helsinki principles of sovereignty, inviolability of borders and human rights. Moscow accepted these over thirty years ago as the basis for security in a common vision of a Europe 'whole and free'.

Russia's war against Ukraine has shattered Germany's post-Cold War identity and left its Russia policy in ruins. Germany's rapid unification after the collapse of the Berlin Wall in 1989 owed much to the Moscow's decision to disengage from Central Europe and instilled a determination in the German political class to achieve reconciliation with Russia as part of an extension of the European integration process that had allowed Germans to normalise relations with former enemies. Their idealistic goal was the creation of a *Friedensordnung*, a post-modern security order built on peaceful relations rather than power. The main instruments for fashioning the new relationship with Russia were dialogue, trade and bilateral cooperation. Germany invested heavily in all three areas while re-purposing its armed forces to perform non-combat roles in international crisis management operations. Contributing to NATO's collective defence mission was no longer a priority as the Alliance's focus shifted to out-of-area challenges. The underlying assumption of this policy was that Russia accepted Germany's logic that the dark days of power relationships and spheres of influence in Europe belonged to the past in a globalising world. Increased German dependency on imports of natural gas from Russia were a by-product of this thinking. The gas was cheap, and from Berlin's perspective, larger imports increased mutual dependency and contributed to stable relations. The security of these gas supplies was not considered a problem, since Moscow had been a reliable gas supplier to West Germany even during the worst days of the Cold War. Russia's deliberate reduction of gas deliveries in the summer of 2022 as Germany and its allies stepped up arms deliveries to Ukraine destroyed the illusion that the gas trade could be an effective insurance policy against war. For German policy makers schooled in the thinking of *Nie wieder Krieg* (War Never Again), the impossible had happened.

At the time of writing, a debate has still to begin among the German policy elite about the responsibility that Germany bears not just for misreading Russia's intentions but for failing to deter it from embarking on a course to dismember the second largest country in Europe. After the annexation of Crimea in 2014, Russian policy makers cannot have failed to note Germany's readiness to make its energy security hostage to Moscow, as well as the continued hollowing out of its armed forces. The concept of *Wandel durch Annäherung* (Change by Getting Closer) that underpinned Germany's approach to Russia for more than two decades proved counter-productive. Russia did indeed change as closer relations between the two countries took shape, but the features it acquired were increasingly negative, as the leadership moved down a path of anti-western authoritarianism backed by re-discovered imperialist instincts. By the time Russia invaded Ukraine in February 2022, it could be considered a fascist state, even if Germans were not inclined to label it as such because of the USSR's role in the defeat of Nazism. However, the brutality of Russia's military operations, including an extraordinary level of violence against Ukrainian civilians, a supposedly 'brotherly people', was deeply shocking for the policy elite and brought accusations of 'genocide' from some quarters.[1] Policy makers had persuaded themselves that Germany's hand of friendship had suppressed Russia's violent tendencies so familiar from history. Berlin's failure to heed the multiple warnings of Poland, the Baltic states and others that Germany's faith in Russia's capacity for positive change was misplaced was a deep source of embarrassment. Germany had not wanted to allow realism to cloud its idealism about Russia.

The coalition of Social Democrats, Greens and Free Democrats that came to power in December 2021 immediately found itself in a highly uncomfortable and challenging situation, as Moscow built up its military forces on Ukraine's borders in a menacing show of force. With western nerves jangling, Moscow invited NATO countries to discuss a fundamental revision of European security arrangements, including not just the prohibition of further NATO enlargement but also the roll-back of NATO's military presence in Central Europe to the situation before the Alliance's first enlargement to the region in 1997. The purpose of these unrealistic proposals was for NATO member states to reject them and make Ukraine's efforts to integrate with NATO a 'casus belli' for Russia. Finland, a country that manages its relations with its Russian neighbour with consummate skill quickly concluded what was at stake for Europe's security. Responding to Moscow's threat of 'serious military and political consequences' if Finland were to join NATO, President Niinisto warned other western countries of the dangers of appeasing Russia and insisted on Finland's right to decide its own security arrangements.[2] Berlin remained silent.

The government was deeply divided on the issue of Russia and how to manage relations with it. The SPD was largely wedded to traditional *Ostpolitik* concepts of preserving close relations with Russia despite tensions and remained committed to bringing into operation the controversial Nord Stream 2 pipeline, while the Greens brought a strong human rights focus to Russia policy and a more sympathetic view of Ukraine. They were opposed to the Nord Stream 2 pipeline on environmental and geopolitical grounds. The Free Democrats were closer to the Greens in their condemnation of the increasing repression in Russia but were divided on the issue of Nord Stream 2.

The growing crisis immediately revealed the government's inexperience and its inability to lead a European response to Russia's increasing pressure. Germany no longer possessed the diplomatic weight that had allowed it to fashion the western response to Russia's annexation of Crimea and its destabilisation of south-eastern Ukraine in 2014. Understandably, Chancellor Scholz could not compete with Angela Merkel's mastery of the issues in the 'east'. Annalena Baerbock, the new Foreign Minister, had not previously served in government and had no specialist knowledge of the region. President Putin had chosen his timing well and his skilful sabre-rattling exposed two deep-seated specifically German vulnerabilities that defined the limits of a European response to a Russian invasion. First, Germany's instinctive discomfort with hard power and its lack of capacity for deploying it. Second, Germany's unprocessed history in relations with Ukraine, marked by its tendency to feel guilt for Hitler's war crimes on the Eastern Front towards Russia rather than Ukraine. This despite the fact that Ukrainians suffered more than Russians at the hands of the German invaders. This reflex made German policymakers particularly cautious about boosting Ukraine's defences, because weapon supplies necessarily meant bringing Germany into indirect military conflict with Russia. Britain, Poland, the Baltic states and others had no such hesitation in arming the victim of Russia's aggression.

Germany's hesitation in supplying weapons reinforced suspicions in Kyiv that Germans shared with Russians a colonial attitude to their country and regarded them as people whose fate along with that of other Central European countries can be decided jointly by Berlin and Moscow. The Ukrainians could point to recent history to support this view. The Minsk Agreements that froze the conflict manufactured by Moscow in Donbas in 2014 to Russia's advantage bore heavy German influence. In the years that followed, Kyiv often felt itself under pressure from Berlin to show flexibility on their implementation in the absence of concessions from Moscow. This contributed to the sense that Germany saw Ukraine as *Verhandlungsmasse*, a bargaining chip for settling relations between Europe and Russia.

Seemingly insensitive to understandable Ukrainian fears, the new German government caused dismay in Kyiv by not immediately threatening to prohibit the operation of the new Nord Stream 2 gas pipeline if Russia invaded Ukraine. Admittedly, there was no evidence to support Ukrainian suspicions that Scholz might be cut from the same cloth as the SPD *Russlandversteher*. He did not hail from the same group in the SPD as former Chancellor Schröder, President Steinmeier and former Minister of the Economy and Foreign Minister Sigmar Gabriel. As Mayor of Hamburg (2011–18), he had kept his distance from his counterparts in the twin city of St Petersburg. However, he did not dissent from the standard SPD line towards Russia and as Vice Chancellor and Finance Minister (2018–21) was part of the Grand Coalition that backed the Nord Stream 2 project and continued to underfund the armed forces.

The Chancellor and his Defence Minister, in particular, did not help themselves during the early months in office by their disastrous communication on weapons deliveries to Ukraine. The government's apparent inability to decide on which weapons Germany would or would not send to Ukraine reflected divisions within both the SPD as well as the Greens on the issue. Defence Minister Lambrecht's announcement in January 2022 that Germany would supply 5,000 helmets as a gesture of solidarity provoked ridicule at home and abroad. Later decisions to supply light weapons and then small amounts of heavy weapons were shrouded in secrecy and confusion, as it emerged that the promised weapons would in some cases take months to reach Ukraine. It quickly became clear that the Bundeswehr was desperately short of equipment and that Germany had precious few weapons systems to give Ukraine. In addition to the weapons debacle, Scholz appeared unmoved by the destruction and loss of life in Ukraine and showed no urgency to visit Kyiv even after the signal that President Steinmeier was welcome. The Ukrainian government had initially caused offence in Germany by indicating that Steinmeier should not visit because of his perceived record as a *Russlandversteher*. The Chancellor finally visited Kyiv in June 2022, together with the French and Romanian Presidents and the Italian Prime Minister.

For all Scholz's instinctive caution, his speech to parliament on 27 February 2022 showed genuine boldness and an impressive command of the issues. It has anchored the word *Zeitenwende* in the English language. The reference to the change of an era reflected Gemany's understanding of the significance of Putin's decision to go to war with Ukraine. This was not a repeat of 2014, when Russia had plucked Crimea from Ukraine's grasp without firing a shot. Moscow had now triggered the first major military conflict in Europe since 1945. Scholz stated clearly that Putin did not just intend to wipe Ukraine from the map – he was building a Russian empire and destroying the European security order.[3] The Chancellor stated Germany's unequivocal support for Ukraine and proceeded with a string of announcements that left commentators aghast at the apparent speed of change. The government would immediately invest €100bn in the Bundeswehr and increase defence spending to 2 per cent. It would invest in building a new generation of aircraft and tanks together with European partners. It would devote resources to improving its resilience to cyber attacks and disinformation. It would also invest in two liquefied natural gas terminals to reduce dependency on gas imports from Russia. Putin had seemingly succeeded where President Trump had failed in persuading Germany that it needed both to invest in defence and reduce its gas dependency on Russia.

Scholz went out his way to brand Russia's aggression against Ukraine as 'Putin's war', concluding that there was no readiness on Putin's part for real dialogue. While Germany would keep communication channels open to Russia, there would be no talking for the sake of talking. He explained the need to differentiate Putin from the Russian people, who had 'not decided in favour of the war', by referring to the historical importance of the reconciliation achieved after 1945 between Germans and Russians. In line with his NATO counterparts after the start of Russia's invasion, Scholz stuck studiously to the message that NATO member states were not at war with Russia and wished to avoid Russia's war against Ukraine from escalating beyond Ukraine's borders. Yet his argumentation in the *Zeitenwende* speech indicated his understanding that Putin was at war with NATO, including Germany. The sanction measures adopted by Germany and its allies against Russia are unquestionably an instrument of economic war, and Russia views them as such. It is difficult to escape the view that Germany, in light of its history, cannot consider itself to be at war with Russia and thinks of the conflict in Ukraine as a crisis to be managed. With one eye to the *Russlandversteher* and pacifist sentiments in his party, Scholz consistently refused to say that Ukraine must prevail in the war with Russia, limiting himself only to stating that Russia must not win and Ukraine must continue to exist. At the same time, the Chancellor warned repeatedly of the risk of the war escalating and drawing in NATO, alluding in particular to the dangers of nuclear conflict.[4] This reference was not by chance. For decades, Russian messaging has played on Germans' anti-nuclear sentiments, which date back to the controversies over the deployment of US nuclear weapons in West Germany.

Even if an inquest into the failings of Germany's Russia policy had not begun four months into the war, two of its chief authors from the SPD had the humility to admit that they had been wrong. President Steinmeier, who had defended Nord Stream to the very end, describing energy relations as 'almost the last bridge between Europe and Russia',[5] said simply:

> We held on to bridges that Russia no longer believed in and that our partners warned us about. My holding on to Nord Stream 2, that was clearly a mistake.

He conceded that he had underestimated Putin's readiness to pay for his 'imperialist delusion' with the 'complete economic political and moral ruin'[6] of Russia. If these arguments were indisputable, his assertion that 'we failed with the project to tie Russia into a common security architecture'[7] was questionable. It presupposed that this idea was feasible in the first place, given the fundamental differences between NATO countries and Russia on the nature of security and how to provide it.

Sigmar Gabriel went further, admitting that Germans were wrong in thinking that they knew better than the Eastern European countries how to deal with Moscow based on their *Ostpolitik* experience and that Germany's attitude towards them was arrogant and paternalistic.

> The idea was that stronger links between the German and the Soviet – or Russian – economy would help us more effectively maintain stability and peace in Europe. Then Vladimir Putin arrived, a man who had no interest in economic success and used a different currency, the currency of power. To be honest, we Germans never

believed the war in Ukraine would happen, until it did. The success of Germany's economy and society is founded on successful economic integration and the conviction that the closer the economic ties are, the safer the world will be. That was obviously a gross misjudgement.[8]

Gabriel also admitted that the previous government's decision to let the market to determine the best source of gas was a mistake and that it should have reduced Germany's reliance on Russian gas after 2014.[9] Robert Habeck, the new Minister for Economic Affairs and Climate Action, reportedly identified a pro-Gazprom lobby in his Ministry, previously led by Gabriel, that had opposed the construction of LNG terminals.[10] Gabriel said that he had personally erred by not listening to the objections of the 'East Europeans' to the Nord Stream 2 pipeline that he lobbied for so vigorously. By contrast, former Chancellor Schröder showed not the slightest regret either for his unflinching support for Putin over more than twenty years or for his considerable influence over the two Nord Stream projects. Only in response to a chorus of public condemnation did he step down from his role as chair of the board of the Russian state oil company Rosneft nearly three months after the war had started. Parliament had earlier voted to strip him of his parliamentary privileges. Beforehand, Schröder had given an unapologetic interview to the New York Times in which he defended the policy of increasing Germany's energy dependency on Russia and predicted that Germany would go back to doing business with Russia after the war as it had done in the past because of its need for raw materials.[11]

Former Chancellor Merkel made her first media appearances in June 2022, six months after leaving office. Clearly shocked by the war in Ukraine, she nevertheless refused to admit any policy mistakes and stood by her earlier decisions to resist granting Ukraine a NATO Membership Action Plan in 2008 as well as her support for the Nord Stream 2 project. She claimed that the project had not increased the risk of the invasion of Ukraine by

Russia [12] and did not take responsibility for the decision to bring forward the closure of Germany's nuclear power plants that led to Germany's increased dependence on gas imports. Nor did she acknowledge that the chronic underfunding of the Bundeswehr during her time in office had weakened Germany's hand in dealing with Russia. Yet she observed that during all her years of dealing with Putin, it had not been possible 'to really bring the Cold War to an end'.[13] At the same time, she noted that she had long made it clear to others that Putin hated the West and that his goal was to destroy the EU because he saw it as the 'entry step' to NATO. Nevertheless, she argued that it was in Germany's interest to seek a 'modus vivendi' with Russia in which the two sides could try to coexist peacefully despite all their differences.[14] She did not believe in the old Ostpolitik mantra of *Wandel durch Handel* (Change through Trade) but instead in *Wandel durch Verbindung* (Change through Connectivity) 'with the second largest nuclear power in the world'.[15]

The combination of sanctions and Germany's commitment to reduce its dependency on Russian oil and gas imports as fast as possible has led to a rapid unravelling of the bilateral trade relationship. Although in June 2022, German companies such as Bayer, Liebherr and Metro continued to operate in Russia, an overwhelming majority had either scaled back or suspended their activities, while a smaller number had announced that they are leaving the country. The departures included major brands such as Aldi, BASF, Deutsche Bank, Deutsche Telekom, Grohe and Siemens.[16] The latter had been in the Russian market for nearly 170 years. The exodus of German companies is highly significant, since the voice of business was a critical factor in influencing the Russia policy of successive governments and sustaining belief in trade as a stabilising force in relations with Russia. The heads of some of Germany's largest companies regularly praised the Russian government despite the worsening business environment in Russia and the increasing tensions with the West.

Afterword

By the summer of 2022, much of Germany's impressive civil society connectivity and other linkages with Russia lay inactive because of the war. Fearful of greater domestic repression, many representatives of Russia's liberal intelligentsia who had contributed heavily to these ties were also now outside the country. Another pillar of Germany's relationship with Russia had disintegrated.

While it is impossible in mid-summer 2022 to predict how long and in what form Russia's war with Ukraine will last or what the outcome will be, it is clear that Europe has already entered a new phase of confrontation with Russia. This phase could last decades and significantly alter the balance of power on the continent if the EU meets its commitment to wean itself off Russian oil and gas and NATO countries, bolstered by the admission to the Alliance of Finland and Sweden, re-invest in defence. Germany will need time to find its feet in this rapidly changing situation that will force it both to re-assess its approach to Russia and pay greater respect to its allies who demonstrated a far better understanding of Moscow's intentions. US–China tensions and German concerns about the future access of German exports to the Chinese market as well as the possible re-election of Donald Trump as US President will make the coming years especially challenging for German diplomacy. Hopefully, there will be an opportunity for Germany to play a leading role both in the reconstruction of post-war Ukraine as well as the process of preparing Ukraine for eventual EU accession. In this scenario, Ukraine will become the key focus of Germany's engagement in its 'east'. An opinion poll conducted in June 2022 indicated that Germans believed by a factor of 2:1 that peace in cooperation Russia was no longer possible and that Europe must stand up to Putin. At the same time, there were signs of increasing support for admitting Ukraine to NATO and overwhelming backing for Ukraine joining the EU.[17] There is little doubt that the hundreds of thousands of Ukrainians who fled to Germany in the early months of the war contributed to changing perceptions of their country, which had previously been framed by Russian propaganda as 'nationalist' and 'neo-Nazi' – terms that left many Germans cold towards Ukraine.

For the foreseeable future, Russia is likely to continue deploying a range of tools to divide the West and break its influence on global affairs. Germany will find itself a major target of this effort and will need to create much greater resilience to guard against Russian attempts to manipulate its public opinion, undermine its government and destabilise its political system. At the same time, Russia's economy will continue to decline under the twin pressures of a harsh sanctions regime that is likely to stay in place for many years and a declining market for hydrocarbons. Sanctions will starve Russia of a range of western technologies and know-how that will be difficult to replace. Poverty and inequality will grow and the transfer of power from Putin to his successor may have the potential to de-stabilise Russia internally with powerful effects on its neighbourhood. Calibrating the pressure on Moscow to revise its policies and neutralise the military threat to its neighbours without causing a breakdown of authority will present a serious challenge to western policymakers.

Scholz has spoken of an 'ice age'[18] in relations with Russia, while also describing Russia's war against Ukraine as a 'caesura' for German diplomacy. Future historians may debate whether the 'caesura' was in fact the preceding three decades separating two eras of confrontation, when Germany flirted with the vision of a reforming Russia that would bring peace and stability to Europe.

Tragically for Ukraine, German policy makers did not equip themselves for the alternative scenario of a Russia set not on reform at home but on re-fashioning the European security system by war.

Notes

INTRODUCTION

1 Popp, M, and von Rohr, M, 'Das ist leider das Ende für die Idee strategischer Partnerschaft', *Der Spiegel*, 31 August 2020, www.spiegel.de/politik/ausland/wolfgang-ischinger-wir-muessen-gegenueber-maennern-wie-wladimir-putin-weniger-erpressbar-werden-a-00000000–0002–0001–0000–0 00172728797 (accessed 25 February 2021).
2 Von Fritsch, R, *Russlands Weg*, Aufbruch (2020), p. 48.
3 Ibid.
4 Scherbakowa I, 'Theodor-Heuss-Gedächtnisvorlesung', 12 December 2019.
5 See, for example, Stürmer M, 'Russland verstehen', 8 July 2016, www.welt.de/print/die_welt/debatte/article156892508/Russland-verstehen.html (accessed 25 February 2021).

CHAPTER 1

1 Quoted in *Unsere Russen, Unsere Deutschen, Bilder vom anderen 1800 bis 2000*, Catalogue of exhibition at Schloss Charlottenburg, December 2007–March 2008. Ch.Links Verlag.
2 Rezvykh, P, 'Die Rezeption der Philosophie Schellings in Russland', *Philosophisches Jahrbuch* 110:2 (January 2003), pp. 350–1.
3 *Geschichte der Deutschen Literatur*, Bayerischer Schulbuch-Verlag (1961), p. 279.
4 Kreuzer, D, *Der Einfluss des Deutschen auf das Russische seit 1700*, MA thesis, München, GRIN Verlag (2007), www.grin.com/document/203835 (accessed 25 February 2021).
5 Von Fritsch, R, *Russlands Weg*, Aufbau (2020), p. 20.
6 Fleischhauer, I, *Die Deutschen im Zarenreich*, Deutsche Verlags-Anstalt (1986), p. 24.

7 Ibid., p. 26.

8 Ibid., p. 40.

9 Ibid., p. 43.

10 Ibid., p. 49.

11 Hecker, H, *Die Deutschen im Russischen Reich, in der Sowjetunion und ihren Nachfolgestaaten* (Historische Landeskunde, Deutsche Geschichte im Osten), Band 2 (1996), p. 15.

12 Ibid., p. 157.

13 Ibid., p. 197.

14 Ibid. pp. 199–200.

15 Ibid., p. 212.

16 Ibid., p. 213.

17 Герцен, A, 'Русские немцы и немецкие русские' (1958), pp. 263–308 http://az.lib.ru/g/gercen_a_i/text_0180.shtml (accessed 25 February 2021).

18 Fleischhauer, p. 225.

19 Ibid., p. 238.

20 Ibid., p. 241.

21 Ibid., p. 250.

22 Ibid., p. 256.

23 *Unsere Russen, Unsere Deutschen*, p. 194.

24 Fleischhauer, p. 266.

25 Ibid., p. 266.

26 Ibid., p. 271.

27 Rjabowa, J, 'Otto von Bismarcks russische Spuren', 3 April 2015, https://de.rbth.com/kultur/2015/04/03/otto_von_bismarcks_russische_spuren_33309 (accessed 25 February 2021).

28 Ibid.

29 Wittram, R, 'Russlandpolitik nach der Reichsgründung', *Historische Zeitschrift*, October 1958, p. 262.

30 Ibid., p. 263.

31 Rjabowa, J.

32 Fleischhauer, p. 352.

33 Oppel, B, 'The waning of a traditional alliance: Russia and Germany after the Portsmouth Peace Conference', *Central European History*, 5:4 (December 1972), p. 327.

34 Happel, J and Mirsechanow, W, *Sankt Petersburg–Berlin, Jubiläen und imperiale Bilanzen 1912/1913*, p. 332, http://inion.ru/site/assets/files/1165/happel_mirzechanow.pdf (accessed 27 February 2021).

35 Ibid., p. 356.

36 Fleischhauer, p. 488.

37 Ibid., p. 461.

38 Ibid., p. 462.

39 Fleischhauer, I, *Das Dritte Reich und die Sowjetunion*, Deutsche Verlags-Anstalt (1983), p. 12.

40 Merridale, C, *Lenin on the Train*, Penguin Random House (2016).

41 *История России, XX Век 1894–1939*, Астрель (2009), p. 501.

42 Fleischhauer, *Die Russen im Zarenreich*, p. 583.

43 Ibid., p. 591.

44 Krieger V, 'Eine Bilanz des Schreckens, Geschichte der Deutschen aus Russland', https://deutscheausrussland.de/2017/03/27/eine-bilanz-des-schreckens/ (accessed 27 February 2021). At least 100,000 Germans died during the Bolsheviks' collectivisation of agriculture while the Germans in cities, typically, first generation arrivals from before the war, suffered marginalisation and a loss of social status followed by exile in 1941.

45 Koenen, G, *Der Russland-Komplex, Die Deutschen und der Osten*, C.H. Beck (2005), p. 172.

46 Kennan, G, *Russia and the West*, Mentor (1967), p. 210.

47 Ibid., p. 201.

48 Kotkin S, *Stalin, Vol: 1 Paradoxes of Power, 1878–1928*, Allen Lane (2014), p. 446.

49 *История России*, p. 788.

50 Pogge von Strandmann, H, 'Großindustrie und Rapallopolitik. Deutsch-Sowjetische Handelsbeziehungen in der Weimarer Republik', *Historische Zeitschrift* (April 1976), p. 270.

51 Ibid., p. 325.

52 Ibid., p. 331.

53 Ibid., p. 331.

54 Ibid., p. 333.

55 Ibid., p. 340.

56 Орлов, Б, Тиммерманн, X (составители), 'Россия и Германия в Европе', *Институт Европы РАН* (1998), p. 41.

57 Ströbinger, R, *Stalin enthauptet die rote Armee. Der Fall Tuchatschewskij*, Deutsche Verlags-Anstalt (1990), p. 270.

58 *История России*, p. 867.

59 Schattenberg, S, 'Der Hitler-Stalin-Pakt: Der Krieg und die europäische Erinnerung' *Osteuropa*, Vol. 59, No. 7/8 (July–August 2009), p. 29.

60 Stupnikova, T, *Die Wahrheit, die reine Wahrheit und nichts als die Wahrheit*, Frank & Timme (2014), p. 119.

61 Ibid.

62 Petersen, A, *Die Moskauer*, S. Fischer (2019), p. 93.

63 *История России XX Век: 1939–2007*, АСТ (2009), p. 34.

64 Buber-Neumann, M, *Als Gefangene bei Stalin und Hitler*, Deutsche Verlags-Anstalt (1962), p. 239.

65 Ibid., p. 24.

66 Радзинский, Э, *Сталин*, Вагриус (1997), p. 472.

67 Ibid., p. 25.

68 European Parliament resolution on the importance of European remembrance for the future of Europe (2019/2819(RSP), www.europarl.europa.eu/doceo/document/RC-9–2019–0097_EN.html (accessed 27 February 2021).

69 'Неформальный саммит СНГ', 20 December 2019 www.kremlin.ru/events/president/news/62376.

70 Moorhouse, R, *Devil's Alliance, Hitler's Pact with Stalin 1939–1941*, Vintage (2016), p. 73.

71 Laqueur, W, *Deutschland und Russland*, Verlag Ullstein (1965), p. 202.

72 *История России XX Век*, p. 27.

73 'Der Generalplan Ost', *Vierteljahrshefte für Zeitgeschichte* (July 1958), p. 299.

74 Аллилуева, С, *Только Один Год*, Hutchinson (1969), pp. 339–40.

75 Snyder, T, 'Lecture at a conference on Germany's historical responsibility towards Ukraine in the German Bundestag', 20 June 2017, www.youtube.com/watch?v=wDjHw_uXeKU (accessed 27 February 2021).

76 *История России XX Век*, p. 112.

77 Ibid., p. 113.

78 Ibid., p. 111.

79 *Für immer gezeichnet, Die Geschichte der 'Ostarbeiter' in Briefen, Erinnerungen und Interviews* (Hrsg. Von Memorial International, Moskau und der Heinrich-Böll Stiftung, Berlin, Ch.Links Verlag (2019), p. 27.

80 'Nichts vergessen', *Der Spiegel*, 4 July 1983, www.spiegel.de/spiegel/print/d-14019863.html (accessed 27 February 2021).

81 'Zwangsarbeit im NS-Staat', www.bundesarchiv.de/zwangsarbeit/geschichte/auslaendisch/russlandfeldzug/index.html (accessed 27 February 2021).

82 Für immer gezeichnet, Die Geschichte der 'Ostarbeiter' in Briefen, Erinnerungen und Interviews, p. 27.

83 Miller, J, 'Germany's Continental was "pillar" of Nazi war effort, study finds', *Financial Times*, 27 August 2020, www.ft.com/content/ddf5a02c-ce3e-445c-816b-1312b6c2ea38 (accessed 27 February 2021).

84 Gebhardt, M, *Wir Kinder Der Gewalt*, Deutsche Verlags-Anstalt (2019), p. 16.

85 Poutrus, K, 'Ein fixiertes Trauma – Massenvergewaltigungen bei Kriegsende in Berlin', *Feministische Studien* 13/2, 17 March 2017, www.degruyter.com/view/journals/fs/13/2/article-p120.xml (accessed 27 February 2021).

Notes

86 Pohlmann, S, 'Die Frau hinter dem Panzer', 13 June 2011, www.zeit.de/kultur/2011–06/biografie-hannelore-kohl (accessed 27 February 2021).

87 Koenen, *Der Russland-Komplex*, p. 452.

88 *История России XX Век*, p. 163.

89 Jähner, H, *Wolfszeit, Deutschland und die Deutschen 1945–1955*, Rowohlt (2019), p. 312.

90 Koehler, J, *Stasi, The Untold Story of the East German Secret Police*, Westview Press (1999), p. 52.

91 Schattenberg, S, '"Gespräch zweier Taubstummer"? Die Kultur der Außenpolitik Chruščevs und Adenauers Moskaureise 1955', *Osteuropa* (7/2007), p. 44.

92 Kempe, F, *Berlin 1961*, Putnam (2011), p. 247.

93 Ibid., p. 376.

94 Juneau, J-F, 'The limits of linkage: The Nixon administration and Willy Brandt's Ostpolitik', *The International History Review* (June 2011), p. 281.

95 Bösch, F, '1973: Energiewende nach Osten', *Die Zeit*, 10 October 2013, www.zeit.de/2013/42/1973-gas-pipeline-sowjetunion-gazprom (accessed 27 February 2021).

96 Bösch, F, 'Energy diplomacy: West Germany, the Soviet Union and the oil crises of the 1970s', *Historische Sozialforschung* (4/2014), pp. 165–6.

97 Gloger, K, *Fremde Freunde, Deutsche und Russen, Die Geschichte einer schicksalhaften Beziehung*, Berlin Verlag (2017), p. 356.

98 Stent, A, *Russia and Germany Reborn*, Princeton University Press (1999), p. 40.

99 Kornblum, J, 'Reagan's Brandenburg Concerto', *The American Interest*, Summer 2007, p. 27.

100 Macintyre, B, *The Spy and the Traitor*, Viking (2018), pp. 181–6.

101 Mehnert, K, 'Bundeskanzler Helmut Kohl in der UdSSR', *Osteuropa*, Vol. 33, No. 10 (October 1983), p. 752.

102 Kevorkov, V, *Der geheime Kanal: Moskau, der KGB und die Bonner Ostpolitik*, Rowohlt (1995).

103 Wehner, M, 'Zorn und Schmerz', 26 June 2020, www.faz.net/aktuell/politik/ausland/angela-merkels-beziehung-zu-russland-zorn-und-schmerz-16829187.html?premium (accessed 27 February 2021).

104 Morina, C, 'Vernichtungskrieg, Kalter Krieg und politisches Gedächtnis: Zum Umgang mit dem Krieg gegen die Sowjetunion im geteilten Deutschland', *Geschichte und Gesellschaft*, 2/2008, p. 263.

CHAPTER 2

1 Von Herberstein, S, *Rerum Moscoviticarum Commentarii*, translated by R. H, Major (Notes Upon Russia) (1900), Vol. 1, p. 32.

Notes

2 Ibid., p. 32.

3 Geier, W, 'Russische Kulturgeschichte in diplomatischen Reiseberichten aus vier Jahrhunderten', *Studien der Forschungsstelle Ostmitteleuropa an der Universität Dortmund*, Vol. 37, p. 58.

4 Ibid., p. 63.

5 Ibid., p. 94.

6 Mensch Putin!, *ZDF*, 14. March 2015 (17 mins) www.youtube.com/watch?v=r9TM8eoX2Mg (accessed 27 February 2021).

7 See, for example, Scheidegger, G, 'Das Eigene im Bild vom Anderen: Quellenkritische Überlegungen zur russisch-abendländischen Begegnung im 16. und 17. Jahrhundert', *Jahrbücher für Geschichte Osteuropas*, Neue Folge, 3/1987), p. 354.

8 Gloger, p. 68.

9 Schiemann, Th, *Rußland, Polen und Livland bis ins 17.* Jahrhundert (1887), Band 2, p. 294 (G Grotesche Verlagsbuchhandlung).

10 Mangold, C, *Stereotype Darstellung der Russen. Untersuchung des Russlandbildes in Adam Olearius' Reisebericht*, Grin (2015), p. 12.

11 Weber, F. C, *Das veränderte Russland* (1744), p. a3.

12 Jahn, P, *Essay in Unsere Russen Unsere Deutschen*, CH.Links, pp. 16–17.

13 Ibid., p. 17.

14 Ibid., p. 96.

15 Stammler, H, 'Wandlungen des deutschen Bildes vom russischen Menschen', *Jahrbücher für Geschichte Osteuropas*, Neue Folge Bd 5, H 3 (1957), p. 280.

16 De Custine, A, *Letters from Russia*, New York Review Books (2002), p. 101.

17 Ibid., p. 102.

18 Ibid., p. 280.

19 Ibid., p. 138.

20 Starr, S. F, 'August von Haxthausen and Russia', *The Slavonic and East European Review*, Vol. 46, No. 107 (1968), p. 467.

21 Ibid., p. 472.

22 Ibid., p. 146.

23 Von Seydlitz, E, *Geographie: Ausgabe B.* Kleines Lehrbuch (1908), p. 243, quoted in *Unsere Russen Unsere Deutschen*, pp. 25–6.

24 Stammler, p. 290.

25 Koenen, *Der Russland-Komplex,*, p. 44.

26 Decker, G, *Ernst Barlach: Der Schwebende: Eine Biographie*, Siedler (2019), p. 81.

27 Koenen, p. 44.

28 Ibid., p. 139.

29 Ibid., p. 353.

30 Koenen, p. 72.

Notes

31 Social Democrat Friedrich Stampfer's article in Vorwärts published in the summer of 1914 quoted in Kruse, V, *Kriegsgesellschaftliche Moderne. Zur strukturbildenden Dynamik großer Kriege*, Herbert von Halem (2017), p. 132.

32 Paddock, T, 'Creating an Oriental Feindbild', *Central European History*, Vol. 39, No. 2 (2006), p. 239.

33 *Unsere Russen Unsere Deutschen*, p. 29.

34 Koenen, p. 43.

35 Schlögel, K, 'Von der Vergeblichkeit eines Professorenlebens: Otto Hoetzsch und die deutsche Rußlandkunde', *Osteuropa*, 12/2005, p. 9.

36 Koenen, p. 185.

37 Ibid., p. 289.

38 Ibid., p. 350.

39 Достоевский Ф.М, Дневник писателя за 1877 г. (май-июнь), https://fedordostoevsky.ru/works/diary/1877/05-06/07/ (accessed 27 February 2021).

40 Weiss, V, in *Das Alte Denken Der Neuen Rechten*, Zentrum Liberale Moderne (2019), p. 56–7.

41 Templin, W, in *Das Alte Denken Der Neuen Rechten*, Zentrum Liberale Moderne (2019), p. 67.

42 Von Klemperer, K, *Germany's New Conservatism: Its History and Dilemma in the Twentieth Century*, Princeton (1968), p. 213.

43 Koenen, pp. 272–3.

44 Ibid., p. 273.

45 Hitler, A, *Mein Kampf*, Zentralverlag der NSDAP (1943), Vol. 2, p. 742.

46 Ibid., p. 743.

47 Ibid., p. 750.

48 Hoppe, B, *Iron Revolutionaries and Salon Socialists, in Fascination and Enmity*, University of Pittsburgh Press (2012), p. 59.

49 Fritzsche, P, 'Return to Soviet Russia: Edwin Erich Dwinger and the narrative of Barbarossa', in *Fascination and Enmity*, p. 121.

50 Connelly, J, 'Nazis and Slavs: From racial theory to racist practice', *Central European History*, Vol. 32, No. 1 (1999), p. 14.

51 Ibid., p. 16.

52 Zeilmann, K, 'Im Kessel von Stalingrad: Der Krieg am Wendepunkt', *Focus*, 1. September 2014, www.focus.de/wissen/mensch/geschichte/tid-22719/wende-vor-70-jahren-im-kessel-von-stalingrad-der-krieg-am-wendepunkt_aid_638924.html (accessed 27 February).

53 *Unsere Russen Unsere Deutschen*, p. 136.

54 Connelly, p. 18.

55 Koenen, p. 430.

56 Anonyma, *Eine Frau in Berlin*, btb (2005), p. 10.

57 Mehnert, K, *Der Sowjetmensch*, Fischer (1958), p. 30.

58 Konsalik, H, *Der Arzt von Stalingrad*, Kindler Verlag München (1956), p. 21.

59 Crawford, D, 'Dresdner's man in Russia', *Wall Street Journal*, 26 April 2000.

60 Weller, C, *Die Öffentliche Meinung*, Westdeutscher Verlag (2000), p. 22.

61 Winkler, H, *Der lange Weg nach Westen: Deutsche Geschichte vom Dritten Reich bis zur Wiedervereinigung*, C.H. Beck (2002), Vol. 2, pp. 450–1.

62 Koenen, p. 456.

63 Ibid., p. 457.

64 Fücks, R, *Freiheit verteidigen*, Carl Hanser Verlag (2017), p. 25.

Chapter 3

1 See, for example, the arguments of Horst Teltschik, Kohl's foreign policy adviser: Teltschik, H, *Russisches Roulette Vom Kalten Krieg zum Kalten Frieden*, C.H. Beck (2019), pp. 224–33.

2 Spohr, K, 'German re-unification: between official history, academic scholarship and political memoirs', *The Historical Journal* 43:3 (2000).

3 Menge, M, *'Ohne uns läuft nichts mehr' Die Revolution in der DDR*, Deutsche Verlags-Anstalt, Stuttgart (1990), p. 13.

4 Литовкин, В, 'Уроки августа 1994-го. Пришли как победители и освободители, уходили как нежеланные гости', 30 August 2019, https://tass.ru/opinions/6786952 (accessed 27 February).

5 Kohl, H, *Erinnerungen 1990–1994*, Droemer (2007), p. 182.

6 Prokhanov, A, quoted in *Уткин А, Измена генсека: бегство из Европы*, pp. 76–8 of eBook.

7 Ibid., pp. 90–1.

8 'Путин: разделение Германии не имело исторической перспективы', 8 November 2009, www.vesti.ru/doc.html?id=324665 (accessed 27 February).

9 Putin has refused to say what he would have done differently.

10 Primakov, Y, *Годы в Большой Политике*, совершенно секретно (1999), p. 234.

11 *От Первого Лица, Разговоры с Владимиром Путиным*, Москва Вагриус (2000), p. 74.

12 Ibid., p. 70.

13 Ibid. pp. 71–2.

14 'Послание Федеральному Собранию Российской Федерации', 25 April 2005 http://kremlin.ru/events/president/transcripts/22931 (accessed 27 February).

15 Hertle, H-H, *Sofort, unverzüglich, Die Chronik des Mauerfalls*, Ch.Links Verlag, Berlin (2019), Interview mit Mikhail Gorbatschow, p. 47.

16 Adomeit, H, *Imperial Overstretch: Germany in Soviet Policy from Stalin to Gorbachev*, Nomos Verlagsgesellschaft (2016), pp. 206–8.

17 Ibid., p. 153.

18 Hertle, p. 23.

19 Ibid., p. 63.

20 Ibid., p. 65.

21 Sarotte, M E, 'Perpetuating US preeminence: the 1990 deals to "Bribe the Soviets Out" and Move NATO In', *International Security*, 35:1, p. 115.

22 Kohl, p. 164.

23 Schaefer, B, *Mensch Genscher*, Edition Latimeria (2018), p. 116.

24 Stent A, *Russia and Germany Reborn*, Princeton (1999), p. 66.

25 Hertle, p. 17.

26 Ibid. p. 36.

27 Stent, p. 76.

28 Adomeit, p. 389.

29 Sarotte, M. E, *The Collapse, The Accidental Opening of the Berlin Wall*, Basic Books (2014), p. 107.

30 Hertle, p. 97 (Interview with Igor Maksimyshchev, Minister-Counsellor in the Soviet Embassy in East Berlin in November 1989); Ibid., p. 97.

31 Ibid., p. 96.

32 Ibid., p. 108.

33 Sarotte, *The Collapse*, p. 140.

34 Gorbachev told Krenz on 1 November 1989 that Kohl was 'no intellectual luminary, but a petty bourgeois … but nevertheless a skilled and stubborn politician', Hertle, p. 67.

35 Kohl, H, *Erinnerungen 1982–1990*, Droemer (2005), pp. 889–91.

36 Weidenfeld. W, 'Aussenpolitik für die Deutsche Einheit: die Entscheidungsjahre 1989/90' (Band IV) quoted in Spohr, K, p. 875.

37 Ibid., p. 877.

38 Kohl, pp. 181–2.

39 Ibid., p. 183.

40 Adomeit, p. 654.

41 Gaidar, Ye, *Гибель империи*, Российская политическая энциклопедия (2006), p. 212, www.yeltsincenter.ru/sites/default/files/gibel-imperii.pdf (accessed 27 February).

42 G7 pledges Russia $43.4bn, Reuters reported cited in OECD press review, 15 April 1993, www.oecd.org/officialdocuments/publicdisplay documentpdf/?cote=SG/PRB/D(93)71&docLanguage=bi (accessed 27 February).

43 G7 Chairmen's statement on support for Russian reform, Tokyo, 15 April 1993, http://www.g7.utoronto.ca/adhoc/g7chair93.htm (accessed 27 February).

Notes

44 Graham T, *Russia's Decline and Uncertain Recovery*, *Carnegie Endowment for International Peace* (2002), p. 45, https://carnegieendowment.org/files/RussiasDecline.pdf (accessed 27 February 2021).

45 Satter, D, *Darkness at Dawn, The Rise of the Russian Criminal State*, Yale University Press (2003), p. 203.

46 Krone-Schmalz, G, *Russland verstehen, Der Kampf um die Ukraine und Arroganz des Westens'*, C. H. Beck (2015), p. 100.

47 Sarotte M. E, 'A broken promise? What the West really told Moscow about NATO expansion', *Foreign Affairs*, Vol. 93, No. 5, 2014, p. 96.

48 Rühe, V, *Opening NATO's Door, in Open Door NATO and Euro-Atlantic Security After the Cold War*, eds Hamilton and Spohr, SAIS, Johns Hopkins University (2019), p. 224.

49 Interview with John Kornblum, US Ambassador to Germany 1997–2001, February 2020.

50 'Путин рассказал, как Гельмут Коль повлиял на его взгляды', 18 June 2017 www.ntv.ru/novosti/1821780/ (accessed 27 February 2021).

51 Литовкин, В, 'Уроки августа 1994-го. Пришли как победители и освободители, уходили как нежеланные гости', 30 August 2019, https://tass.ru/opinions/6786952 (accessed 27 February 2021).

52 Winkler, H, 'Von der deutschen zur europäischen Frage', *VfZ* 63 (2015), H. 4, p. 478.

53 Von Fritsch, p. 333.

CHAPTER 4

1 Kohl, p. 656.

2 Bresselau von Bressensdorf, A, *Frieden durch Kommunikation, Das System Genscher und die Entspannungspolitik im Zweiten Kalten Krieg 1979–1982/3*, De Gruyter Oldenbourg (2015), pp. 89–90.

3 Deutsch-Russische Städtepartnerschaften im Überblick, www.deutsch-russisches-forum.de/deutsch-russische-staedtepartnerschaften-im-ueber blick/1726141 (accessed 27 February 2021).

4 https://russische-botschaft.ru/de/information/bilaterale-beziehungen/zusammenarbeit-auf-dem-gebiet-der-bildung-forschung-und-innovation en/langfristige-fuer-beide-seiten-vorteilhafte-partnerschaft/ (accessed 27 February 2021).

5 Kohl, H, 'Das vereinte Deutschland und Europas Architektur' ('A united Germany and Europe's Architecture'), *Financial Times*, 29 October 1990, www.helmut-kohl-kas.de (accessed 27 February 2021).

6 Kohl, H, 'Ansprache bei einem Abendessen zu Ehren des russichen Präsidenten Boris N. Jelzin im Palais Schaumburg in Bonn', 21 November 1991, www.helmut-kohl-kas.de (accessed 27 February 2021).

Notes

7   Report by Committee on Legal Affairs and Human Rights on Russia's application for membership of the Council of Europe, doc 7463, 18 January 1996, https://assembly.coe.int/nw/xml/XRef/X2H-Xref-Vie wHTML.asp?FileID=7397&lang=EN (accessed 27 February 2021).

8   Kohl, *Erinnerungen*, p. 719.

9   'Erklärung auf der internationalen Pressekonferenz in Moskau zum Besuch in der Russischen Föderation', 20 February 1996.

10 Yeltsin, B, *Boris Yeltsin, The View From The Kremlin*, HarperCollins (1994), p. 135.

11 'Nein, nein, nein', *Der Spiegel*, 3/1995 pp. 25 and 26.

12 Kohl, Erinnerungen, p. 671.

13 Ibid., p. 672.

14 Erklärung, 20 February 1996.

15 Kohl, *Erinnerungen*, p. 644.

16 Agreement on Partnership. and Co-operation, *Official Journal of the European Communities*, L 327/3, 28 November 1997.

17 Ibid.

18 Гайдар, Е, *Дни поражений и побед*, Вагриус (1997), p. 9.

19 Kohl, *Erinnerungen*, p. 467.

20 Talbott, S, *The Russia Hand*, Random House (2003), p. 224.

21 Kovalev, A, *Russia's Dead End, An Insider's Testimony from Gorbachev to Putin*, Potomac Books (2017), p. 123.

22 At a meeting attended by the author on 22 March 1996 between Russia's Defence Minister Pavel Grachev and the NATO Secretary General Javier Solana, Grachev drew a map. showing the countries between Germany and Russia in what he described as a 'grey zone'.

23 Kohl, H, 'Rede anlässlich des Kolloquiums der Alfred Herrhausen Gesellschaft für internationalen Dialog zum Thema "Russland – was tun?"', 4 July 1997, www.helmut-kohl-kas.de (accessed 27 February 2021).

24 Ibid.

25 Загорский, А, 'От партнёрства к равнодушию? Россия и Германия в Европе', *Институт Европы РАН* (1998), p. 268.

26 Ibid., p. 271.

27 Koalitionsvereinbarung zwischen der Sozialdemokratischen Partei Deutschlands und Bündnis 90/Die Grünen, 20 October 1998 p. 47.

28 'Югославия, далее – везде', https://eurasia.film/2017/03/yugoslaviya-dalee-vezde/ (accessed 27 February 2021).

29 'Wir verraten keinen', Interview with Werner Grossmann, Deputy Head of the GDR State Security Ministry and Head of the Main Directorate Intelligence (HVA) 1986–90, *Der Spiegel*, 5 February 2001, www.spiegel. de/spiegel/print/d-18423339.html (accessed 27 February 2021).

30 Mensch Putin!, *ZDF*, 14 March 2015 (18 mins), www.youtube.com/watch?v=r9TM8eoX2Mg (accessed 27 February 2021).

31 Interview mit Alfred Biolek anlässlich der deutsch-russischen Regierungskonsultationen (ARD), 9 April 2002 (official transcript provided by the Federal Press office).

32 Schröder, G, 'Deutsche Russlandpolitik – europäische Ostpolitik', *Die Zeit*, 5 April 2001.

33 Ibid.

34 Путин В. В. 'Г.Шрёдер и международная политика, Статья Президента России В.Путина. Опубликована в журнале "Форвертс" ("Vorwaerts"), ФРГ', 30 November 2005, http://kremlin.ru/events/president/transcripts/articles/23309 (accessed 28 February 2021).

35 According to one account, he learned the art of recruitment to perfection, see Belton, C, *Putin's People, How the KGB Took Back Russia and Then Took on the West*, William Collins (2020), p. 141.

36 Латухина, К, 'Путин рассказал об опыте работы в КГБ', *Российская Газета*, 10 March 2018, https://rg.ru/2018/03/10/putin-rasskazal-ob-opyte-raboty-v-kgb.html (accessed 27 February 2021).

37 Interview mit Alfred Biolek.

38 Ibid.

39 'Wortprotokoll der Rede Wladimir Putins im Deutschen Bundestag am 25.09.2001', www.bundestag.de/parlament/geschichte/gastredner/putin/putin_wort-244966 (accessed 27 February 2021).

40 'Schröder sieht Russland langfristig in der Nato', 9 August 2001, www.welt.de/print-welt/article466722/Schroeder-sieht-Russland-langfristig-in-der-Nato.html (accessed 27 February 2021).

41 'Der Irak Konflikt – Der Weg in den Krieg (Archiv), Regierungserklärung am 13 February 2003 vor dem Bundestag', www.lpb-bw.de/irak-konflikt (accessed 27 February 2021).

42 Gordon, P, '"Punish France, Ignore Germany, Forgive Russia" No Longer Fits', 1 September 2007, www.brookings.edu/opinions/punish-france-ignore-germany-forgive-russia-no-longer-fits/ (accessed 27 February 2021).

43 'Gerhard Schroeder's dangerous liaison', *Spiegel Online*, 1 December 2004, www.spiegel.de/international/moscow-mon-amour-gerhard-schroeders-dangerous-liaison-a-330461.html (accessed 27 February 2021).

44 'Schröder stärkt Putin den Rücken: "Verstehe die Aufregung um Yukos nicht"', *Frankfurter Allgemeine Zeitung*, 9 July 2004.

45 'Lobbyistin im Land der Zaren', *Der Spiegel*, 12 December 2003, www.spiegel.de/wirtschaft/russland-lobbyistin-im-land-der-zaren-a-277994.html (accessed 27 February 2021).

Notes

46 Rede von Bundeskanzler Gerhard Schröder auf der Deutsch-Russischen Investitionskonferenz am 28. Oktober 2004 in Stuttgart.

47 *Hamburger Abendblatt*, 23 November 2004, www.abendblatt.de/politik/ deutschland/article106930893/Schroeder-Putin-ist-lupenreiner-Demok rat.html (accessed 27 February 2021).

48 *Die Zeit*, 5 April 2001.

49 Загорский, А, 'Россия и Германия: преемственность и перемены', *IFRI,Russia.Cei.Visions* n°6(a), 2005, p. 9.

50 See Schröder's statement in Parliament on 24 November 2004, pp. 13022–23.

51 Spanger, p. 7.

52 The Schröders adopted a 3-year-old girl in 2004 and a baby boy in 2006, www.faz.net/aktuell/gesellschaft/menschen/persoenlich-ehepaar-schroeder-adoptiert-zweites-russisches-kind-1356851.html (accessed 27 February 2021).

53 Beunderman, M, 'Germany and Lithuania clash over Russian gas pipeline', *EU Observer*, 26 October 2005, https://euobserver.com/eco nomic/20183 (accessed 27 February 2021).

54 'Schröder defends pipeline project', *Deutsche Welle*, 26 October 2005, www.dw.com/en/schr%C3%B6der-defends-pipeline-project/a-1753658 (accessed 27 February).

55 'Regierungsprogramm Deutschlands', www.kas.de/upload/ACDP/CD U/Programme_Bundestag/2005–2009_Regierungsprogramm_Deutsch lands-Chancen-nutzen_Wachstum-Arbeit-Sicherheit.pdf (accessed 27 February).

56 'Gemeinsam für Deutschland – mit Mut und Menschlichkeit, Koalitionsvertrag zwischen CDU, CSU und SPD', www.kas.de/upload/ ACDP/CDU/Koalitionsvertraege/Koalitionsvertrag2005.pdf (accessed 27 February).

57 Rede von Bundeskanzlerin Dr. 'Angela Merkel in der Plenarveranstaltung des 'Petersburger Dialogs', 10 October 2006.

58 Gutschker, T, 'Nüchterne Ostpolitik', *Die Politische Meinung* (445), December 2006, p. 9.

59 Ibid.

60 Rahr, A, 'Germany and Russia: a special relationship', *The Washington Quarterly* (Spring 2007), p. 141.

61 Lough, J, 'Russia's energy diplomacy', Chatham House Briefing Paper, May 2011, www.chathamhouse.org/sites/default/files/19352_0511bp_ lough.pdf (accessed 27 February 2021).

62 Weiland, S, 'Merkel macht Kaczynski Zugeständnisse im Gas-Streit', *Der Spiegel*, 30 October 2006, www.spiegel.de/jahreschronik/a-451961.html (accessed 27 February 2021).

63 Путин, В, 'Выступление и дискуссия на Мюнхенской конференции по вопросам политики безопасности', 10 February 2007, http://krem lin.ru/events/president/transcripts/24034 (accessed 27 February 2021).

64 'Rede des Außenministers Frank-Walter Steinmeier am Institut für internationale Beziehungen der Ural-Universität in Jekaterinburg', 13 May 2008, www.auswaertiges-amt.de/de/newsroom/080513-bm-russ land/219750 (accessed 27 February 2021).

65 Ibid.

66 'Merkel says Russia's actions in Georgia "Disproportionate"', www.dw. com/en/merkel-says-russias-actions-in-georgia-disproportionate/a-356 5127 (accessed 27 February 2021).

67 'Выступление на встрече с представителями политических, парламентских и общественных кругов Германии', 5 June 2008, http://kremlin.ru/events/president/transcripts/320 (accessed 27 February 2021).

68 'Steinmeier will keine Sanktionen', *Frankfurter Allgemeine Zeitung*, 28 August 2008.

69 'Kritik ja, aber Sanktionen?', *Die Zeit*, 1 September 2008, www.zeit. de/online/2008/36/russland-georgien-eu-gipfel (accessed 27 February 2021).

70 'Independent International Fact-Finding Mission on the Conflict in Georgia' (2009), p. 24, www.echr.coe.int/Documents/HUDOC_38263_ 08_Annexes_ENG.pdf (accessed 27 February 2021).

71 'Rede von Bundeskanzlerin Dr. Angela Merkel im Rahmen der Plenarveranstaltung des achten Petersburger Dialogs, 2 October 2008', www.bundesregierung.de/breg-de/service/bulletin/rede-von-bundeska nzlerin-dr-angela-merkel-796262 (accessed 27 February 2021).

72 'The Russo-Ukrainian gas dispute of January 2009: a comprehensive assessment', Oxford Institute for Energy Studies, February 2009, p. 22.

73 'Koalitionsvertrag zwischen CDU, CSU und FDP', 17. Legislaturperiode, p. 120.

74 'Russland bleibt strategischer Partner', *Handelsblatt*, 20 November 2009, www.handelsblatt.com/politik/international/westerwelle-in-mos kau-russland-bleibt-strategischer-partner/3308460.html?ticket=ST-905 6392-Ut2GUNJfhaErUNbBDpdH-ap3 (accessed 27 February 2021).

75 See, for example, 'Rede von Außenminister Guido Westerwelle zur Eröffnung des ersten Walter-Scheel-Forums', 4 December 2012, www. auswaertiges-amt.de/de/newsroom/121204-bm-w-scheel-forum/252688 (accessed 27 February 2021).

76 Fix, L, 'A new German power in Europe?', unpublished doctoral dissertation (2019), p. 97.

77 Meister, S, 'An alienated partnership, German–Russian relations after Putin's return', The Finish Institute of International Affairs (2012), p. 7.

78 'Koalitionsvertrag zwischen CDU, CSU und SPD', 18. Legislaturperiode, p. 118, www.cdu.de/sites/default/files/media/dokumente/koalitionsvertrag.pdf (accessed 27 February 2021).

79 Ibid., p. 118.

80 'Rede von Bundeskanzlerin Angela Merkel anlässlich der Jubiläumsveranstaltung "60 Jahre Ost-Ausschuss der Deutschen Wirtschaft"', 25 October 2012, www.bundesregierung.de/ContentArchiv/DE/Archiv17/Reden/2012/10/2012–10–25-merkel-60-jahre-ostausschuss.html (accessed 27 February 2021).

81 'Antrag der Fraktionen der CDU/CSU und FDP, Durch Zusammenarbeit Zivilgesellschaft und Rechstaatlichkeit in Russland stärken', 6 November 2012.

82 '"Russland braucht keine verordneten Vereine"', Spiegel Online, 10 July 2007, www.spiegel.de/politik/deutschland/russland-beauftragter-schockenhoff-russland-braucht-keine-verordneten-vereine-a-425349.html (accessed 27 February 2021).

83 'Заседание международного дискуссионного клуба "Валдай"', 19 September 2013, http://kremlin.ru/events/president/news/19243 (accessed 27 February 2021).

84 Grant, C, 'Is the EU to blame for the crisis in Ukraine?', 1 June 2016, www.cer.eu/insights/eu-blame-crisis-ukraine (accessed 27 February 2021).

85 Medvedev, D, interviews to television channels Channel One, Russia, and NTV, 31 August 2008, http://en.kremlin.ru/events/president/transcripts/48301 (accessed 27 February 2021).

86 Lough, J, 'The place of Russia's "Near Abroad"', F32 Conflict Studies Research Centre, January 1993.

87 'Стенографический отчет о встрече с участниками международного клуба "Валдай"', 12 September 2008, http://kremlin.ru/events/president/transcripts/1383 (accessed 27 February 2021).

88 Bucharest Summit Declaration, 3 April 2008, www.nato.int/cps/ua/natohq/official_texts_8443.htm (accessed 27 February 2021).

89 'Barroso: Without EU enlargement, Russia would have gobbled up Bulgaria, the Baltics', Euractiv, 29 October 2014, www.euractiv.com/section/global-europe/news/barroso-without-eu-enlargement-russia-would-have-gobbled-up-bulgaria-the-baltics/ (accessed 27 February 2021).

90 'Ответы на вопросы Альфреда Биолека во время совместного с Федеральным канцлером ФРГ Герхардом Шредером интервью в эфире программы "Бульвар Био" телеканала АРД', 9 April 2002,

http://special.kremlin.ru/events/president/transcripts/24576 (accessed 27 February 2021).

91 See for example, 'Strategie ist möglich: Diplomat Huterer über Deutschlands Ostpolitik', *Osteuropa* (2013), Vol. 63, No. 2/3, p. 271.

92 Pörzgen, G, 'Auf der Suche nach der verlorenen Kompetenz', *Osteuropa*, 59 Jg., 9/2009 p. 7.

93 'Von der Leyen beendet Ära der Abrüstung', *Handelsblatt*, 20 May 2016, www.handelsblatt.com/politik/deutschland/bundeswehr-von-der-leyen-beendet-aera-der-abruestung/13573068.html?ticket=ST-9554766-bELM p7fNvo6QedX9fGb1-ap3 (accessed 27 February 2021).

94 Pörzgen, G, 'Das Russlandbild in den deutschen Medien', 9 May 2018 www.bpb.de/internationales/europa/russland/47998/russlandbild-deu tscher-medien (accessed 27 February 2021).

CHAPTER 5

1 'Янукович пожаловался Меркель на "очень сильную Россию"', 29 November 2013 https://lb.ua/news/2013/11/29/243250_yanukovich_ pozhalovalsya_merkel.html (accessed 27 February 2021).

2 'Politics of brutal pressure', *The Economist*, www.economist.com/ea stern-approaches/2013/11/22/politics-of-brutal-pressure (accessed 27 February 2021).

3 Мишка, Я, Умланд, А, 'ЕС и российско-украинский конфликт', *Экономика*, 28 January 2014, http://economica.com.ua/vlast/arti cle/24738475.html (accessed 27 February 2021).

4 'Rede von Außenminister Frank-Walter Steinmeier bei der Amtsübergabe im Auswärtigen Amt am 17 December 2013', www.auswaertiges-amt.de/ de/newsroom/131217-bm-antrittsrede/258728 (accessed 28 February 2021).

5 'Deutschlands Rolle in der Welt: Anmerkungen zu Verantwortung, Normen und Bündnissen', Opening speech at the Munich Security Conference, 31 January 2014, www.bundespraesident.de/SharedDocs/ Reden/DE/Joachim-Gauck/Reden/2014/01/140131-Muenchner-Siche rheitskonferenz.html (accessed 28 February 2021).

6 'О вводе и выводах, Владимир Путин изложил свою позицию по событиям на Украине', 5 March 2014, https://rg.ru/2014/03/04/ putin-site.html (accessed 28 February 2021).

7 Umland, A, 'Sind die rechtsradikalen Minister der ukrainischen Regierung "Faschisten"?', 28 March 2014, www.boell.de/de/2014/03/28/ rechtsradikalen-minister-ukrainischen-regierung-faschisten (accessed 28 February 2021).

8 'Жириновский предложил Польше поделить Украину', *BBC News Русская Служба*, 24 March 2014, www.bbc.com/russian/intern

ational/2014/03/140324_zhirinovsky_poland_ukraine (accessed 28 February 2021).

9 'Regierungserklärung von Bundeskanzlerin Merkel', 13 March 2014, www.bundeskanzlerin.de/bkin-de/aktuelles/regierungserklaerung-von-bundeskanzlerin-merkel-443682 (accessed 28 February 2021).

10 Ibid.

11 'Ukraine – Es gibt nur den Weg der Diplomatie, Rede von Gregor Gysi', 13 March 2014, www.linksfraktion.de/parlament/reden/detail/ukraine-es-gibt-nur-den-weg-der-diplomatie/ (accessed 28 February 2021).

12 'Ohne Russland geht es nicht, Beitrag von Außenminister Frank-Walter Steinmeier zur Münchner Sicherheitskonferenz. Erschienen in der Zeitschrift Focus', 27 January 2014, www.auswaertiges-amt.de/de/newsroom/140127-bm-focus-muesiko/259394 (accessed 28 February 2021).

13 Council Regulation (EU) No. 833/2014, 31 July 2014 concerning restrictive measures in view of Russia's actions destabilising the situation in Ukraine, https://eur-lex.europa.eu/legal-content/EN/TXT/?uri=uriserv:OJ.L_.2014.229.01.0001.01.ENG (accessed 28 February 2021).

14 'US sanctions on Russia, Congressional Research Service', 17 January 2020, p. 33, https://fas.org/sgp/crs/row/R45415.pdf (accessed 28 February 2021).

15 'Diskussion mit Bundeskanzlerin Merkel am Lowy Institut für Internationale Politik', 17 November 2014, www.bundeskanzlerin.de/bkin-de/aktuelles/diskussion-mit-bundeskanzlerin-merkel-am-lowy-institut-fuer-internationale-politik-844530 (accessed 28 February 2021).

16 *Financial Times*, 2 February 2015.

17 Ibid.

18 Ibid.

19 Report on the human rights situation in Ukraine, 15 December 2014, Office of the United Nations High Commissioner for Human Rights, pp. 4 and 8, www.ohchr.org/Documents/Countries/UA/OHCHR_eighth_report_on_Ukraine.pdf (accessed 28 February 2021).

20 'Rede von Außenminister Frank-Walter Steinmeier an der Ural Federal University, Jekaterinburg: "Deutsche und Russen – Vergangenheit, Gegenwart, Zukunft"', 9 December 2014.

21 'Putins Vorgehen ist verständlich', *Die Zeit*, 27 March 2014, www.zeit.de/2014/14/helmut-schmidt-russland/komplettansicht (accessed 28 February 2021).

22 'Kohl kritisiert Isolation Russlands', *FAZ.net*, 2 November 2014, www.faz.net/aktuell/politik/ausland/ukraine-konflikt-kohl-kritisiert-isolation-russlands-13243364.html (accessed 28 February 2021).

23 Genscher, H-D, 'Ukraine-Krise: Von Entschärfung weit entfernt', *Handelsblatt* (244), 20. November 2014, p. 4.

24 'Sanktionen und Isolation bringen nichts', Interview mit SonntagsBlick (Schweiz) und Welt am Sonntag (Deutschland), 11 May 2014, https://ger hard-schroeder.de/2014/05/11/russland-ukraine/ (accessed 28 February 2021).

25 Sirleschtov, A, 'Verbotene Liebe: Das große Geschäft mit Russland', *Der Tagesspiegel*, 6 May 2014, www.tagesspiegel.de/themen/agenda/ukraine-krise-und-die-wirtschaft-verbotene-liebe-das-grosse-geschaeft-mit-russla nd/9847288.html (accessed 28 February 2021).

26 'Ulrich Grillo: Sanktionen sind geboten', *Handelsblatt*, 28 August 2014.

27 Gersemann, O, Jost, S, 'Es gilt das Primat der Politik', *Die Welt*, 18 May 2014, www.welt.de/print/wams/wirtschaft/article128129431/Es-gilt-das-Primat-der-Politik.html (accessed 28 February 2021).

28 'Der nächste Putin-Versteher', *Handelsblatt*, 27 March 2014, www. handelsblatt.com/politik/international/siemens-chef-kaeser-in-der-kri tik-der-naechste-putin-versteher/9674620.html (accessed 28 February 2021).

29 'Battle for Ukraine: How the west lost Putin', *Financial Times*, 2 February 2015, www.ft.com/content/e3ace220-a252-11e4-9630-00144feab7de (accessed 28 February 2021).

30 'Иловайский котел, пять лет спустя. Что нужно знать об одной из самых трагичных страниц войны на Донбассе', *Новое Время*, 20 August 2019 https://nv.ua/ukraine/events/ato-donbass-ilovayskiy-kotel-godovshchina-tragedii-50037442.html (accessed 28 February 2021).

31 See Forensic Architecture's investigation, 19 August 2019, https://fo rensic-architecture.org/investigation/the-battle-of-ilovaisk (accessed 28 February 2021).

32 German diplomatic sources.

33 Allan, D, 'The Minsk Conundrum: Western Policy and Russia's War in Eastern Ukraine' (2020), p. 10, www.chathamhouse.org/publication/ minsk-conundrum-allan (accessed 28 February 2021).

34 Traynor, I, 'Putin claims Russian forces 'could conquer Ukraine capi-tal in two weeks', *Guardian*, 1 September 2015, www.theguardian.com/ world/2014/sep/02/putin-russian-forces-could-conquer-ukraine-capital-kiev-fortnight (accessed 28 February 2021).

35 'ATO troops destroy rebels' TOS-1 "Buratino" heavy flamethrower system', *ATO News* (Ministry of Defence of Ukraine), 2 February 2015, www.mil.gov.ua/en/news/2015/02/04/ato-news-ato-troops-destroy-re bels-tos-1-%E2%80%98buratino-heavy-flamethrower-system/ (accessed 28 February 2021).

36 Wagstyl, S, Chassany, A-S and Hille, K, 'Merkel and Hollande fly to Kiev and Moscow', *Financial Times*, www.ft.com/content/6a80c702-ad5d-11e4-a5c1-00144feab7de (accessed 28 February 2021).

37 Giles, K, Sherr, J and Seaboyer, A, 'Russian reflexive control', report prepared for Defence Research and Development Canada, October 2018, p. 19.

38 Baev, P, 'Ukraine: a test for Russian military reforms', *Russie.Nei.Reports*, No. 19 (2015), p. 13.

39 'Wieder Krieg in Europa? Nicht in unserem Namen!', *Die Zeit*, 5 December 2014, www.zeit.de/politik/2014–12/aufruf-russland-dialog (accessed 28 February 2021).

40 'Friedenssicherung statt Expansionsbelohnung', *Die Zeit*, 11 December 2014, www.zeit.de/politik/2014–12/aufruf-friedenssicherung-statt-expa nsionsbelohnung (accessed 28 February 2021).

41 Beyer, S, "Ein schamloser Angriff", *Der Spiegel*, 5 May 2014, www.spiegel. de/spiegel/print/d-126830940.html (accessed 28 February 2021).

42 Allan, p. 13.

43 von Salzen, C, 'Neue Alte Ostpolitik', *Der Tagesspiegel*, 12 January 2016, www.tagesspiegel.de/themen/agenda/deutscher-vorsitz-in-der-osze-ne ue-alte-ostpolitik/12816054.html (accessed 28 February 2021).

44 von Salzen, C, 'Diplomatischer Eklat in Kiew', *Der Tagesspeigel*, 8 February 2015, www.tagesspiegel.de/politik/ukraine-und-deutschland-diplomati scher-eklat-in-kiew/19365674.html (accessed 28 February 2021).

45 von Salzen, C, "Ein politischer Schaden", *Zeit Online*, 4 February 2016, www.zeit.de/politik/2016–02/ein-politischer-schaden (accessed 28 February 2021).

46 Issig, P, 'In Moskau wird Seehofer zum Putin-Versteher', *Die Welt*, 3 February 2016, www.welt.de/politik/deutschland/article151819684/ In-Moskau-wird-Seehofer-zum-Putin-Versteher.html (accessed 28 February 2021).

47 'Steinmeier kritisiert Nato-Militärübung', *Zeit Online*, 18 June 2016, www. zeit.de/politik/ausland/2016–06/frank-walter-steinmeier-nato-manoev er-russland-abruestung (accessed 28 February 2021).

48 'Politik überschattet Wirtschaftsgespräche in Moskau', *DW*, 22 September 2016, www.dw.com/de/politik-%C3%BCberschattet-wirtsc haftsgespr%C3%A4che-in-moskau/a-19568448 (accessed 28 February 2021).

49 Ibid.

50 Hoffmann, C and Schult, C, 'Wer ist gefährlicher für den Weltfrieden: Trump oder Putin?' *Der Spiegel*, 14 April 2018, www.spiegel.de/spie gel/heiko-maas-kritisiert-donald-trump-a-1202784.html (accessed 28 February 2021).

51 'Reducing European Dependence on Russian Gas: distinguishing nat ural gas security from geopolitics', The Oxford Institute For Energy Studies, October 2014 p. 3.

Notes

52 'Встреча с вице-канцлером, министром экономики и энергетики ФРГ Зигмаром Габриэлем', 28 October 2015, www.kremlin.ru/events/president/news/50582 (accessed 28 February 2021).

53 Wehner, M, 'Ein äußerst politisches Projekt', *FAZ.net*, 15 April 2018 www.faz.net/aktuell/politik/merkels-sinneswandel-im-fall-der-gasleitung-nord-stream-2–15540994.html?premium (accessed 28 February 2021).

54 Naftogaz data: https://naftogaz-europe.com/article/en/naturalgastransitviaukraine2018 (accessed 28 February 2021).

55 Arbeitsgemeinschaft Energiebilanzen e.V, Evaluation Tables of the Energy Balance for Germany (March 2020), p. 10.

56 BP Statistical Review 2019 – UK Energy Market in 2018, www.bp.com/content/dam/bp/business-sites/en/global/corporate/pdfs/energy-economics/statistical-review/bp-stats-review-2019-uk-insights.pdf (accessed 28 February 2021).

57 'Arbeitsgemeinschaft Energiebilanzen e.V', Energy Consumption in Germany in 2018, p. 14.

58 Ibid., p. 4.

59 Neumann, A, Göke, L, Holz, F, Kemfert, C, and von Hirschhausen, C, 'Natural gas supply: no need for another Baltic Sea pipeline', *DIW Weekly Report*, 4 July 2018, www.diw.de/documents/publikationen/73/diw_01.c.593663.de/dwr-18–27–1.pdf (accessed 28 February 2021).

60 Brügmann, M, 'Sberbank entlässt Analysten nach kritischem Bericht über Gazprom', *Handelsblatt*, 24 May 2018, www.handelsblatt.com/finanzen/banken-versicherungen/russisches-geldhaus-sberbank-entlaesst-analysten-nach-kritischem-bericht-ueber-gazprom/22598516.html (accessed 28 February 2021).

61 'Во сколько обойдется России и Европе "Северный поток-2"', *DW*, 7 March 2018.

62 Roth, A, 'Ukraine walks out of Europe human rights body as Russia returns', *Guardian*, 25 June 2019, www.theguardian.com/law/2019/jun/25/ukraine-walks-out-council-europe-human-rights-assembly-protest-russia-return (accessed 28 February 2021).

63 Foreign Affairs Council, 14 March 2016, www.consilium.europa.eu/en/meetings/fac/2016/03/14/# (accessed 28 February 2021).

64 International Monetary Fund, Russian Federation, Staff Report for the 2015 Article IV Consultation, July 2 2015, p. 5, www.imf.org/external/pubs/ft/scr/2015/cr15211.pdf (accessed 28 February 2021). Four years after its publication, the Swedish economist Anders Aslund stated that the IMF estimate remained the best estimate of the impact of sanctions. Aslund A, 'Putin finally tells Russians the truth (sort of)', UkraineAlert, 27 June 2019, www.atlanticcouncil.org/blogs/ukrainealert/putin-finally-tells-russians-the-truth-sort-of/.

Notes

65 'Путин заявил, что санкции мешают развитию России в сфере энергетики', *РИА Новости*, 9 April 2019, ria.ru/20190409/1552518677. html (accessed 28 February 2021).

66 'Das steckt hinter dem Hackerangriff aufs Regierungsnetz', *Der Spiegel*, 1 March 2018, www.spiegel.de/netzwelt/netzpolitik/regierungsnetz-geha ckt-wer-steckt-dahinter-und-was-passiert-jetzt-a-1195914.html (accessed 28 February 2021).

67 'Suspected assassin in the Berlin killing used fake identity documents', *Bellingcat*, 30 August 2019, www.bellingcat.com/news/uk-and-europe/2019/08/30/suspected-assassin-in-the-berlin-killing-used-fa ke-identity-documents/ (accessed 28 February 2021).

68 Jansen, F, and von Salzen, C, 'Merkel rechtfertigt Ausweisung russis-cher Diplomaten', *Tagesspiegel*, 4 December 2019, www.tagesspiegel.de/ politik/mord-an-georgier-in-berlin-merkel-rechtfertigt-ausweisung-russi scher-diplomaten/25298820.html (accessed 28 February 2021).

69 Krone-Schmalz, G, *Russland verstehen*, C.H. Beck (2015), p. 28.

70 Teltschik, H, *Russisches Roulette*, C.H. Beck (2019), p. 211.

71 Ibid, p. 224.

72 Ibid. p. 223.

73 Ibid. p. 160.

74 'Fool me once', *The Economist*, 23 April 2016, www.economist.com/ europe/2016/04/23/fool-me-once (accessed 28 February 2021).

75 Traynor, I and Wintour, P, 'Ukraine crisis: Vladimir Putin has lost the plot, says German Chancellor', 3 March 2014, www.theguardi an.com/world/2014/mar/03/ukraine-vladimir-putin-angela-merkel-ru ssian (accessed 28 February 2021).

76 Von Fritsch, R, *Russlands Weg*, Aufbau (2020), p. 113.

77 'Merkel stellt Bedingungen für Nord Stream 2', *ntv*, 10 April 2018, www.n-tv.de/wirtschaft/Merkel-stellt-Bedingungen-fuer-Nord-Stream-2-article20377801.html (accessed 28 February 2021).

78 Chazan, G, 'Angela Merkel stands firm on Nord Stream 2 despite Navalny poisoning', *Financial Times*, 23 September 2020, www.ft.com/ content/a26cacdf-7238–4417-b0b7–696eeeeb239c (accessed 28 February 2021).

79 Karntischnig, M, 'Trump, Biden and the "f****** Germans"', *Politico*, 20 October 2020, www.politico.eu/article/donald-trump-joe-biden-angela-merkel-us-germany-transatlantic-relationship/ (accessed 28 February 2021).

80 Presentation during Chatham House discussion on Nord Stream 2 on 27 October 2020.

81 Sherr, J, 'Memorandum submitted to the Defence Committee Inquiry of the UK Parliament "Russia: a new confrontation?"', 23 February

Notes

2009, https://publications.parliament.uk/pa/cm200809/cmselect/cmd fence/memo/russia/ucr1302.htm (accessed 28 February 2021).

82 See, for example, 'Белоруссия прекратила реэкспорт санкционной продукции в Россию', *Ведомости*, 1 April 2019, www.vedomosti.ru/business/news/2019/04/01/797966-belorussiya (accessed 28 February 2021).

CHAPTER 6

1 Calculations based on data quoted by the Ost-Auschuss Osteuropaverein, www.oaoev.de/sites/default/files/page_files/Deutscher%20Osthandel%202019.pdf (accessed 28 February 2021).

2 Calculations based on World Bank Group data.

3 Королева, А, 'Доля сырья в российской экономике достигла абсолютного рекорда', *Эксперт Online*, 18 February 2020.

4 'Треть доходов бюджетной системы России оказалась связана с нефтью и газом', 22 August 2019, www.rbc.ru/economics/22/08/2019/5d555e4b9a7947aed7a185de (accessed 28 February 2021).

5 Russland-Update, Ost-Ausschuss Osteuropaverein, December 2019, p. 6, www.oaoev.de/sites/default/files/page_files/OAOEV_Russland-Update-Dez2019.pdf (accessed 28 February 2021).

6 Ibid., p. 6.

7 'Handel mit der Sowjetunion', *Die Zeit*, 7 July 1955, www.zeit.de/1955/27/handel-mit-der-sowjetunion (accessed 28 February 2021).

8 Spaulding, R, 'German trade policy in Eastern Europe, 1890–1990: preconditions for applying international trade leverage', *International Organization*, 1991 (45/3), p. 346.

9 Calculation based on Gazprom Export data, www.gazpromexport.ru/statistics/.

10 Calculation based on Fitch estimates. See Титова, Ю, 'Цунами для «Газпрома»: как компания лишилась более $10 млрд за пять месяцев', *Forbes.ru*, 9 July 2020, www.forbes.ru/biznes/404655-cunami-dlya-gazproma-kak-kompaniya-lishilas-bolee-10-mlrd-za-pyat-mesyacev (accessed 28 February 2021).

11 See Szabo, F, *Germany, Russia and the Rise of Geo-Economics*, Bloomsbury (2015).

12 'Der deutsche Außenhandel im Jahr 2012', *Statistisches Bundesamt, Wirtschaft und Statistik*, May 2013, p. 349.

13 Ibid. p. 351.

14 Statistisches Bundesamt (Destatis) 2020, www.oaoev.de/sites/default/files/page_files/Top-20-Handelspartner%20Deutschlands%202019.pdf (accessed 28 February 2021).

15 Domínguez-Jiménez, M and Poitiers, N, 'FDI another day: Russian reliance on European investment, Policy Contribution 03/2020', *Bruegel*, www.bruegel.org/wp-content/uploads/2020/02/PC-03_2020_-1.pdf (accessed 28 February 2021).

16 World Bank data, https://data.worldbank.org/indicator/NY.GDP.MKTP.KD.ZG?locations=RU (accessed 28 February 2021).

17 'Доля государства в экономике РФ превысила 50% и препятствует развитию конкуренции, ТАСС', 6 May 2019, https://fas.gov.ru/publications/18306 (accessed 28 February 2021).

18 See, for example, 'Кудрин заявил о застое в экономике России', 11 July 2020, www.rbc.ru/economics/11/07/2020/5f09bc599a794712f299 75c5 (accessed 28 February 2021).

19 'Счетная палата раскритиковала проект бюджета на три года', 14 October 2019, www.rbc.ru/economics/14/10/2019/5da448199a794741e ae1180b (accessed 28 February 2021).

20 Calculations based on data quoted by the Ost-Auschuss Osteuropaverein, www.oaoev.de/sites/default/files/page_files/Deutscher%20Osthandel %202019.pdf (accessed 28 February 2021).

21 Calculation from data in 2019 BP Statistical Review, www.bp.com/ content/dam/bp/business-sites/en/global/corporate/pdfs/energy-eco nomics/statistical-review/bp-stats-review-2019-full-report.pdf (accessed 28 February 2021).

22 'Verteilung der Erdgasbezugsquellen Deutschlands im Jahr 2017', *destatis*, 13 September 2018, https://de.statista.com/statistik/daten/ studie/151871/umfrage/erdgasbezug-deutschlands-aus-verschiedenen-la endern/ (accessed 28 February 2021).

23 These volumes peaked in 2019 at around 1.2 million tonnes, 'Import von Flüssiggas nach Deutschland in den Jahren 1995 bis 2019', *destatis*, 7 April 2020, https://de.statista.com/statistik/daten/studie/28824/umfrage/ import-von-fluessiggas-in-deutschland-seit-1995/ (accessed 28 February 2021).

24 Gustafson, T, *The Bridge*, Harvard University Press (2020), p. 360.

25 Bros, A, Mitrova, T and Westphal, K, 'German-Russian Gas Relations, A Special Relationship in Troubled Waters', *Stiftung Wissenschaft und Politik*, December 2017, p. 30, www.swp-berlin.org/fileadmin/contents/prod ucts/research_papers/2017RP13_wep_EtAl.pdf (accessed 28 February 2021).

26 'Выступление на IV ежегодном экономическом Форуме руководителей и топ-менеджеров ведущих германских компаний', 26 November 2010, http://archive.premier.gov.ru/events/news/13118/ (accessed 28 February 2021).

27 Putin, W, 'Von Lissabon bis Wladiwostok', *Süddeutsche Zeitung*, 25 November 2010, www.sueddeutsche.de/wirtschaft/putin-plaedoyer-fu er-wirtschaftsgemeinschaft-von-lissabon-bis-wladiwostok-1.1027908-0# seite-4 (accessed 28 February 2021).

28 Ibid.

29 'Misstöne überschatten Putins Berlin-Besuch', *Handelsblatt*, 26. November 2011, www.handelsblatt.com/politik/international/sackga sse-bei-kooperation-misstoene-ueberschatten-putins-berlin-besuch/364 8840.html (accessed 28 February 2021).

30 Gustafson, p. 371.

31 See, for example, Павел Одеров: 'От Европы до Азии', 'Газпром', *ноябрь*, 2012, p. 11.

32 Eich, R, 'Das sowjetische Öl auf dem Weltmarkt', *Ost-Probleme*, Vol. 14, No. 8 (1962), p. 237.

33 Ibid., p. 178.

34 'RWE sieht Gasversorgung der Ukraine weiter kritisch', *Handelsblatt*, 26 May 2014, www.handelsblatt.com/unternehmen/energie/nach-praesidentschaftswahl-rwe-sieht-gasversorgung-der-ukraine-weiter-kriti sch/9949140.html (accessed 28 February 2021).

35 Stratmann, S, 'Deutsche helfen Russen beim Energiesparen', *Handelsblatt*, 25 February 2009.

36 Willershausen, F, 'Energiesparen für Anfänger', *Handelsblatt*, 29 November 2011, www.handelsblatt.com/technik/energie-umwelt/russl and-energiesparen-fuer-anfaenger/5870558-all.html (accessed 28 February 2021).

37 'Russische Föderation – Wirtschaftliche Beziehungen, Bundesministerium für Wirtschaft und Energie', www.bmwi.de/Redaktion/DE/Artikel/ Aussenwirtschaft/laendervermerk-russische-foerderation.html (accessed 28 February 2021).

38 Positionspapier: Schrittweise aus der Krise, Ost-Ausschuss, 25 June 2017.

39 Russische Föderation – Wirtschaftliche Beziehungen (BMWi).

40 'Weniger deutsche Firmen in Russland', *AHK Russland Pressemeldung*, 9 January 2020, https://russland.ahk.de/infothek/news/detail/weniger-deutsche-firmen-in-russland (accessed 28 February 2021).

41 Positionspapier: Gemeinsame Interessen definieren – gemeinsame Projekte umsetzen, Ost-Ausschuss/Osteuropaverein der Deutschen Wirtschaft (2019).

42 Crawford, D, 'Geheimsache Korruption', *Correctiv* (2020), p. 63.

43 'Five charged in German-Russian money-laundering case', *Reuters*, 14 December 2011.

44 Kehoe Down, A, 'Deutsche Bank: Lawbreaking Likely in Russian Laundromat', 17 April 2019, www.occrp.org/en/daily/9588-deutsche-

bank-lawbreaking-likely-in-russian-laundromat-2 (accessed 28 February 2021).

45 Financial Conduct Authority (FCA) press release: FCA fines Deutsche Bank £163 million for serious anti-money laundering controls failings, 31 January 2017, www.fca.org.uk/news/press-releases/fca-fines-deutsche-bank-163-million-anti-money-laundering-controls-failure (accessed 28 February 2021).

46 Ostrovsky, A, 'Putin aide calls Yukos asset sale "scam of the year"', *Financial Times*, 28 December 2004, www.ft.com/content/f2709f22-590b-11d9-89a5-00000e2511c8 (accessed 28 February 2021).

47 'Complaint by the United States Securities and Exchange Commission v Siemens AG', 12 December 2008, www.sec.gov/litigation/compl aints/2008/comp20829.pdf (accessed 28 February 2021).

48 Ibid.

49 'Wirtschaft steht hinter Merkels Sanktionsdrohungen (dpa)', *Handelsblatt*, 14 March 2014, www.handelsblatt.com/politik/deutschland/krim-krise-wirtschaft-steht-hinter-merkels-sanktionsdrohungen/9618764.html (accessed 28 February 2021).

50 Words spoken to US President Carter at a meeting on 5 March 1980, in Bösch. F, p. 166.

51 Минфин подсчитал долю доходов бюджета РФ от нефти и газа в 2020–2022 годах, 19 September 2019, https://1prime.ru/state_regula tion/20190919/830338839.html (accessed 28 February 2021).

CHAPTER 7

1 Petersen, F, 'Die Grenzen der Propaganda', *FAZ.net*, 18 March 2015, www.faz.net/aktuell/politik/inland/allensbach-studie-die-grenzen-der-russischen-propaganda-13489238.html?printPagedArticle=true#pageIn dex_2 (accessed 28 February 2021).

2 Wergin, C, 'Der deutsche Russland-Tick', *Die Welt*, 4 December 2019, www.welt.de/print/die_welt/article204029090/Kommentar-Der-deuts che-Russland-Tick.html (accessed 28 February 2021).

3 Ibid.

4 Gloger, p. 372.

5 Von Knoop, A, 'Deutsch-Russische Auslandshandelskammer (AHK)', *Verband erfährt verdiente Aufwertung*, 5 June 2006, https://russland.ahk. de/infothek/news/detail/deutsch-russische-auslandshandelskammer-ahk (accessed 28 February 2021).

6 See, for example, the article 'Sanktionen gegen Russland: Eine imaginäre Stabilisierung' prepared by the Russian International Affairs Council on the outlook for western sanctions in its publication *Osteuropa Informationen*,

3 April 2020, pp. 12–13. www.ost-ausschuss.de/de/osteuropa-informa tionen (accessed 28 February 2021).

7   Hoffman, M, 'Wir verlieren Russland', *Der Tagesspiegel*, 18 November 2014, www.tagesspiegel.de/meinung/plaedoyer-fuer-einen-neuanfang-der-beziehungen-wir-verlieren-russland/10992794.html (accessed 28 February 2021).

8   'Владимир Путин наградил члена правления, исполнительного директора форума "Петербургский диалог" Мартина Хоффманна орденом Дружбы', 5 October 2007, http://kremlin.ru/events/presi dent/news/42895 (accessed 28 February 2021).

9   Stelzenmüller, C, 'The Impact of Russian Interference on Germany's 2017 Elections, Testimony before the US Select Committee on Intelligence', 28 June 2017, www.brookings.edu/testimonies/the-impact-of-russian-interference-on-germanys-2017-elections/ (accessed 28 February 2021).

10 'Abkommen zwischen der Regierung der Bundesrepublik Deutschland und der Regeierung der Russischen Föderation über jugendpolitische Zusammenarbeit', www.stiftung-drja.de/_Resources/Persistent/bfa006 a984d9f56cbb4a8e35387f2be43cc405f5/Reg.%20Abkommen%202004-deutsch%20(mit%20unterschriften).pdf (accessed 28 February 2021).

11 www.russisches-haus.de/impressum (accessed 28 February 2021).

12 www.berlin.de/kultur-und-tickets/tipps/multikulti/institutionen/22259 08–2929798-russisches-haus-der-wissenschaft-und-kul.html (accessed 28 February 2021).

13 www.russisches-haus.de/landsleute?lang=de (accessed 28 February 2021).

14 Ibid.

15 Ibid.

16 See Russkiy Mir's explanation of its ideology to German speakers: https://russkiymir.ru/languages/germany/Ideologia.htm (accessed 28 February 2021).

17 Interview in September 2020.

18 Banse, D, and Müller, U, 'Die Russen kommen', *Die Welt*, 17 June 2008, www.welt.de/welt_print/article2113068/Die-Russen-kommen.html (accessed 28 February 2021).

19 Ibid.

20 Ibid. and interview with Dmitri Khmelnytsky, Berlin, September 2020.

21 'Ominöse Orden aus Moskau', 14 November 2011, www.focus.de/poli tik/ausland/peter-der-grosse-ominoese-orden-aus-moskau_aid_316158. html (accessed 28 February 2021).

22 Wehner, M, 'Die Maulwürfe im deutschen Garten', *FAZ.net*, 12 January 2013, www.faz.net/aktuell/prozess-um-russisches-agenten paar-die-maulwuerfe-im-deutschen-garten-12022971.html (accessed 28 February 2021).

23 Schmid, F and Stark, H, 'Spies Strain German-Russian Ties', *Spiegel Online*, 2 July 2013, www.spiegel.de/international/world/trial-of-russian-spies-in-germany-strains-diplomatic-relations-a-908975.html (accessed 28 February 2021).

24 Müller, U and Nagel, L-M, 'Die Eheleute Anschlag müssen für Jahre in Haft', *Die Welt*, 2. Juli 2013, www.welt.de/politik/deutschland/arti cle117645693/Die-Eheleute-Anschlag-muessen-fuer-Jahre-in-Haft.html (accessed 28 February 2021).

25 'Germany frees Russian spy', *DW*, 22 November, www.dw.com/en/germany-frees-russian-spy/a-18080455 (accessed 28 February 2021).

26 'Russischer Spion in Heimat abgeschoben', *FAZ.net*, 3 June 2016, www.faz.net/aktuell/rhein-main/russischer-spion-aus-hessen-in-heimat-abge schoben-13628370.html (accessed 28 February 2021).

27 Hufelschulte, J, 'Würgen, schlagen, töten lernen', *Focus Magazin* Nr 22/14, www.focus.de/magazin/archiv/report-wuergen-schlagen-toeten-lernen_id_3870339.html (accessed 28 February 2021).

28 Even, B, 'Propaganda und politische Einflussnahme als strategische Handlungsoption ausländischer Nachrichtendienste, Neue Gefahren für Informationssicherheit und Informationshoheit, 10. Sicherheitstagung BfV und ASW Bundesverband am 9. Juni 2016, p. 30.

29 Pörzgen, G, 'Informationskrieg in Deutschland? Zur Gefahr russischer Desinformation im Bundestagswahljahr', 19 May 2017, www.bpb.de/apuz/248506/informationskrieg-in-deutschland-zur-gefahr-russis cher-desinformation-im-bundestagswahljahr (accessed 28 February 2021).

30 Ibid.

31 Spahn, S, *Das Ukraine-Bild in Deutschland*, Verlag Dr. Kovic (2016), p. 23.

32 Ibid. pp. 27–34.

33 Meisner, M and von Salzen, C, 'Linken-Abgeordnete auf Abenteuertour im Kriegsgebiet', 20 February 2015, www.tagesspiegel.de/politik/wolf gang-gehrcke-und-andrej-hunko-in-der-ostukraine-linken-abgeordnete-auf-abenteuertour-im-kriegsgebiet/11400156.html (accessed 28 February 2021).

34 Von Salzen, C, 'Die Krim ist jetzt die russische Krim', 18 April 2019, www.tagesspiegel.de/politik/die-russland-reisen-der-afd-die-krim-ist-jet zt-die-russische-krim/24232604.html (accessed 28 February 2021).

35 Spahn, p. 105.

36 Klimeniouk, N, 'Nationalismus und Rassismus bei "Russlanddeutschen"?' www.bpb.de/politik/extremismus/rechtsextre mismus/260496/nationalismus-und-rassismus-bei-russlanddeutschen (accessed 28 February 2021).

37 Beitzer, H, 'Russlanddeutsche mögen die Linkspartei lieber als die AfD', 8 March 2018, www.sueddeutsche.de/politik/bundestagswahl-russland deutsche-moegen-die-linkspartei-lieber-als-die-afd-1.3897458.

38 Fiedler, M and Von Salzen, C, 'Russlands Spiel mit den Rechten', 9 April 2019.

39 Sasse, G, 'Russland: Russlandbilder in Ost- und Westdeutschland', ZOiS Report 05/2020 www.zois-berlin.de/fileadmin/media/Dateien/ZOiS_ Reports/ZOiS_Report_5_2020.pdf (accessed 28 February 2021).

40 Klimeniouk.

41 'Сергей Лавров о Лизе, русской девочке изнасилованной мигрантами', 26 January 2016, www.youtube.com/watch?v=cbYadxb2VI8 (accessed 28 February 2021).

42 Jolkver, N, 'Der "Fall Lisa" ein Jahr danach. War da was?', *DW*, 11 January 2017, www.dw.com/de/der-fall-lisa-ein-jahr-danach-war-da-was/a-37079923 (accessed 28 February 2021).

43 'Neue Gefahren für Informationssicherheit und Informationshoheit, 10. Sicherheitstagung BfV und ASW', Bundesverband am 9. Juni 2016, p. 30.

44 'Merkel droht Russland wegen Hackerangriff mit Konsequenzen', 13 May 2020, www.faz.net/aktuell/politik/ausland/merkel-droht-russland-wegen-hackerangriff-mit-konsequenzen-16767763.html.

45 Verfassungsschutzbericht 2019 (annual report by the domestic intelligence agency), p. 283.

46 Heil, G, Malcher, I and Musharbash, Y, 'In zweifelhafter Gesellschaft', *Zeit Online*, 6 June 2019, www.zeit.de/2019/24/cyber-sicherheitsrat-ev-hans-wilhelm-duenn-russland-kontakte (accessed 28 February 2021).

47 Ibid.

48 Private Russian sources.

49 DOC website, https://doc-research.org/about-us/ (accessed 28 February 2021).

50 See, for example the investigation by the Foundation for the Fight Against Corruption, 'Как Пилят в РЖД', 16 July 2013.

51 Шлейнов, Р, 'В каких коррупционных делах фигурировал Siemens', *Ведомости*, 2 December 2013, www.vedomosti.ru/library/articles/2013/12/02/v-kakih-korrupcionnyh-delah-figuriroval-siemens (accessed 28 February 2021).

52 Siemens press release, 'Russische Eisenbahnen vergeben zwei Aufträge an Siemens und Partner', 7 September 2009.

53 Von Rapp, T, 'Nähe zum Kreml', *Der Spiegel*, 2 July 2017, www.spiegel. de/kultur/naehe-zum-kreml-a-7120079f-0002-0001-0000-000145638325 (accessed 28 February 2021).

54 DOC Research Institute Annual Report 2019, pp. 12–13, https://doc-

research.org/wp-content/uploads/2020/08/DOC-annualreport2019_200717_RZ.pdf (accessed 28 February 2021).

55   Ibid. p. 46.
56   Ibid. p. 58.
57   'Putin-Freund Wladimir Jakunin bekommt Arbeitsvisum für Deutschland', *DW*, 23 August 2018, www.dw.com/de/putin-freund-wladimir-jakunin-bekommt-arbeitsvisum-f%C3%BCr-deutschland/a-45195652 (accessed 28 February 2021).
58   Müller, U, Nagel, L-M and Smirnova, J, 'Deutschland im Visier von Moskaus Agenten', *Die Welt*, 10 February 2013, www.welt.de/politik/deutschland/article113505450/Deutschland-im-Visier-von-Moskaus-Agenten.html (accessed 28 February 2021).
59   Von Fritsch, p. 85.
60   Verfassungsschutzbericht 2019, p. 283.
61   Private Russian sources.
62   Even, B, pp. 24–32.
63   'Verleihung der russischen Staatsbürgerschaft an die Ehrenpräsidentin der AHK Russland', 8 November 2016, https://russland.ahk.de/infothek/news/detail/verleihung-der-russischen-staatsbuergerschaft-an-die-ehrenpraesidentin-der-ahk-russland (accessed 28 February 2021).

Chapter 8

1   'Кукловодство к действию. Николай Патрушев – о методах "цветных революций"', *Аргументы и Факты* 24, 10 June 2020.
2   'Путин обвиняет США в провоцировании протестов', *Би-Би-Си*, 8 December 2011, www.bbc.com/russian/mobile/russia/2011/12/111208_putin_opposition_protests (accessed 28 February 2021).
3   See for example the comments of the Secretary of the Russian Security Council, Nikolay Patrushev, 'За дестабилизацией Украины скрывается попытка радикального ослабления России', *Коммерсант*, 22 June 2015, www.kommersant.ru/doc/2752250 (accessed 28 February 2021).
4   'Глава СВР заявил об участии ЦРУ и Пентагона в подготовке протестов в Белоруссии', 29 September 2020, https://tass.ru/politika/9580909.
5   Quoted in Kundnani, H, *The Paradox of German Power*, Hurst & Company (2014), p. 68.
6   'AKK: Rede zur Verleihung des Medienpreises', 23 October 2020, www.bmvg.de/de/aktuelles/akk-rede-medienpreis-steuben-schurz-3816700 (accessed 28 February 2021).
7   Barber, L, Foy, H, and Barker, A, 'Vladimir Putin says liberalism has

"become obsolete"', 28 June 2019, www.ft.com/content/670039ec-98f3–11e9–9573-ee5cbb98ed36 (accessed 28 February 2021).

8 Путин, В., '75 лет Великой Победы: общая ответственность перед историей и будущим', 19 June 2020, http://kremlin.ru/events/presi dent/news/63527 (accessed 28 February 2021).

9 Gates, R, *Duty*, WH Allen (2014), p. 193.

10 Von Krause, U, 'The 2-Percent Objective and the Bundeswehr: Discussion about the German Defence Budget, Federal Academy for Security Policy', Security Policy Working Paper, No. 23/2018, p. 3.

11 Fakten zum deutschen Außenhandel, Bundesministerium für Wirtschaft und Energie (BMWi), September 2020, p. 2.

12 'Discours du Président Emmanuel Macron sur la stratégie de défense et de dissuasion devant les stagiaires de la 27ème promotion de l'école de guerre', 7 February 2020.

13 Stelzenmüller C, 'German lessons', November 2019, www.brookings.edu/essay/german-lessons/ (accessed 28 February 2021).

14 'Vladimir Putin and Angela Merkel: Through good times and bad', 18 August 2018, www.dw.com/en/vladimir-putin-and-angela-merkel-through-good-times-and-bad/g-45129235 (accessed 28 February 2021).

15 Snyder, T, 'Vladimir Putin's politics of eternity', *Guardian*, 16 March 2018, www.theguardian.com/news/2018/mar/16/vladimir-putin-rus sia-politics-of-eternity-timothy-snyder (accessed 28 February 2021).

16 Von Fritsch, p. 105.

17 'Merkel schickt Putin manchmal sächsisches Bier', *Leipziger Volkszeitung*, 11 March 2018, www.lvz.de/Region/Mitteldeutschland/Merkel-schickt-Putin-manchmal-saechsisches-Bier (accessed 28 February 2021).

18 Wehner, M, 'Zorn und Schmerz', *FAZ.net*, 26 June 2020, www.faz.net/aktuell/politik/ausland/angela-merkels-beziehung-zu-russland-zorn-und-s chmerz-16829187.html?GEPC=s53&premium (accessed 28 February 2021).

19 See, for example, 'Merkels Kuschel-Treffen mit Putin im Kreml', 11 January 2020, *Bild am Sonntag*, www.bild.de/politik/2020/politik/merkel-in-moskau-merkels-kuschel-treffen-mit-putin-im-kreml-67258096.bild.html (accessed 28 February 2021).

20 Pressekonferenz von Bundeskanzlerin Merkel und dem Präsidenten von Russland, Wladimir Putin, 11 January 2020, www.bundeskanzlerin.de/bkin-de/aktuelles/pressekonferenz-von-bundeskanzlerin-merkel-und-dem-praesidenten-von-russland-wladimir-putin-1711802 (accessed 28 February 2021).

21 'Merkel verurteilt "versuchten Giftmord"', *Tagesschau*, 2 September 2020, www.tagesschau.de/inland/nawalny-merkel-101.html (accessed 28 February 2021).

22 Pressekonferenz von Bundeskanzlerin Merkel und Staatspräsident

Putin am 10. Mai 2015 in Moskau, www.bundesregierung.de/breg-
de/aktuelles/pressekonferenzen/pressekonferenz-von-bundeskanzlerin-
merkel-und-staatspraesident-putin-am-10-mai-2015-in-moskau-848730
(accessed 28 February 2021).

23 'О вызове в МИД России Чрезвычайного и Полномочного Посла
ФРГ в Москве Г. фон Гайра', 9 September 2020, www.mid.ru/ru/for
eign_policy/news/-/asset_publisher/cKNonkJE02Bw/content/id/432
9721 (accessed 28 February 2021).

24 Fücks, R, p. 134.

25 Giles, K, *Moscow Rules*, Brookings Institution Press/Chatham House,
2019, p. 140.

Conclusion

1 'Dialog-Vertrauen-Sicherheit, Beschluss der SPD-Bundestagsfraktion', 9
October 2018, p. 6.

2 Kundnani, H, 'Die Ost-Politik Illusion', *Internationale Politik*, January/
February 2014, p. 79.

3 Huterer, M, 'Sicherheit vor und mit Russland', *Osteuropa* 9–10/2017,
p. 115.

4 'Zeitenwende|Wendezeiten, Sonderausgabe des Munich Security Report
zur deutschen Außen- und Sicherheitspolitik', October 2020, p. 159.

5 'Discours du Président de la République Emmanuel Macron à la
Conférence des Ambassadeurs et des Ambassadrices de 2019', 27 August
2019, p. 8.

6 National Security Strategy of the United States of America, December
2017, p. 25.

7 Techau, J, "Ohne Russland gibt es keine europäische Sicherheit",
Internationale Politik, May/June 2020, p. 13.

8 'Europa muss künftig stärker selbst sehen, was es für seine eigene
Sicherheit machen kann', Außenminister Heiko Maas im Interview mit
der Rheinischen Post, 27 July 2020, www.auswaertiges-amt.de/de/news
room/maas-rp/2371018 (accessed 28 February 2021).

9 Techau, J, 'No Trust In Self, No Money For Defense', *The American
Interest*, Vol. 15, No. 3, 4 October 2019, www.the-american-interest.
com/2019/10/04/no-trust-in-self-no-money-for-defense/ (accessed 28
February 2021).

10 World Bank data.

Notes

Afterword

1 See, for example, the tweet by the former Green Member of Parliament Marieluise Beck from 23 April 2022, https://twitter.com/MarieluiseBeck /status/1517882598659436547 (accessed 18 July 2022).

2 Milne, R, 'Finland insists on its right to join Nato in defiance of Russia', *Financial Times*, 2 January 2022.

3 'Regierungserklärung von Bundeskanzler Olaf Scholz am 27. Februar 2022', www.bundesregierung.de/breg-de/suche/regierungserklaerung -von-bundeskanzler-olaf-scholz-am-27-februar-2022-2008356 (accessed 18 July 2022).

4 Amann, M and Knobbe, M, 'Es darf keinen Atomkrieg geben', *Der Spiegel*, 22 April 2022 www.spiegel.de/politik/olaf-scholz-und-der-ukra ine-krieg-interview-es-darf-keinen-atomkrieg-geben-a-ae2acfbf-8125-4b f5-a273-fbcd0bd8791c.

5 'Interview mit der Tageszeitung Rheinische Post, 6. Februar 2022', www .bundespraesident.de/SharedDocs/Reden/DE/Frank-Walter-Steinme ier/Interviews/2021/210206-Interview-Rheinische-Post.html (accessed 18 July 2022).

6 Ismar, G, 'In Putins imperialem Wahn habe ich mich geirrt', 5 April 2022, www.tagesspiegel.de/politik/steinmeiers-fehleranalyse-in-bellevue-in-pu tins-imperialem-wahn-habe-ich-mich-geirrt/28226810.html (accessed 18 July 2022).

7 Ibid.

8 'Nord Stream 2 war ein Fehler. Und auf die Osteuropäer haben wir schlicht nicht gehört', Interview mit dem Vorsitzenden der Atlantik-Brücke, Sigmar Gabriel, www.atlantik-bruecke.org/nord-stream-2-war-ein-feh ler-und-auf-die-osteuropaeer-haben-wir-schlicht-nicht-gehoert (accessed 18 July 2022).

9 Gabriel räumt Fehler bei Nord Stream 2 ein, 19 April 2022, www. tagesschau.de/newsticker/liveblog-ukraine-dienstag-117.html#Gabriel (accessed 18 July 2022).

10 Private sources.

11 Bennhold, K, 'The Former Chancellor Who Became Putin's Man in Germany', *New York Times*, 23 April 2022, www.nytimes.com/2022/04 /23/world/europe/schroder-germany-russia-gas-ukraine-war-energy .html (accessed 18 July 2022).

12 Ibid.

13 '„Was also ist mein Land?“: Altkanzlerin Merkel im Live-Gespräch mit Schriftsteller Alexander Osang', 7 June 2022, www.youtube.com/watch ?v=hiwnD00kV0w (accessed 18 July 2022).

14 Phoenix, 9 June 2022 https://mobile.twitter.com/phoenix_de/status/15 34458127369785344 (accessed 18 July 2022).

15 'Jetzt bin ich frei', *Der Spiegel*, 18 June 2022, www.spiegel.de/politik/
    deutschland/angela-merkel-ueber-kanzlerschaft-und-ruhestand-jetzt-bin
    -ich-frei-a-913bd7c5-9155-472d-a9bb-34d809858767 (accessed 18 July
    2022).

16 Yale CELI List of Companies Leaving and Staying in Russia, www.yaler
    ussianbusinessretreat.com (accessed 18 July 2022)..

17 Petersen, T, 'Wunsch nach starkem Europa', *Frankfurter Allgemeine Zeitung*,
    22 June 2022 (142), p. 8.

18 'Scholz sieht Eiszeit mit Moskau aufziehen', 22 June 2022, www.ta
    gesschau.de/inland/regierungserklaerung-scholz-gipfeltreffen-103.html
    (accessed 18 July 2022).

Index

Index

Index

Index